Defence
without
the Bomb

Defence without the Bomb

The Report of the Alternative Defence Commission

Set up by the Lansbury House Trust Fund

Taylor & Francis Ltd
London and New York
1983

First published 1983 by Taylor & Francis Ltd,
4 John Street, London WC1N 2ET

© 1983 Lansbury House Trust Fund

Phototypesetting by Georgia Origination, Liverpool
Printed and bound in Great Britain by Redwood Burn Ltd, Trowbridge

Distributed in the USA and Canada by International Publications Service
Taylor and Francis Inc., 114 East 32nd Street, New York, NY 10016

British Library Cataloguing in Publication Data
Alternative Defence Commission
  Defence without the bomb.
  1. Great Britain—Military policy
  I. Title
  355'.0335'41   UA647

ISBN 0-85066-240-0

Contents

Preface

The idea behind the setting up of the Alternative Defence Commission was a simple one. An increasing number of people in Britain (also in other parts of Europe, and in the United States and Japan) have been coming to the conclusion that they have to say No to nuclear weapons: it would never be right to use, or threaten to use, these weapons, or indeed any other weapons of mass destruction.

However, to say No to nuclear weapons is not a defence policy. The question then arises: if Britain does renounce nuclear weapons, what defence policy should it adopt? The remit of the Commission was to address itself to this question, and to review a wide range of alternative non-nuclear defence policies for Britain. (This is, of course, not simply a British problem. It is a problem for most nations in the world: most nations do not have nuclear weapons deployed on their soil.)

The persons who were invited to serve on the Commission had one tenet in common: they all accepted the initial premise – that Britain should renounce the use, or deployment on its territory, of nuclear weapons. But the Commission members came from various backgrounds and held a wide variety of views. During the course of the work the people involved developed, and in some cases changed, their original ideas, and the Commission did reach agreement on many important issues; some differences, however, obviously do remain. The Report therefore represents a general consensus: clearly each member does not agree with every word, but all are in agreement with the general lines of the report. In any case, its main purpose is to encourage serious debate, rather than to present hard and fast conclusions.

The initiative for setting up the Commission came from the Trustees of the Lansbury House Trust Fund, a charitable educational trust set up to promote research into means of resolving conflict in national and international affairs; this Trust was also responsible for raising the funds to meet the Commission's costs. The University of Bradford sponsored the project by setting up a Fellowship in the School of Peace Studies specifically for it, thus enabling the research fellow to make use of the facilities of the School.

Thanks are due to the many individuals who made donations – some very generous indeed – to the project. A special debt of gratitude is owed to the Joseph Rowntree Charitable Trust and the Barrow and Geraldine S. Cadbury Trust, whose major grants made the project possible at all. Thanks, too, to other charitable trusts and organisations who have assisted with donations, including the Cheney Peace Settlement, the Godshill Trust, Quaker Peace Studies, and a number of Meetings of the Society of Friends.

The Commission met for the first time on 4 October 1980 and held 16 meetings. After I had accepted the chair, I was appointed to the directorship of the Stockholm International Peace Research Institute, and left for Sweden in mid-September 1981; from then on the chair rotated between members of the Commission. SIPRI is, of course, not committed to the conclusions of this report.

The members of the Commission owe a deep debt of gratitude to their co-ordinator, Michael Randle, for his unremitting work to get the report out in reasonable time. They are grateful too to his assistants, Lisa Foley, Anne Randle and Howard Clark. A great many people helped the Commission with comments and advice, but are of course in no way committed to the Commission's conclusions. The Commission is especially grateful to Colonel Jonathan Alford, Dr Ken Booth, Professor Michael Howard, Dr David Holloway, Dr Wolf Mendl, Professor Peter Nailor and Dr Paul Rogers, and to Adam Roberts, who served on the Commission from October 1981 to September 1982 and made an important contribution to its work.

This is, I think, a report whose time has come. A Britain without nuclear weapons is now a serious political possibility, and deserves serious study. Here is a substantial contribution to that study.

Frank Blackaby
Stockholm International Peace Research Institute

December 1982

Introduction

British defence policy is at a turning point. The Trident decision has given a new impetus to the debate about the wisdom of trying to maintain an independent British deterrent, and the proposed deployment of US cruise missiles in Britain and elsewhere in Europe in 1983 has resurrected controversy over US nuclear bases and facilities in this country; finally the Falklands war has highlighted the issue of what role British defence should seek to play outside Europe, and the kind of conventional forces it should maintain.

The British decision in 1947 to manufacture its own bomb occurred at a time when Britain saw its role in the world in very different terms to what it does today, and when the creation of an independent deterrent seemed a viable goal. Ten years later when the Defence White Paper of 1957 formulated the policy of making nuclear weapons the cornerstone of British defence, this still looked like a relatively cheap and painless option, permitting a cut-back in conventional forces and the phasing out of conscription.

Today the situation has radically altered. Despite the Falklands war, Britain no longer sees itself as playing a major global role in a military sense, and with the dissolving of the Empire, and subsequently the policy of withdrawal East of Suez announced in 1967, it has drastically curtailed its commitments outside Europe. At the same time the technology associated with maintaining a credible nuclear option has become so complex and costly that since the early 1960s Britain has had to rely heavily on US back-up to sustain it. We do not in fact have an independent deterrent in the sense that its originators intended.

The wisdom of Britain's retaining its own Bomb has been increasingly called into question in recent years, and there is a growing public awareness of the dangers of this policy. First, the credibility of the British deterrent is questionable, because if Britain ever used these weapons against a superpower it would be courting its own certain destruction; if the use of nuclear weapons in war would not be rational, the threat to use them may not be believed. Second, there is the problem of proliferation. The arguments Britain uses in support of its Bomb are also dangerously available to other states with the capacity to produce nuclear weapons, and as long as Britain remains a nuclear power it will not be in a position to contribute effectively to the major effort that is now urgently required to make the Nuclear Non-Proliferation Treaty more effective. Third, there is the moral argument that the use of weapons of mass destruction can never be justified; they violate the notion of discrimination in the conduct of war, and no cause, however worthy, could justify the devastation that would be involved. The moral argument was once again convincingly stated in the report of the Church of England Working Party published in 1982, *The Church and the Bomb*.

The nuclear emphasis in Britain's own defence policy, and that of its European partners in NATO, is now widely challenged. Thus the decision to replace Polaris in the 1990s with the far more powerful and expensive Trident has been criticised even by people in, or close to, the defence establishment, and the main opposition parties are against the project. Other aspects of NATO policy, especially the declared intention to use nuclear weapons first if necessary to halt a Soviet conventional attack, and the related deployment of battlefield nuclear weapons which increases the danger that any military clash will escalate rapidly to nuclear war, have come under fire from prominent figures in the political and strategic community on both sides of the Atlantic.

But it has undoubtedly been the resurgence of the nuclear disarmament movement, in Europe particularly, but also in other countries including the United States and Japan, that has been crucial in putting the question of disarmament and security back into the centre of the political stage, and exerting pressure on the leaders of the major powers to take these issues more seriously. In June 1982, over a million people took part in a peace demonstration in New York during the second UN Special Session on Disarmament, and there were mass demonstrations involving up to 300,000 people in favour of nuclear disarmament and against the deployment of cruise and Pershing II missiles in several European countries during 1981–82, including those in London in October 1981 and June 1982. The last two years have also seen the emergence of small but significant independent peace movements in Eastern Europe, notably in East Germany. The disarmament movements are raising, among other things, the fundamental question of whether it could ever be justified to use weapons of mass destruction, and whether it makes either moral or strategic sense to fashion a defence policy around a threat to do so. They are thus challenging the very basis of the notion of nuclear deterrence.

However, the rising cost of both nuclear and conventional weapons, especially as high technology has come to play a predominant role, requires a review of defence assumptions and strategies that goes beyond a simple rejection of nuclear policies. At the global level the diversion of resources for military purposes has become a major scandal, costing indirectly millions of lives. According to UN estimates, armaments spending worldwide in 1981 amounted to over US $500 billion compared with $400 billion ten years previously (at constant prices); over the last 20 years military expenditure has approximately doubled. Nearly three quarters of these sums are spent by the two main military blocs, NATO and the Warsaw Pact. Nor do these figures give an adequate picture of the waste of talent and resources involved; some 500,000 scientists and engineers, for instance, are estimated to be engaged in military research and development throughout the world.

Expense is in fact an important constraint on the defence decisions of any individual country, and for Britain and other Western European countries whose economies are experiencing a prolonged period of decline, this constraint is likely to become more noticeable. The Trident debate is showing that judgements about priorities in defence spending are inescapable, and it is important that these judgements should be made in the context of an overall review of British defence objectives and needs.

The proposition underlying the work of the Alternative Defence Commission is that Britain should get rid of its own nuclear weapons and secure the removal of nuclear weapons and bases from British territory. It accepts the unilateralist approach in so far as it does not think these measures should be dependent on reaching an agreement with the Soviet Union — though pressure for it to take reciprocal steps should be exerted. However, by concentrating on the question of alternative defence strategies, the Commission hopes to shift somewhat the focus of the disarmament debate.

We have examined a range of possible approaches from those involving the maintenance of strong conventional forces to radical proposals for defence by nonviolent, civil, resistance. Some of these could be adopted by a government within the next few years; others involve a major shift in the way questions of security and defence are regarded and handled, and perhaps also political and social changes, and do not constitute immediate options. The Commission, though concerned about long-term possibilities, has focused mainly on the short and medium term. For those committed to more radical propositions, including pacifists on the Commission, these options can nonetheless be welcomed for the most part as steps away from the existing policy and towards more fundamental change.

We regard this report as a contribution to a continuing discussion, and there is of course no suggestion that it exhausts the possibilities of alternative strategies. When the various permutations and sub-options are taken into account, some of which involve significant shifts of emphasis, the range of alternatives is very large. We hope, however, that in reviewing the major considerations involved, and raising possibilities that have not generally been given much attention, we may succeed in broadening the horizons of the debate.

Summary of Conclusions and Main Recommendations

The Commission's brief was to explore the defence options that would be available to Britain if it gave up its own Bomb and asked the United States to remove all nuclear bases from this country. The main emphasis of the Report therefore is on examining the full range of conventional and unconventional military strategies that Britain alone, or Western Europe as a whole, could adopt. The Report also gives serious attention to the more radical options of making either guerrilla warfare or nonviolent resistance a central element in its defence policy. However, in addition to presenting a range of strategies the Commission has also tried to reach agreement about a number of specific recommendations.

There are in fact a variety of defence options open to a nuclear disarmed Britain. The Commission believes that nuclear disarmament by Britain (and Western Europe) would reduce the danger of nuclear war and of a major war in Europe, especially if it was accompanied by moves to secure political settlements and wider measures of disarmament. A constructive stress upon unilateral initiatives is more likely, in the Commission's view, to lead to agreement than the policy of 'negotiation from strength' which in fact has tended to reinforce the arms race. However, the policy of nuclear disarmament does necessitate giving due weight to the problems of a non-nuclear defence.

The Commission considers that the main threats to Britain stem from the two great powers, directly or indirectly. It concurs with the majority of political and strategic analysts that a Soviet invasion of Western Europe is unlikely, and it sees no balance of political or economic interests that might incline the Soviet Union to undertake such an invasion. Nevertheless it would be wrong to conclude that Britain, or Western Europe, need give no consideration to defending itself, if only because the Soviet Union, like every other major power in history, could be tempted to try to extend the area under its control if there appeared to be no obstacles. In some circumstances a nonnuclear Britain could also face pressure of various kinds from the United States.

Britain, NATO and Europe

The Commission is unanimous that a nuclear disarmed Britain could not accept NATO's current nuclear-based strategy. It debated at length whether it would be better for Britain to stay in NATO and seek to influence its policy in a non-nuclear direction, or to leave the Alliance altogether. The majority reached the conclusion that Britain should seek to initiate a process of nuclear disarmament in Europe by staying in the Alliance subject to the condition that NATO does move decisively towards abandoning any reliance on a nuclear strategy. The goal of de-nuclearising NATO strategy implies the following steps:

(1) Acceptance by NATO of a policy of no-first-use of nuclear weapons.

(2) Withdrawal of short-range, 'battlefield', nuclear weapons.

(3) Withdrawal of 'theatre' nuclear weapons.

(4) The decoupling of the US strategic nuclear deterrent from NATO by ending reliance on US nuclear weapons as an element in NATO strategy.

As part of this process, NATO would obviously seek reciprocal measures of disarmament by the Soviet Union. But the commitment to de-nuclearise NATO strategy should be unconditional and therefore not dependent on Soviet reciprocation.

A conditional membership of NATO must imply some kind of time scale for achieving the above goals if it is to have any force. But since the purpose of this approach is to give Britain diplomatic leverage, there are difficulties in being too rigid. We provisionally suggest that Britain should tell its allies that it places a special importance on a no-first-use policy and that it will leave NATO within a year unless the Alliance adopts this policy as a signal of its commitment to move away from reliance on nuclear weapons.

Britain could set a definite time limit, say three years, for the removal of US nuclear weapons from its territory, and seek the removal of the battlefield and theatre weapons based in Europe within three to four years. We suggest that unless there has been substantial progress towards the removal of these weapons from Europe within three years, Britain should consider withdrawing from the Alliance.

We recognise that decoupling NATO from the US nuclear force is a more complex and even more controversial aim, but consider it as an essential goal for a coherent non-nuclear strategy.

The Commission is completely opposed to the deployment of cruise, Pershing II and neutron weapons in Europe. If any of these have been deployed by the time a unilateralist government is elected in Britain, priority should be given to securing their removal. The Commission also opposes the deployment of binary nerve gas weapons in Europe.

If NATO was not willing to renounce nuclear strategies, Britain should withdraw from the Alliance. It could then explore the possibility of alternative approaches to collective security in Europe, or adopt a non-aligned position. Some Commission members thought that from the outset Britain should adopt a non-aligned approach.

Provision could also be made for countries to help each other in nonviolent resistance to occupation or to other enforced limitations of political and economic rights.

Alternative strategies

The military posture which is in general favoured by the Commission is one of 'defensive deterrence'; this means having the capacity to inflict heavy losses on any invading force, but at most only a limited capacity to mount offensive operations in the opponent's territory. Renouncing nuclear weapons is itself a major step in this direction; it could be extended by, for instance, emphasising territorial defence, by limiting the numbers of tanks, and by eliminating long range bombers. How far Britain or Western Europe should go in this direction is a matter for further debate.

In so far as the Soviet Union is the main potential adversary, a nuclear-disarmed Britain, or Western Europe, could confront a nuclear opponent. But the possession by an opponent of nuclear weapons (or of other indiscriminate weapons or weapons of mass destruction such as chemical or biological weapons) does not nullify preparations for conventional military defence. A powerful state might be tempted to move against a country that was militarily undefended, but might not think the stakes involved warranted a serious military campaign, or the political and moral opprobrium, and other hazards and penalties, of having to invoke the nuclear threat, or of actually using nuclear weapons. Most of the members of the Commission therefore favoured Britain and Western Europe retaining a sizeable conventional military deterrent at least in the short to medium term, or pending negotiated arms reductions. But to meet the possible contingency of nuclear escalation or blackmail, the Commission recommends that military defence policies should have a fall-back strategy of defence by civil, nonviolent resistance.

Within NATO or a European alliance

A conventional defence strategy in Western Europe must take account of political and economic as well as purely military factors. The political goal of a reorganised defence should be to avoid a conventional arms build-up in Central Europe and to maximise the possibility of arms limitation. A European defence policy must also recognise the West German government's anxiety to retain a convincing multinational frontier defence of its territory. Finally, the economic constraints of European countries, especially in a period of recession, rule out major increases in defence spending. Therefore the preferable policy would be to switch the emphasis throughout Europe towards in-depth defence. The greater dispersal of forces involved in this approach means fewer military concentrations that might merit a nuclear attack. In principle a strategy of pure in-depth defence could be adopted involving the total re-deployment in depth of regular forces in Germany or elsewhere in mainland Europe, perhaps supplemented by territorial forces, but the Commission favoured the argument that mobile regular forces would be necessary to 'seal off' border incidents, or to mount counter-offensives within the territory under attack. Maintaining such a force could at least partially meet West German concern about the security of its borders.

In the near future, NATO seems likely to prefer a frontier-based defence, concentrating on holding any Soviet attack as far East as possible with regular NATO forces. There are three main options here:

(1) to maintain approximately existing force levels. (Many experts think there is scope for improved effectiveness within these levels.)

(2) to strengthen existing defences by more systematic preparations for territorial defence.

(3) to increase to some extent the size of regular conventional forces.

The Commission would prefer to avoid any increase in conventional forces, but recognises that certain non-nuclear strategies might involve this to a limited extent. Under any of the above options, Britain would continue to maintain ground forces with the British Army of the Rhine (BAOR) in Germany, possibly strengthening them to some degree as part of a re-organisation within NATO as a whole upon the withdrawal of battlefield nuclear weapons; it would not substantially alter its existing preparations for the defence of the UK home territory except possibly under option (2) in which territorial forces might be strengthened along with others in Western Europe.

Outside NATO

Britain outside NATO (or any alternative European alliance) could adopt a 'high entry price' policy, concentrated on the defence of the home territory. This would involve strong coastal and anti-aircraft defences, an air force with a strong emphasis on fighter air-craft, a navy comprising mainly submarines and small to medium-sized craft which would operate principally in and around British waters, and a highly mobile regular army. Territorial forces might also be increased to provide in-depth resistance in support of operations by regular forces.

Guerrilla tactics could be used by territorial units in this supportive role. However, the Commission does not think the conditions in Britain favour *protracted* guerrilla warfare against an occupying power and it is totally opposed to a campaign of political assassination or the random killing of military personnel.

In the British context the Commission favours nonviolent civil resistance as a fall-back anti-occupation strategy. This type of resistance aims at depriving an occupying force or client regime of its authority and control through mass non-co-operation and other forms of political struggle, and at undermining the authority of the aggressor's own regime. Nonviolent defence might also be employed, in preference to military methods, in particular circum-stances; some Commission members thought that the longer-term goal should be to make nonviolent resistance the central element in a defence policy.

Variations of the strategies outlined here are clearly possible, and some of these are discussed in the body of the Report.

The political dimension

The Commission's proposals would tend to accelerate the process of British withdrawal from military commitments outside the

European area. There are problems relating to this process, but, despite the fact that Britain was prepared to go to war over the Falklands, it has been a steady and inevitable one as Britain's global military capacity has declined. The Commission recognises, however, that the process of transferring responsibility for remaining overseas territories and defence commitments could take time.

The foreign policy of a nuclear-disarmed Britain was not considered in detail by the Commission, though it is well aware of its vital importance to security. The general thrust of the policy should be to promote detente and disarmament, for instance by supporting the demand for a European nuclear-free zone and efforts to bring about a new political settlement in Europe to make possible the dissolution of the two military pacts. Britain should use the occasion of its renunciation of nuclear weapons to press for the strengthening of the Non-Proliferation Treaty, and the signing of a Comprehensive Test Ban Treaty.

Chapter 1
Thinking about defence

The fundamental purpose of defence is to protect the lives and rights of a community from outside attack. In a democratic society this implies the right of the community to frame its own institutions and determine the political, cultural, economic and other aspects of life. Defence as such cannot guarantee these rights, but it can help to protect them from certain kinds of threat.

Implied in the claim to have a right to defend one's own society is a recognition that other states and communities have a similar right. Another aspect of defence therefore may be to defend through a system of mutual security the rights of other communities under attack.

Finally, defence has an internal function, legitimate in so far as its aim is to prevent the seizure of power in a democratic society by an armed minority or to protect the community from attack by armed groups, illegitimate if its aim is to repress freedom of association or political expression.

How are these general goals to be translated into a defence policy? For this we need to define specific objectives and to have an understanding of the international system in which policy operates. There is an analogy here with economic policy, where those who decide on such matters as changes in the tax rates or exchange rates need to have enough knowledge of the working of the economic system to enable them to estimate the effects of their policies. Thus considerable space is devoted in this report to evaluating the international repercussions of particular strategies and to considering ways of implementing them. We can consider the principal objectives under a number of headings.

Preventing nuclear war

Nuclear war would be such an absolute disaster that preventing it must rank as the first and overriding objective of defence. This much the advocates of nuclear deterrence and its opponents often agree about. The question is how it is to be achieved.

Britain's own bomb and the presence of US nuclear bases in this country make it a prime target for nuclear attack in the event of war. It is true that, with or without nuclear weapons, Britain would be at risk in a nuclear war and would suffer severe consequences even if it was not the target of direct nuclear attack. But if nuclear weapons were removed entirely from the national territory, the danger of an all-out nuclear attack on Britain would be somewhat diminished, just as today countries like Sweden and Yugoslavia — or Canada which is a member of NATO but which no longer has nuclear weapons on its territory — are generally deemed less likely than Britain to face a major nuclear attack should the deterrent fail.

The more important question is whether British nuclear disarmament and the removal of US bases would make nuclear war as such less likely. This is not something that can be proved conclusively either way, but in our view if it was part of a much broader initiative there is a strong case for thinking that it would. Thus British nuclear disarmament ought to be accompanied by a major effort to secure the removal of tactical nuclear weapons from Europe, East and West, and the establishment, if possible, of a nuclear-free zone covering the whole of Europe. The growing peace movements in Europe and the United States are particularly important in trying to achieve these goals and other measures that are urgently required to halt the nuclear arms race. In addition the development of alternative defence policies by Britain could add to the significance of British nuclear disarmament and make it more likely that its initiative would be seen by other states as providing a model worth serious consideration.

Catastrophic consequences would also flow from chemical or biological warfare. While the Commission has concentrated on the nuclear issue, it is acutely aware of the hazards of these forms of warfare and is totally opposed to the manufacture, deployment or use of chemical or biological weapons. Thus our definition of conventional defence excludes any reliance on these weapons. It is important to make this point clear at a time when the science of genetic engineering could make new biological weapons available, and when technological developments have made the storage and use of chemical weapons much simpler than in the past.[1]

Preventing invasion and occupation

This is important in several respects: in protecting the lives of people who would be at risk in the event of occupation; in permitting the national community to have continued access to the resources of the territory it inhabits; and to allow the community to maintain its institutions and values. Moreover, if the territory becomes the subject of foreign interventions and adventures, this could make it the focus of international tension and even wider war.

The right of access to territorial resources raises the issue of national sovereignty. The problem is to define what constitutes the national community and what territory it can be said legitimately to inhabit. Existing national boundaries are often the result of past wars and aggressions and in ex-colonies especially the national boundaries may cut right across ethnic and linguistic communities.

But while there are grey areas here, sharply illustrated by the conflict in Northern Ireland, the issue itself is unavoidable. It would clearly be wrong for Britain to attempt to seize territory in the Middle East for its oil resources, and no less wrong for another country to seize territory in and around Britain. And if this was attempted, Britain would have the right to resist.

The ability to resist invasion, or to frustrate the process of occupation, is central also in the sense that many of the lesser threats and pressures to which a country may be subjected imply ultimately a threat of occupation. They can therefore be more confidently resisted if there is a convincing anti-invasion or anti-occupation strategy.

Accepting the need for defence does not of course mean a commitment to maintaining society exactly as it is. Radical critics of British society have in fact sometimes queried whether it is worth defending. But occupation frequently results in the establishment of a much more repressive and dictatorial regime, and the ability to resist occupation can be an important part of keeping open the possibility of creative change and development.

Defending values and human rights

Recognizing the right of people to resist occupation implies a commitment to principles and values which are essential to human freedom and the possibility of a civilised existence. During World War II the struggle against Nazi Germany was reinforced by an entirely justified belief that Nazi doctrine and practice were evil and so individuals and communities were prepared to make great sacrifices to combat them. The example shows that it is not enough simply to list defence objectives; an order of priorities between the various objectives is also necessary. Moreover because no defence policy is equally good at doing everything, the choice of policy is itself to some extent an expression of priorities.

Civilised values may also be put at risk by internal factors, including the defence system itself. The use of torture by the French army in Algeria, and the killing of civilians in reprisal for guerrilla attacks by the FLN, or for acts of terrorism, had a profoundly corrupting influence on French political life. Although it is not an exact parallel, the possession of nuclear weapons, which involves at least a conditional willingness to kill millions of people, similarly erodes the acceptance of the imperative to respect the lives and rights of individuals and communities.

The secrecy surrounding defence decisions can also lead to a loss of democratic control in a vital area of national policy. In Britain even the decision in 1947 to manufacture nuclear weapons was taken in secret by an inner group in the Cabinet, and it was not until some time later that Parliament was informed.[2] Again the decision of a Labour government in the mid-1970s to modernise the warheads of the Polaris missiles, giving them manoeuvrability to evade the Soviet Anti-Ballistic Missile (ABM) defences around Moscow (the 'Chevaline' programme) was taken without the knowledge or approval of Parliament.[3]

Responsibilities to British overseas territories and former colonies

The issue of Britain's responsibility for overseas outposts and dependencies has been highlighted by the Falklands war. In a sense the issue here is how far British territory extends, but the central question is Britain's responsibility to people who find themselves in a vulnerable position as a result of its imperial past, and this arises in connection not only with territories that Britain still directly controls but with some former colonies such as Belize which find themselves under threat from neighbouring states and to whom Britain has made certain defence commitments.

Complex moral and constitutional issues are raised by some of the territorial disputes relating to British overseas territories or former colonies, and it was clearly beyond the brief of the Commission to examine these in detail. But it recognised that Britain may need to retain a capacity for some level of military intervention outside the European area if it is to honour genuine overseas responsibilities, or to contribute effectively to UN or other multinational peacekeeping operations.

Nevertheless, it would be wrong to foster illusions about the extent to which Britain can continue to defend territories many thousands of miles from its shores. It must be doubted, for instance, whether British naval forces can sustain indefinitely a capacity to mount operations on the scale of the Falklands Task Force. The Commission itself suggests the possibility of drastically reducing the size of Britain's surface fleet (see Chapter 4 and Appendix 2), though such a policy is not of course necessitated by a commitment to nuclear disarmament, and the extent of cuts would have to take account of existing overseas commitments. But some cut-backs in the size of the surface fleet seem likely whatever government is in office.

The political implications of Britain's declining capability to intervene in distant territories are that it will have either to transfer or share responsibilities for remaining territorial outposts and other overseas defence commitments. In the case of Hong Kong, the most populous and important of Britain's overseas territories, it is clearly essential to reach agreement with China; elsewhere too, in the Falklands and Gibraltar, the search for political settlements which would take account of the rights of the inhabitants must continue. In the case of commitments to former colonies such as Belize, Britain might attempt to share responsibility with a number of other powers.

The wishes of the inhabitants must be the most important single consideration in determining the future of Britain's overseas territories, but cannot always be the sole and overriding factor. The historical, geographical and economic context has to be taken into account, and certain options, such as indefinite British sovereignty, may simply have to be ruled out. On the other hand there can be no justification for the action taken by a previous British government in relation to the Indian Ocean island of Diego Garcia whose inhabitants were deported without their consent to Mauritius to make way for an extension of US military facilities.

Sometimes, however, an ideal or just solution is not possible to achieve, especially if one has regard for the need for proportionality in the use of force even for legitimate ends. The Argentine invasion of the Falklands was unjustified and violated the rights of the inhabitants, but this does not suffice to show that Britain's military response was right, and it may turn out to have done little for the long-term prospects of the islanders, since a satisfactory compromise with Argentina may now be harder than ever to reach, and Britain's ability to defend a territory 8,000 miles away can only decline.

In the longer term, the general solution to problems of this kind may be to strengthen the peacekeeping and collective security roles of the UN. The difficulties of UN peacekeeping are considerable, as the war in the Lebanon has tragically illustrated, and stem to a great extent from the division between the superpowers. But the possibility of the UN playing a more extensive peacekeeping role is worth exploring, particularly in cases where the interests of the two superpowers are not involved in a direct or important way.

One issue which the Falklands war has highlighted is that Britain, along with many other states, has been supplying major weapons to military dictatorships which may be used for external aggression or for repressing their own populations. If Britain's declining capacity to play a global role would mean that in future it might be unable on its own to prevent certain injustices occurring in other parts of the world, its commitment to freedom and human rights can at least be expressed by putting an end to this practice. Such unilateral action by Britain would not of course solve the problem, which will have to be tackled at an international level. While in no way underestimating the difficulties involved, the Commission believes that an international effort to solve the problem must be made.

Resisting economic threats

Britain, as a densely populated island heavily dependent on trade for access to food and raw materials, would be particularly hard hit by an economic blockade. An attempt to impose such a blockade would be an act of war and could legitimately be resisted. However, a blockade is more often a prelude to invasion than a substitute for it. It can be used as a means of extracting concessions from a country or weakening it in preparation for an invasion, but it is too inflexible and cumbersome a weapon to provide a substitute for occupation if the aim is to control the overall policy of a government. So Britain's vulnerability to blockade does not make preparations for the defence of the territory, or for resisting occupation, irrelevant.

Resisting a blockade is one thing. A proposition of quite a different character, however, is that of establishing a British or NATO rapid deployment force, especially if its purpose is to ensure access to raw materials such as oil produced in other countries. Countries, like individuals, tend to exaggerate both their interests and the threats to them — witness for instance the absolute conviction of many British politicians in 1956 that the Egyptians could never operate the Suez Canal. Moreover such a rapid deployment force could easily become the instrument of a new imperialism. Most countries are not in any position to threaten or use armed force to secure access to raw materials and markets and must perforce rely upon the mutually beneficial effects of trade to secure their needs. Interestingly it is generally the larger states, or states with an imperial history, that tend to see their interests as dependent on being able to control events in distant countries — leading them often to clash with powerful rivals who view the world in a similar way.

Resisting internal threats

Threats to democratic self-government and even to autonomy can come from within a state, for instance from armed groups who may be supported by an outside power or from the military itself. Traditionally one of the functions of the military has been to 'aid the civil power' in maintaining order during civil unrest. It is the most dubious and controversial of its duties and clearly open to abuse. Yet there is sometimes a case for using military forces internally, for instance to prevent the seizure of power by an armed faction, or to help control riots that threaten a serious loss of life.

In practice the role of the military in conducting such internal functions tends at best to be ambiguous. Northern Ireland illustrates the point. The British Army was sent there in 1969 in response to pleas from the leaders of the Catholic community and as a means of preventing communal bloodshed. In the early days they probably did help to control the situation and indeed if they were now withdrawn the risk of an escalation in the level of violence is a real one, possibly even leading to a civil war. On the other hand they have also been instrumental in carrying out repressive policies, especially during the period of political internment, and there is certainly room for argument about the wisdom of retaining them there.

The Commission has not, however, attempted to deal with the complex moral, social, political and constitutional problems surrounding the question of Northern Ireland, and nor has it considered how the security problem there might best be handled. The security problem and the political and constitutional problems are in fact so closely interwoven that an attempt to deal with the security problem on its own would be artificial and likely to produce misleading conclusions. Since the Commission has concentrated mainly on defence against external threats, and on reducing the risks of nuclear war, most of the strategies we discuss are not affected by whatever decision is eventually made about the political future of the province.

Assisting in European defence

Wars and invasions occurring in the region in which a country is situated can pose an immediate and acute threat to its security. This is the logic behind the regional security pacts and military alliances we find in many parts of the world.

For Britain the security of Western Europe is a matter of legitimate concern. Firstly, if Western Europe were occupied or controlled by a hostile power, Britain would be placed in a vulnerable situation. Secondly, there are cultural, political, economic — and at present of course military — ties with Western Europe. Britain's military commitment is expressed through membership of NATO and a substantial military presence in West Germany in the shape of the British Army of the Rhine (BAOR).

Membership of NATO while it retains its present strategy with regard to nuclear weapons raises serious problems for a nuclear-disarmed Britain. These are discussed in Chapter 3, along with possible alternative approaches. But Britain's interests in Western Europe should be recognised.

Contributing to global collective security

Although countries have an immediate concern for the security of the region in which they are situated, developments in quite distant areas are also important. In the end the security of any one country cannot be isolated from what is happening elsewhere. Moreover, countries do have some moral obligations to help those whose independence is threatened by external aggression, or who face the threat of genocide. This does not necessarily mean that military action is always the appropriate response, and in some situations it could make matters infinitely worse — for instance if NATO had intervened militarily to resist the Soviet intervention in Hungary in 1956 or Czechoslovakia in 1968, or if the Soviet Union had attempted to expel the United States by force from Vietnam.

It is the United Nations which in principle provides the framework for collective security; in practice it has proved largely ineffective in tackling major problems, to a considerable extent because of the rivalry and antagonism between the superpowers. It has carried out some useful peacekeeping operations, but only in Korea was it involved in a serious conflict to enforce collective security, and then only as a result of a temporary Soviet boycott of the Security Council. Moreover, it was one of the superpowers, the United States, which in practice was in charge of running the war, though formally responsible to the UN.

Various steps have been suggested to make the UN a more effective instrument for collective security and peacekeeping. The Olof Palme Commission on Disarmament and Security Issues, for instance, put forward a number of suggestions designed to make the UN more effective, at least in dealing with disputes and acts of aggression in the Third World.[4] A concordat would be necessary among the major powers not to vote against proposals for UN action to settle disputes and enforce collective security in Third World countries, and the support of the non-aligned movement would be crucial.

Collective security procedures, the Palme Commission suggests, would be designed to anticipate and prevent aggression and armed conflict, as well as enforcing the peace where necessary; thus it would include provision for sending military observations teams, and for deploying forces in advance of a conflict at the invitation of one or both parties as a means of deterring aggression. Where hostilities had broken out before a UN force had been deployed, the objective would be to bring about a cease-fire, and to station a UN force between the combatants, until the state that had crossed the recognized boundary withdrew. Where an aggressor refused to withdraw, the Security Council would consider ways of enforcing its will, including the imposition of mandatory economic sanctions, and in addition the UN forces would of course have the right to defend themselves if attacked. Full-scale collective security enforcement action would imply the use of military means to restore the status quo that existed before the attack, but the Palme Commission recognized that this was not a realisable goal in the immediate future; however it saw it as one towards which the international community should work.

As part of the process of strengthening UN collective security and peacekeeping operations, the Palme Commission proposes the creation of permanent stand-by forces which could be deployed regionally and would be particularly important in regions where enforcement action was likely to be required. Regional security organisations would be encouraged to co-operate in this process, and individual member states to include provision for the training of their forces for such operations. Appropriate means of automatic funding would also have to be established.

Probably the greatest difficulty in this proposal would be in persuading the major powers to agree to the suggested concordat. The Third World has become very much the battleground for the rivalry between the superpowers, and the latter have shown themselves willing on various occasions to give covert or open support to the territorial ambitions of regimes which they regard as friendly. Thus the United States, far from restraining the Suharto regime in Indonesia when it invaded the former Portuguese colony of East Timor in 1975, continued supplying it with arms and equipment, including a squadron of OV-10 counter-insurgency aircraft that was vital to the operation.[5] Similarly, it is hard to see how the UN could enforce collective security in one of the world's most dangerous trouble spots, the Middle East, while the superpowers (among others) continue to pour arms into the area and to give diplomatic support to friendly or client states.

There is, moreover, the question as to whether it would even be desirable for the UN to become engaged in major military operations, on the scale of, for instance, the Korean war, to enforce collective security. It may be that the approach of using the UN as a means of exercising diplomatic, political and economic pressure, and engaging in peacekeeping and limited collective security operations is the best that can be achieved at the present time.

The Commission however supports in general the notion that the UN role should be strengthened. An important objective of British policy therefore should be to bring this about, and Britain should be prepared to increase its contribution to UN peacekeeping operations.

II. Framing a defence policy

Having established the main objectives of defence, what are the considerations that should influence the framing of a policy, or the restructuring of an existing one?

First it has to be recognized that there is no ideal, and certainly no risk-free policy. Moreover, as any given strategy will be more effective in some respects than others, the choice of strategy reflects value judgements about defence priorities, and about the risks and opportunities afforded by different approaches. A nuclear-based strategy largely reflects the judgement that the threat of massive retaliation is the best way to prevent nuclear war, but it involves a willingness to wage it and to countenance a nuclear holocaust should the deterrent fail. A non-nuclear policy lowers the level of threat, but for that reason may be more credible.

Second, there is an element of deterrence in any defence policy, not simply in nuclear-based defence. A distinction can, however, be drawn between retaliatory deterrence which threatens destruction of the opponent's society in the event of war, and defensive deterrence which directly threatens mainly the forces that are used in an attack.

Third, there is an important political dimension to security which defence planners have to take into account. Clearly, political settlements provide a more secure foundation for peace than any military threats; the security situation within Western Europe for instance has been transformed by the integration of West Germany in the Western economic and political system.

However, political settlements are not always possible, and so countries have to take precautions against outside attack; moreover, a sound security policy may provide the basis for political agreement. But it is important to avoid as far as possible postures which could be interpreted as provocative and threatening by other states, thereby diminishing the prospects of political understanding and agreements upon which security ultimately depends. Defensive deterrence aims to be non-provocative in this way.

Defence itself may also take on a political form. Propaganda, for instance, aimed at affecting the morale of the opponent or influencing third parties, has become a central feature of modern war. Plans for non-co-operation by the civilian population could also threaten to deny to a potential aggressor the economic and political objectives that would motivate an attack. This is the basis of the concept of defence by civil, nonviolent, resistance which is discussed in Chapter 7.

Political factors may also inhibit the use of certain weapons, including nuclear weapons. But if one possesses these weapons oneself, though one may gain military deterrence, one may reduce the psychological and political constraints on their use by an opponent. Again a defence strategy has to take this into account and try to avoid steps which would tend to remove inhibitions on certain forms of warfare or make measures of disarmament more difficult to achieve; the aim indeed should be to fashion a defence policy that is conducive to disarmament rather than one that is likely to lead to an escalation of the arms race.

A related consideration is the cost of defence. Excessive military expenditure may in time undermine both the economy and social stability of a country and thus itself pose a threat to society and to its ability to defend itself effectively. In addition, the vast diversion of resources to military purposes worldwide serves to prevent the solution of some of the world's most pressing problems. And if these problems are not solved, especially that of world hunger, and of narrowing the gap between the rich and poor countries, instability and war may be the consequence. Thus the goal of drastically reducing military expenditure is a vital one, even if it is not immediately realisable.

Fourth, there is the asymmetry in warfare between defence and attack in so far as the defence has certain inherent advantages. A nation under attack has the advantage that its defenders have a better knowledge of the terrain and the way the society operates, have shorter supply lines, and generally better possibilities for mobilisation than the attacker. Therefore one does not necessarily need in a defensive strategy to match the forces of the other side but only to see that one's forces are sufficiently strong to frustrate an attack. This could be important in bringing the arms race under control, since one of the problems has always been that of defining balance where so many elements are not directly comparable. Stability, rather than exact balance, should be the goal.

Finally a non-nuclear defence strategy should seek to minimise the military advantage of the nuclear weapons that the other side may still possess. This implies decentralisation of command, and the dispersal of forces. Guerrilla warfare probably represents the ultimate form of a dispersal strategy, and in Vietnam US nuclear weapons were irrelevant in the conduct of hostilities, just as those of the Soviet Union are today in Afghanistan. Whether Britain should adopt a guerrilla strategy depends on broader considerations which are dealt with later in the report. A dispersal strategy would not of course prevent the political use of nuclear weapons, for instance bombing or threatening to bomb cities to secure capitulation; here it is the political constraints that are paramount.

III. *The rationale for rejecting nuclear weapons*

The pros and cons of nuclear deterrence, and of Britain's retaining a nuclear capacity, have been widely debated.[6] It is not therefore our intention here to repeat all these arguments, but simply to indicate some of the principal reasons why the Commission's work is based on the proposition that Britain should reject a nuclear-based defence, and look towards alternative strategies.

There are various interpretations of what is implied by a non-nuclear defence of Britain. This can be taken to mean simply that Britain should renounce its own nuclear weapons. A second proposition is that it should, in addition to this, ask the United States to remove nuclear weapons from British territory. Finally there is the view — which the Commission accepts — that for strategic and moral reasons Britain should go still further and should seek to avoid any reliance on the nuclear weapons of other states. There are strong arguments in favour of Britain's abandoning the attempt to maintain an independent deterrent, and seeking the removal of US nuclear bases from this country. Although the Commission believes that Britain has to take the logic of rejecting nuclear weapons further than this, many of the points made in this section apply to the more limited interpretations of British nuclear disarmament.

The strategic argument

The British Bomb

The strategic argument for Britain's retaining its own nuclear deterrent falls into three parts: first, that it enhances the deterrent posture of the Western Alliance; second, that it could be used in the last resort to deter Soviet nuclear attack or nuclear blackmail if at some future time Britain found itself on its own confronting the Soviet Union; third, that we must look to a future in which there are many nuclear powers and Britain would be vulnerable to nuclear blackmail or attack if it had given up its own Bomb.

Britain's nuclear arsenal, though small by comparision with the superpowers, is formidable. Its strategic deterrent comprises four submarines each carrying 16 missiles with three warheads; the missiles are supplied by the United States and depend on US satellites for targeting; the submarines and warheads are British. The force is assigned to NATO, but Britain reserves the right to use its weapons independently in its own defence in an emergency; how far it would be capable of doing so without the assistance of the USA in providing targeting information has been questioned but need not detain us here.

In the 1990s Polaris is due to be replaced by the Trident D5 submarine-launched missile system under a similar arrangement with the USA. It will mean a quantum leap in Britain's nuclear capability. Each submarine will carry 16 missiles, but each of these will be capable of carrying up to 14 warheads which, unlike the three warheads on each existing Polaris missile, are independently target-able. With such a system Britain would have the capacity to destroy 200 or more Soviet cities, thus greatly exceeding the criterion of a capacity to inflict unacceptable damage in a retaliatory second strike.

In addition, Britain has a wide-ranging theatre and tactical nuclear capacity. The RAF has some 200 strike aircraft, including Vulcans, Buccaneers and Jaguars equipped with British nuclear bombs and Nimrods equipped with US nuclear depth bombs. 48 Vulcans and 36 Buccaneers are being replaced by 220 of the strike version of the Tornado multi-role combat aircraft during the 1980s. In addition the RAF will deploy 60 nuclear-capable Harrier GR5 aircraft from 1984 onwards. There are reports that the Tornados could be adapted to carry air-launched cruise missiles and thus provide a possible alternative to the Trident programme as a way of maintaining British strategic nuclear forces.[7]

The British Army of the Rhine has a smaller number of US Lance artillery missiles which can deliver a kiloton-range warhead over a distance of 75 miles. It also has 16 M110 nuclear-capable howitzers and 50 M109 guns. A further 69 M109 guns are now being deployed. The warheads for these three systems are under joint British/US control through a dual key system and are not technically part of Britain's independent deterrent. The Royal Navy deploys over 70 nuclear-capable helicopters — Sea King, Wessex, Wasp and Lynx — able to deliver British nuclear depth bombs, and also has Sea Harriers capable of delivering British free-fall nuclear weapons. Though all this constitutes a formidable armoury, the argument that it enhances NATO's deterrent rests not on the proposition that it increases the overall firepower available, but rather on the claim that Britain's deterrent plays a distinctive role within the Alliance. The claim rests essentially on what is known as the 'second centre' argument. As the 1981 Defence White Paper puts it:

"The crucial role which our nuclear forces play in enhancing Alliance security lies in providing a nuclear deterrent capability committed to the Alliance yet fully under the control of a European member. Even if in some future situation Soviet leaders imagined that the United States might not be prepared to use nuclear weapons, having to take account of enormous destructive power in European hands would compel them to regard the risks of aggression in Europe as still very grave. This additional element of insurance — the 'second centre of decision' — has been a feature of Alliance deterrence for over twenty-five years."[8]

We are dealing here with rather complicated calculations about the perceptions and psychology not only of our potential adversary but also of our allies, and it is hard to know whether the British Bomb does in fact provide additional insurance rather than devaluing the insurance in the shape of the US nuclear guarantee that we already have in the present NATO context. It could be, for instance, that by insisting on having an independent deterrent, we may signal to the Soviet Union that we ourselves do not fully trust the US nuclear guarantee, thereby encouraging them too to question its credibility. Of course there would still be sufficient uncertainty about the situation to deter a Soviet attack under normal circumstances; in a dire emergency, however, or moment of panic, the Soviet Union might be somewhat more willing to risk an attack if there were clear signals that the West European governments did not really believe that the United States would risk its own destruction on their behalf.

Would the Soviet Union in that situation be deterred by what amounts to a British nuclear guarantee to NATO? The argument is that it might be, because Britain's stake in Europe is greater than that of the United States — it has more to lose if Western Europe succumbs to a Soviet attack; against this has to be set the fact that Britain is more vulnerable than the USA to Soviet nuclear attack. It seems scarcely credible therefore that Britain would actually initiate the use of nuclear weapons in response to a Soviet conventional attack on Western Europe. So if the situation was desperate enough to the Soviet Union to gamble on the United States holding back, it would hardly be deterred by a British threat which is somewhat less credible in the first place. In the context of an alliance, two nuclear threats are not necessarily better than one, since they may signal internal confusion and lack of confidence rather than resolve.

Anything which appears to cast doubt on the viability of NATO's decision making process in an emergency, or which complicates that process, could erode the credibility of deterrence rather than enhancing it.[9] At the critical moment, for instance, the USA might be inclined to hold back from using its nuclear weapons because it would prefer Britain to strike the first blow, perhaps in order to avoid the opprobrium of initiating nuclear war, and because it would be anxious to delay, or avoid altogether if possible, a decision that would risk starting the full-scale nuclear exchange between it and the Soviet Union; however, Britain for its part might well hesitate too, knowing what the consequences for itself would be if it resorted to nuclear weapons.[10]

It is sometimes suggested that the British use of nuclear weapons in an emergency would act as a trigger to the US deterrent, ensuring that the USA could not renege on its nuclear commitment to Europe — and that therefore the Soviet Union has to take the US guarantee that much more seriously. But this does not meet the objection that Britain would not want to invite annihilation by initiating the process of nuclear escalation. Moreover, it is far from certain that such a British action if it did occur would result in the USA being prepared to redeem its nuclear pledge to Europe; indeed in these circumstances its leaders, angered by the attempt of a European state to preempt a decision which could cost millions of American lives, might be at pains to let the Soviet Union know exactly where the attack had come from. In that case the British action would have been entirely counter-productive, bringing about exactly the decoupling of the US strategic deterrent from West European defence that it was intended to prevent. For its part the Soviet Union, no less anxious to avoid the final showdown than the USA, might be more than willing to accept the assurances of the US government, and to confine its retaliation in the first instance to Britain.

There are further arguments on both sides, but the proposition that British nuclear weapons enhance NATO deterrence is at best questionable and would certainly not on its own justify a British decision to go on deploying them at a rapidly increasing cost. What of the second argument that they would in the last resort deter a Soviet attack on Britain itself?

The scenario here is usually set at some time in the future when the situation in Western Europe is assumed to have radically changed; NATO for instance might have been dissolved, and the US forces, together with the US nuclear guarantee, have been withdrawn. As Defence Secretary, Mr Nott, for instance, justifying the decision to acquire the Trident D4 missile system, argued that we could not know what the position might be in 30 or 40 years time — though this could also have been a diplomatic way of saying that even as things are Britain must look to its own devices and not place too much trust in the US nuclear umbrella.[11] In the more pessimistic scenarios, the Soviet Union would have taken control of the rest of Western Europe, and would be seeking to complete the task by securing the capitulation of Britain.

If, for whatever reason, Britain did find itself on its own confronting a hostile Soviet Union, it is true that without nuclear weapons it would ultimately be vulnerable to Soviet nuclear escalation or blackmail. The Soviet Union might, for instance, try to neutralise British conventional forces by the threat that unless they surrendered Britain would face an escalating series of nuclear attacks.[12] But in this extreme predicament, how much better off would Britain be if it had nuclear weapons? The threat to use them to deter or halt a Soviet conventional attack would not be very convincing unless one assumes that a British government would actually choose to see

Britain annihilated rather than capitulate. It is true, however, that as long as the British nuclear forces remained invulnerable to a Soviet first strike, they might deter the Soviet Union from attempting nuclear blackmail, or from launching an all-out nuclear attack on Britain which would mean that it would have nothing to lose by retaliating. One would then have an approximate parallel to the nuclear stand-off that exists between the superpowers at the moment.

But given the disparity in the size of the forces on either side and technological developments such as improved missile accuracy and submarine detection and tracking, the invulnerability of Britain's nuclear deterrent cannot be taken for granted. Even if a disarming first strike left Britain with some capacity to retaliate in kind, the Soviet Union could probably prevent this, and secure British capitulation, by threatening the destruction of the population if Britain used its remaining nuclear weapons.

As long ago as 1962 the then US Secretary of State for Defense, Robert McNamara, in the course of his famous speech at Ann Arbor summed up the weakness of secondary powers seeking to have an independent deterrent against a major nuclear power:

> "relatively weak nuclear forces with enemy cities as their targets are not likely to be sufficient to perform even the function of deterrence. If they are small, and perhaps vulnerable on the ground or in the air, or inaccurate, a major antagonist can take a variety of measures to counter them. Indeed, if a major antagonist came to believe there was a substantial likelihood of it being used independently, this force would be inviting a 'pre-emptive' first strike against it. In the event of war, the use of such a force against cities of a major nuclear power would be tantamount to suicide, while its employment against significant military targets would have a negligible effect on the outcome of the conflict . . . In short then, limited nuclear capabilities, operating independently, are dangerous, expensive, prone to obsolescence and lacking in credibility as a deterrent."[13]

If Britain possessed nuclear weapons it could reasonably hope to deter Soviet nuclear attack or blackmail so long as its nuclear forces remained invulnerable. But it could not be confident that they would remain so, and it would risk inviting a pre-emptive nuclear attack that would destroy it as a society. Moreover, leaving aside the question of whether its nuclear forces might become vulnerable to a first strike, the danger of a nuclear war by accident or miscalculation would apply in this situation as it applies today in the confrontation between the superpowers. Simply on grounds of prudence therefore, there is a strong case for saying that Britain should reject the notion of retaining nuclear weapons as an insurance against an eventual confrontation on its own with the Soviet Union.

The third line of argument is that Britain should retain its nuclear weapons because if proliferation continues it may one day need them to prevent nuclear attack or blackmail by a state that had managed to acquire a limited nuclear capacity. Clearly a nuclear-disarmed Britain would be vulnerable in a confrontation with any state possessing nuclear weapons; moreover, if Britain retained nuclear forces, these would probably not be vulnerable to a pre-emptive first strike by a technologically less advanced opponent. This does therefore constitute a reasonable case on strategic grounds for retaining a British nuclear deterrent at some level.

But there are counter considerations. By retaining nuclear weapons Britain may be contributing to the very proliferation that this scenario envisages. Britain's stance in fact is a kind of propaganda by the deed for proliferation, and the more general the arguments advanced for its deterrent, as opposed to those which relate to Britain's specific strategic situation, the more they apply to every other state that might consider acquiring nuclear weapons.

A deterrent against future minor nuclear powers would not of course require or justify Polaris or Trident, and the British deterrent at the moment is clearly directed against a perceived Soviet threat. The cost of remaining in the nuclear club at this level is rising steeply and the question is whether a country of Britain's size and economic capacity can really afford to stay in it, and whether the money and resources would not be better invested elsewhere. Britain has managed to limit somewhat the cost of its nuclear deterrent by co-operation with the US, but this in turn has political consequences which limit Britain's freedom of action. Thus although there is no formal connection between the US co-operation in Britain's deterrent system and the presence of US bases in this country, it is hard to imagine that, if Britain requested their removal, the US co-operation in Britain's deterrent would continue. In this sense Britain's deterrent is not independent.

To sum up then, there are situations in which Britain's possession of nuclear weapons would confer some advantage, particularly if it confronted a minor nuclear power at some time in the future. But Britain's continued possession of nuclear weapons may actually make it more difficult to control nuclear proliferation, and the rationale for the British deterrent in its present form is highly questionable. The British contribution to NATO deterrence is of doubtful worth, and may even be counter-productive; and it is equally doubtful if the British deterrent would be effective in the long run against Soviet nuclear blackmail if Britain in isolation confronted the Soviet Union. Clearly, however, the goal must be to greatly reduce the stocks of nuclear weapons worldwide, and to secure their eventual prohibition; until that is achieved the security of every country will continue to be threatened.

US bases in Britain

The establishment of US Air Force bases and other monitoring and supply facilities in Britain dates back to the decision to grant temporary facilities to the USAF during the Berlin Blockade in 1948. These facilities are now extensive, as Duncan Campbell reported in an article in the *New Statesman* in October 1980:

> "In Britain the US forces have at least 21 air bases used or reserved for them, 9 transportation terminals, 17 weapons dumps and stores, 7 nuclear weapons stores, 38 communications facilities, 10 intelligence bases and three radar and sonar surveillance sites. Of these the majority clearly contribute at least as much to strategic global 'US only' options as to the options for defending Europe."[14]

The arrangement for consultation with Britain over the use of the bases is vague. A joint communique in January 1952 stated that "the use of these bases in an emergency would be a matter for joint decision by H.M. Government and the US Government in the light of circumstances prevailing at the time".[15] However, in October 1973 at the time of the Arab-Israeli war, as the Kissinger memoirs testify, the US bases in Britain — as elsewhere — were put on nuclear alert without prior consultation with the British government.[16]

The presence of US bases and facilities means that Britain would be in the front line of nuclear warfare if deterrence should fail. Moreover, given the looseness of the consultation arrangements, and the fact that some of the facilities relate to the US global role, Britain could find itself facing destruction over a situation in which it felt the US had acted wrongly or irresponsibly.

Accepting some US nuclear bases with a clear agreement that they could be used for war only with prior British agreement would be an honourable and reasonable risk to take if one accepted that the US nuclear umbrella was right and necessary for West European (including British) security, and that this required such bases in Europe. However, the withdrawal of nuclear weapons from outside the territory of the two superpowers would represent a step in the direction of accepting a minimal deterrent posture, and one that the Commission recommends as part of a package of measures aimed at raising the nuclear threshold. We also put the argument in Chapter 3 for the view that, far from seeking a US nuclear guarantee, the European states in NATO should seek to decouple the US strategic deterrent from European defence. Finally, if nuclear weapons are rejected on moral grounds, this implies that one does not ask another country to threaten or wage nuclear war on one's behalf or grant it facilities to do so.

The erosion of deterrence

There is a rational basis to the notion of nuclear deterrence; it is in effect a very old notion writ large. With conventional warfare, however, if deterrence failed there was the possibility of fighting and winning a war, whereas nuclear war would be a catastrophe for all concerned. To this extent the situation has changed fundamentally.

There is no doubt that the existence of nuclear weapons has induced caution in the leaders of the superpowers. It would be surprising if this were not so, for no rational person would lightly risk embroiling the country or the world in nuclear war. We know also from published correspondence that the fear of nuclear war induced Khruschev to back down during the Cuban missile crisis. However, the example is instructive in another sense, for the crisis was very much a product of nuclear deterrence since it arose out of the Soviet wish to have missiles as close to the US heartland as the US already had them to the Soviet Union. It is a reminder that deterrence is only one aspect of maintaining peace, and that it can be pursued to the point of being counter-productive.

Nuclear weapons have inspired suspicion and heightened tensions as well as inducing caution. Perhaps the US monopoly of these weapons in the immediate post-World War II period deterred Stalin from extending his control over Western Europe — that is still a matter of debate among historians and political analysts. It certainly, however, contributed to the suspicion that caused a rapid deterioration of East/West relations at the end of the war and to the onset of the Cold War. This is why the claim, which the 1981 Defence White Paper sees as commonsense, that nuclear weapons have prevented a global conflict since 1945 needs to be treated with caution. But in any case the real question now is whether we can go on taking the appalling risks that nuclear deterrence involves.

Nuclear weapons became a factor of strategic importance as soon as the first atomic bombs were dropped on Hiroshima and Nagasaki in 1945. From then until 1949 the US had a monopoly of atomic weapons and for some years thereafter it retained an undisputed nuclear predominance. Nevertheless, it was not until the 'new look' in defence in 1953 under Eisenhower that the threat of massive retaliation was established as the cornerstone of US policy. The doctrine was formally enunciated in a speech by the US Secretary of State, John Foster Dulles, in January 1954, in which he declared that henceforth the United States would seek to deter the Soviet Union by having "a greater capacity to retaliate, instantly, by means and at places of our own choosing".[17] During the previous year, tactical nuclear weapons were introduced into Europe as a means of strengthening NATO conventional defence.

The problem with the massive retaliation doctrine was to define what level of aggression or subversion would elicit the nuclear response, and this problem became more evident as the Soviet nuclear capability increased. Thermonuclear weapons, which could be made thousands of times more powerful than atomic bombs, were developed by both sides by the mid-1950s, and by the end of the decade each had intercontinental missiles capable of striking the heartland of the opponent. Two new strategic doctrines gradually emerged out of this situation, that of mutual deterrence and that of flexible response.

Mutual deterrence (or mutually assured destruction as it became known) required that each side would have an assured second strike capacity, so that if either were tempted to launch a nuclear attack they would know for certain that this would entail the destruction of their own society. Although the doctrine has been modified by the concept of flexible response, mutual deterrence is still the basis for trying to prevent an all-out nuclear attack by either side. The two SALT treaties (Strategic Arms Limitations Talks) are in effect a formal recognition of the essential strategic parity between the super-powers, and SALT I ABM Treaty (1972) imposes limits on the development of certain kinds of anti-ballistic missile system which in principle could have threatened the concept of mutual deterrence by providing protection against a second strike.

Today it is other technological developments, in conjunction with shifts in strategic doctrine, that are threatening the always precarious stability of this system. The development of extremely accurate missiles, each containing a number of warheads that can be inde-pendently targeted, means that even missiles in specially hardened silos may become vulnerable to attack, while satellite reconnaissance and improvements in submarine detection could mean eventually that no missiles could be concealed without the possibility of detection. The notion of a first strike that would completely disarm the other side at the nuclear level is, and is likely to remain, an illusion. But these developments could mean that the side that struck first might perceive that it had a significant advantage, and the danger is that during a period of exceptional tension, such as the Cuba crisis, each side would be tempted to take the initiative if only in anticipation of a pre-emptive strike by the other side.

The accuracy of missiles and warheads, and the very short warning period if missiles are launched from submarines lying off the coast, or from territories near to the target country, increases the danger of 'accidental' or unpremeditated war, again especially in periods of heightened tension. And whereas strategic bombers could be recalled when mistakes in the interpretation of radar signals had been detected, the same is almost certainly not true of missiles.

Flexible response, formally adopted by NATO in 1967, is an attempt to meet the problem that the threat of massive retaliation in response to any level of attack is not credible in the circumstances of approximate strategic parity. Flexible response envisages that Soviet aggression would be dealt with at the appropriate level, and is based on a triad of forces — conventional, 'theatre' nuclear weapons, and the central strategic deterrent. However, the concept of using 'theatre' weapons (which in this case includes both the short-range 'battlefield' nuclear weapons and the intermediate-range weapons based in Europe),[18] to contain an overwhelming Soviet conventional attack is retained. Today battlefield nuclear weapons are so closely integrated with conventional weapons, on both sides, that there is a danger that any conventional conflict will quickly lead to the use of nuclear weapons and escalate to all-out nuclear war.

The case in favour of current strategy is succinctly put in the 1981 Defence White Paper. The facts of geography, it argues, and the "totalitarian direction of resources" give the Soviet Union a massive preponderance in Europe at the conventional level. For the Western democracies to attempt to match this would impose enormous economic and social costs, and the resulting forces would still not make Western nuclear weapons unnecessary. Nuclear weapons are needed to redress the balance, and it makes sense to have a range of nuclear weapons — presumably because this makes the nuclear threat more credible; escalation from theatre to all-out nuclear war is a matter of human decision "not an inexorable scientific process". Thus it is "perfectly sensible — indeed essential — to make plans which could increase and exploit whatever chance there might be of ending war short of global catastrophe''. But the Statement insists that this does not mean that the West has a 'war-fighting' strategy; theatre and battlefield nuclear weapons are seen as a way of extending the reach of nuclear deterrence to cover conventional aggression, and since ''a non-nuclear war between East and West is by far the likeliest road to nuclear war'', they are a vital element in the deterrence system.

However, the wisdom of threatening nuclear retaliation in response to a Soviet conventional attack is being increasingly questioned, including by those who in other respects accept the need for nuclear deterrence, such as the former British Chief of the Defence Staff, Lord Carver, and the former US Defense Secretary, Robert McNamara;[19] the Defence White Paper also overstates the preponderance of Soviet conventional forces in Europe at the present time, thereby in effect dismissing the possibility of an adequate Western conventional system of defence. However much one may insist that one is not thinking in terms of a nuclear war-fighting option, the logic of deploying battlefield nuclear weapons, and of arguing that escalation to the strategic level is not inevitable, is that one is bound to start doing so. The confusion in fact is only too clear in the conflicting statements in November 1981 by the then US Secretary of State, Alexander Haig, and the US Defense Secretary, Caspar Weinberger, and indeed in statements and retractions by President Reagan himself.[20]

The Defence White Paper is not persuasive either in its defence of what it terms ''non-city target options'' — i.e. weapons aimed at destroying the nuclear weapons or other military targets of the other side. The objective we are told is not to fight a limited nuclear war but ''to help ensure that even if an adversary believed in limited nuclear war (as Soviet writings sometimes suggest) he could not expect actually to win one'' — which sounds remarkably like saying that we are, however reluctantly, considering a war-fighting option. There is no consideration either of how these 'non-city target options', or 'counter-force options' as they are sometimes called, are eroding the concept of mutual deterrence, and no acknowledgement that it is the West that has led the way, and is still far ahead, in developing the technology for a counter-force strategy.

The hazards of current NATO strategy in Europe have led a number of strategic analysts on both sides of the Atlantic to insist on the need for certain changes, notably the adoption of a no-first-use of nuclear weapons policy. On its side the Soviet Union has proposed such an agreement on a number of occasions, most recently at the

UN Special Session on Disarmament in June 1982, where it also declared that it was adopting this policy unilaterally and inviting the West to reciprocate.

The central argument in favour of this step is that the 'firebreak' between nuclear and non-nuclear weapons should be kept as wide and clear as possible because of the probability that any use of nuclear weapons by either side would escalate to all-out nuclear war. The effect would be that nuclear weapons during the period that they continued to be deployed would have the sole function of deterring a nuclear attack by the other side.

In line with this approach, battlefield nuclear weapons should be phased out at an early stage in the process of nuclear disarmament. At present tactical nuclear weapons of diverse types are closely integrated with the weapon systems, force structures and tactical plans of both NATO and the Warsaw Pact. These tactical nuclear weapons include many different kinds of free-fall nuclear bombs, nuclear depth charges, mines, torpedos, stand-off missiles, artillery shells, ground-to-air missiles and even air-to-air missiles.

Whilst the Commission does not support any policies which could involve the waging of a nuclear war, it recognizes that nuclear weapons are not likely to be abolished all at once, and that it is important to reduce some of the most immediate dangers. Thus we argue in Chapter 3 that the most urgent steps needed in Europe are the adoption of a policy of no-first-use of nuclear weapons and the withdrawal of so-called battlefield nuclear weapons. The Commission also supports the efforts to prevent the deployment of new battlefield weapons, such as the neutron bomb, and of the intermediate range cruise and Pershing II missiles. Finally the conclusion of a Comprehensive Test Ban Treaty, by inhibiting the development of new nuclear weapons, would enhance both European and global security.

Deterrence however is perhaps being most seriously undermined by the development of highly accurate long-range missiles and of anti-submarine warfare capabilities. Should it ever become possible to track and destroy the majority of the opponent's missile-carrying submarines, and to locate and destroy enemy missiles in their silos, the temptation to strike first in a moment of acute crisis would become dangerously strong. In such a context nuclear weapons, far from inducing caution and thereby contributing to stability in periods of crisis, could increase the likelihood of a crisis ending in war. The timetable for such a transformation is unclear, but counter-silo missiles such as the modified Minuteman III ICBM are already deployed in small numbers and the Reagan administration is pressing for the deployment of the MX missile system.

It is less clear what Britain and the rest of West Europe can do to halt this process, except to underline the dangers, and use the disarmament initiatives they are prepared to take themselves as a means of creating a more favourable climate for negotiations between the superpowers. The renewed strategic arms talks (START) between the US and the Soviet Union in Geneva in 1982 owe something to the pressure from the European disarmament movements and show that European governments and movements do have some leverage.

Lastly, deterrence is being undermined by the spread of nuclear weapons. India has already exploded a nuclear weapon and it seems likely that Israel (and possibly South Africa) already have nuclear weapons; over the next two decades many others are likely, on present trends, to acquire them. Probable candidates are Argentina, Brazil, Egypt, Iraq, Libya, Pakistan and South Korea. None of these countries is likely to be decisively influenced by a British decision to renounce its nuclear weapons since they have mainly their own regional concerns in mind. But if Britain's action was part of a major international effort to halt proliferation, it would have a chance of exercising some restraining influence. Britain's action could in fact help to give greater credibility to the existing Nuclear Non-Proliferation Treaty, since in principle it obliges those states possessing nuclear weapons to move towards nuclear disarmament as soon as possible. Again it would be important in the context of trying to halt proliferation to press for the adoption of a Comprehensive Test Ban Treaty.

Confronting a nuclear opponent

The central problem about relying purely on conventional defence against a nuclear adversary is that the opponent can in the last analysis deliver a nuclear ultimatum — either surrender or we will take out one or more of your major cities — or can resort to tactical or strategic nuclear attacks to bring about capitulation in the course of a war. It is this possibility of nuclear blackmail or escalation which has led many people who are far from being morally unconcerned to support the notion of nuclear deterrence.

The bombing of Hiroshima and Nagasaki by the United States in 1945 is often cited as proof of the need for a nuclear deterrent. There are in fact two separate issues here. The first is whether in the particular historical circumstances of 1945 the USA would have been deterred from using atomic bombs if Japan had also managed to develop these weapons; the second is whether the US action is a reliable indication of what one can expect in the future of a nuclear power at war with a non-nuclear state.[21]

The first question is finally unanswerable; so much depends on the circumstances surrounding this suggested scenario. Thus it would be fanciful to imagine Japan possessing more than one or two atomic bombs at that date (the US itself had only two), so that one can imagine the possibility of a pre-emptive strike by the United States. And if both sides had been feverishly working on the project in the course of the war, it is quite conceivable that some expected relative advantage in a nuclear exchange might have prompted one side or the other to risk a nuclear attack.

It is the second question that is more pertinent to the present discussion. Here it is important to point out that in 1945 very few people knew of the existence of nuclear weapons and there was no widespread revulsion against their use to act as a restraining influence on the US leadership. Today the extent of this revulsion has become a political factor which any nuclear power has to take into account, especially in its dealings with non-nuclear countries. Nevertheless Hiroshima and Nagasaki are a reminder of the appalling danger of nuclear escalation in a major war at the present time.

Political constraints on the use of nuclear weapons, especially against non-nuclear opponents, have played a part in preventing their use since the end of World War II. The USA did not use them either in Korea or Vietnam (though their use in the Korean war was contemplated), and the Soviet Union is not going to use them against guerrilla fighters in Afghanistan. It is of course particularly difficult to use nuclear weapons against a guerrilla opponent whose forces are dispersed and often to a large extent invisible, and where there may be no obvious centre of political control to be blackmailed into surrender. But these considerations did not apply in Korea, and it was certainly political factors that were of paramount importance. Neither side has wanted, or would in the future lightly risk, the scandal and outrage, and the consequent loss of moral and political authority, that would result from using nuclear weapons against a non-nuclear opponent.

There are also economic reasons in an inter-dependent world economy for avoiding the devastation of important centres of production which are also markets for the sale of one's own products. The destruction of Western Europe, for instance, would cause immense problems throughout Eastern Europe and in the Soviet

Union. The point should not of course be overstated. The destruction of one or two cities and the threat to take out others would probably be sufficient to ensure the capitulation of one or even several countries that had no capacity to retaliate in kind; but considerations of economic self-interest would be an additional brake on any Soviet resort to nuclear weapons.

The problem does nevertheless have to be taken into account because longer-term political developments are unpredictable and because it is a requirement of a defence strategy to consider the response that could be made to any given level of escalation by the potential opponent. British nuclear disarmament, and the renunciation of any reliance on nuclear weapons by other governments in Western Europe, is a possibility if the nuclear disarmament movements continue to gain strength, and the eventual result could be the total withdrawal of nuclear weapons from Western Europe and decoupling of the US strategic nuclear deterrent from European defence. If that happened, or of course if the NATO Alliance itself dissolved, Western Europe could in principle be subjected to nuclear blackmail or attack without a serious likelihood of retaliation (to avoid over-complicating the argument we largely ignore the problem of French nuclear weapons at this point). If Britain alone, and not the rest of Europe, renounced any reliance on nuclear weapons, the likelihood of its being subjected to nuclear blackmail would be small, though it could not be ruled out altogether.

There are a number of possible approaches to defence which non-nuclear states can adopt when their potential adversary is a nuclear power. One approach is to say that a sufficiently strong system of conventional defence should be maintained to deter the opponent from risking a conventional attack in the expectation that political considerations would prevent the opponent from using nuclear weapons or delivering a nuclear ultimatum. Another is to say that there should also be preparations for either guerrilla warfare or non-violent resistance as a fall-back strategy. A more radical option is to say that defence by nonviolent, civil resistance should become the central element in a defence policy.

The case for maintaining strong conventional forces is that it raises the military and political costs to any aggressor. Either the aggressor must be prepared to engage in a conventional war at a disproportionate military cost or to face the unique opprobrium of using, or threatening to use, nuclear weapons against a non-nuclear country. If little or no military opposition was to be expected, the opponent might be tempted to risk a military adventure, for instance seizing areas of some strategic or economic importance to it, or even embarking on a full-scale occupation. Sweden, Switzerland and Yugoslavia maintain a high degree of military readiness; none has taken the view that the Soviet possession of nuclear weapons renders its own military preparations irrelevant. In varying degrees all three countries have fall-back strategies, though these are not principally focused on dealing with the nuclear threat. Yugoslavia has made extensive preparations for conducting a guerrilla war in the event of occupation, and both Sweden and Switzerland envisage at least a limited role for civil resistance.

Later in this Report we consider guerrilla warfare and civil resistance at some length and the roles they might play in an overall defence system. The need to have a fall-back strategy if one is relying principally on conventional defence was recognised by the Commission, and it was agreed also, for reasons discussed in Chapter 6, that guerrilla warfare was less likely to play a major role in the British context, or in highly industrialised societies generally; it tends moreover to be extremely divisive and destructive. How central a role civil resistance might play in defence is a more open question.

Facing a nuclear ultimatum. The response that a country could make if faced with a nuclear ultimatum would vary according to the context and to its own defence policy. A specifically nuclear threat is not very likely against a country or group of countries that had substantially disarmed and had adopted a strategy of nonviolent defence, if only because other forms of military pressure would be available to an opponent. The problem is rather more likely to arise where a country or alliance relies mainly on conventional defence.

Even then a nuclear ultimatum is not likely to come as a bolt out of the blue; it is likely only if there is a war actually in progress or if countries are on the very brink of war. The idea that nuclear black-mail would be applied recurrently to secure political and other concessions does not seem convincing to us and is not suggested by the experience of smaller states dealing with the nuclear powers over more than thirty years.

If the nuclear ultimatum was delivered at a time of acute crisis, but before a war was actually in progress, there would probably be some scope for exerting political pressure on the nuclear opponent to withdraw the threat. This might be done through the UN and other international bodies, or through initiatives by individual states, perhaps even by some states with close links with the nuclear power making the threat.

If it became clear that the opponent was not bluffing and would not respond to moral and political pressure, the countries under threat could finally be forced to capitulate and to accept the terms demanded. This would probably mean having to endure occupation; it is much less likely that a nuclear ultimatum would be used to compel a country to make other political and economic concessions. In principle a nuclear threat could be used to force a country to accept a client regime, or to accede to a set of demands which would limit its independence and freedom of manoeuvre in the future. But client regimes are in a very difficult situation where they command no popular support and are not necessarily able to deliver what is required of them — as Poland has demonstrated. There are also enormous difficulties about repeatedly threatening nuclear destruction to manipulate a country's foreign and domestic policy from outside; thus the Soviet Union does not in reality have the option of using the nuclear threat to crush the popular resistance in Poland.

If occupation did occur, or if a client regime was imposed, the fall-back strategies of guerrilla warfare or civil resistance could be resorted to. The aim would be to deny to a government or occupying force effective political and economic control of the country and it would help to keep alive the spirit of freedom and the possibility of eventual liberation; as we indicate in Chapters 6 and 7, the defeat of the state does not have to mean the surrender of the people.

This is not, however, to suggest that political pressure and non-violent resistance could be counted on to bring a quick or painless victory against an aggressor. But then there simply are no defence options that can guarantee immunity from attack or can guarantee victory. Nuclear deterrence, however, involves a qualitatively different order of risks, and it is only when the measure of these risks has been taken that other risks can be evaluated and confronted.

If a nuclear ultimatum occurred in the course of a European war, the states under threat would probably have to accept the terms demanded without delay. Again a fall-back strategy of guerrilla or nonviolent resistance could be resorted to if an occupation was imposed. The problems of organising such resistance would depend in part on how destructive the war had been.

There is one temptation that a nuclear-disarmed state should firmly resist, namely to gamble on the possibility that while both superpowers have nuclear weapons neither will dare to use, or threaten to use, them anywhere for fear of provoking a nuclear holocaust. Non-aligned countries may at times, and to some degree, have that kind of *de facto* 'nuclear cover', but it is not to be relied upon. Moreover, a country that had rejected nuclear weapons on principle would not want such weapons used on its behalf. A nuclear-disarmed country must therefore plan its defences as if the possibility of this kind of nuclear protection did not exist. It is all the more important for it to do so today when the superpowers have achieved approximate strategic parity with the result that the validity of even explicit nuclear guarantees is very questionable.

Inhibiting the battlefield or other military uses of nuclear weapons. The risk that an opponent might use nuclear or chemical weapons on the battlefield, or more generally against military targets, is another aspect of the overall problem we have been considering, and merits some separate attention.

This report recommends that Britain should seek to persuade NATO to give up intermediate-range, 'theatre' weapons, and short-range 'battlefield' nuclear weapons — as well as chemical weapons — and that any alternative military alliance in Europe that might replace NATO should be non-nuclear. Clearly if Western Europe adopted this non-nuclear approach, the first step would be to use diplomatic means to encourage reciprocal action by the Soviet Union and to try to conclude a formal agreement under which both sides would renounce such weapons. But it is impossible to rely on such an outcome, and at present the Soviet forces are equipped with battlefield nuclear weapons, and the Soviet Union also deploys many intermediate range nuclear weapons such as the SS4, SS5 and SS20 missiles and a variety of medium- and long-range aircraft.

There are military problems associated with the strictly battlefield use of nuclear weapons because of radiation and fall-out — though these problems can be at least partially overcome by the wearing of protective clothing. Moreover, deploying tactical nuclear weapons in the hope of deterring their use by the other side is a policy that could backfire since it might tempt the opponent to make a pre-emptive nuclear strike. Sweden and Switzerland decided against acquiring battlefield nuclear weapons for tactical reasons. Despite the possible military advantages, they concluded that the possession of such weapons would increase the likelihood of an enemy using them first, that their own use of them would invite retaliation, and that in any case to use them on their own territory would be too destructive.

What then could a nuclear-disarmed Western Europe do unilaterally to reduce the danger of Soviet battlefield or other purely military use of nuclear weapons?

First, it could seek to strengthen the political inhibitions on the first use of nuclear weapons of whatever category. This would partly depend on creating an international climate of abhorrence in advance, but NATO, or any alternative European alliance, could issue a public reminder at the outbreak of war, or at a moment of acute crisis when war seemed imminent, that it had no nuclear weapons and would not sanction any use of them on its behalf.

Second, Europe could try to avoid Soviet pre-emptive nuclear action by assuaging genuine fears: advance inspection measures, for instance, could go some way to convincing the Soviet Union that tactical nuclear weapons had indeed been removed. The main problem with this is that such weapons can be concealed without much difficulty so that a foolproof system of inspection is probably not possible. Western Europe could also avoid the use of missiles which can be fitted with conventional explosives but which are especially associated with nuclear warheads, such as cruise missiles.

Third, Europe could adopt a strategy which reduced the numbers of military targets that would warrant a nuclear attack. Since battle-field nuclear weapons would be most effective against concentrations of troops and tanks, the dispersal of forces would minimise the impact of a nuclear attack. Command and control structures could also be de-centralised to reduce the impact of intermediate-range nuclear weapons against military targets.

Clearly none of these measures provides a complete answer to the problem. If war breaks out, the Soviet leaders might not be inhibited by the moral and political pressures against the use of nuclear weapons, and these constraints would in any case be somewhat weakened if France remained a nuclear power. Moreover, the extensive use of intermediate-range nuclear weapons behind the battlelines could strike a terrible blow to any system of defence, and as the attacker would not need to move in troops quickly, the problem of exposing them to fall-out would probably not arise. And however dispersed one's forces, however decentralised one's command and control structures, the effect on morale of the battle-field and other military uses of nuclear weapons by an opponent would still have to be reckoned with, and might be more important than the actual losses of troops and equipment.

Factors which might tend to inhibit the Soviet military use of nuclear weapons are firstly the disadvantages, in the case of short-range weapons, of irradiating areas where one's own troops are operating; and secondly the economic and political problems which a massive destruction of Western Europe would cause the Soviet

Union and Eastern Europe. The fact that the Soviet use of nuclear weapons requires a top-level political decision might also lessen the risk of their rash or unpremeditated use.

An alternative defence strategy cannot remove the threat of nuclear weapons being used on the battlefield or against other military targets, but it can try to strengthen political inhibitions, minimise any threat which may be perceived by the other side, and limit, at least to some degree, the military advantage of the opponent using nuclear weapons. The logic of this position points to a primarily defensive stance and a relatively dispersed, chequer-board deployment of forces, together with a decentralisation of command and control structures.

The moral argument

War always raises moral issues and these are posed in an acute form with weapons of mass destruction. The most critical problems arise where — however strong the reasons for resorting to war — innocent people are maimed and killed. In modern war especially, the loss of civilian life tends to be very high, and many of the combatants themselves may be victims of a coercive machine over which they have little or no control.

One response to this situation is to reject organised war altogether, or to reject it under modern conditions. The pacifist response, which has been a recurring phenomenon down the centuries, claims renewed attention today when war has become so destructive and when collective nonviolent action has shown itself capable of fulfilling at least some of the legitimate functions of armed conflict.

However, the tradition which is more widely supported, and underlies many of the provisions of international law relating to the conduct of war, is that of the just war.[22] This maintains that the cause itself must be just and sufficiently serious, and that the conduct of war must conform to the principles of discrimination and proportionality. The principle of discrimination means that the distinction between combatant and non-combatant must be maintained and that civilians may not be deliberately attacked. The principle of proportionality means that the purpose of the war must be commensurate with the suffering and loss of life that is likely to occur; at another level it implies that if civilian casualties are unavoidable in the course of an attack upon a legitimate military target there must be some reasonable proportion between this legitimate aim and the probable extent of collateral civilian casualties — and indeed there must come a point where the extent of civilian casualties would have to be recognized as inherently indiscriminate and so inherently murderous.

It is impossible to maintain that nuclear warfare conforms to these principles. The scale of destruction in an all-out war between the superpowers would be catastrophic, involving the death of hundreds of millions of people, the widespread destruction of industry and agriculture, and possibly severe and lasting damage to the environment. It would be a disaster quite without precedent in human history. Even the scenarios for 'limited' nuclear warfare, for instance where the superpowers concentrate on destroying the military targets of the other side, or where war is restricted to Europe, would involve many millions of casualties.[23] Moreover, the likelihood of such wars remaining limited is generally agreed to be slight.[24]

Unease about the moral issue is indeed reflected in certain government statements. Thus in the 1981 Defence White Paper we read: "Any readiness by one nation to use nuclear weapons against another, even in self-defence, is terrible. No-one — especially from within the ethical traditions of the free world, with their special respect for individual life — can acquiesce comfortably in it as the basis of international peace for the rest of time."[25] The statement goes on, however, to argue that while we must seek unremittingly through arms control and other means for better ways of ordering the world, "to tear down the present structure, imperfect but effective, before a better one is firmly within our grasp would be an immensely dangerous and irresponsible act."

This last comment attempts to turn the tables on the critics of nuclear policy who have consistently maintained that it is the preparation to wage nuclear war which constitutes the immensely dangerous and irresponsible act. In effect the proponents of nuclear deterrence, presssed by their critics to say what possible political ends could justify a willingness to wage nuclear war, have latterly responded by saying it is justified as a means of preventing such a war from occurring.

There is more than a hint of sophistry about the reply. It is the policy of relying on nuclear weapons that has brought us to the situation where a nuclear holocaust is possible, and those who have supported this policy must accept the prime responsibility for the hazards we are now facing. It is, however, true that now that thousands of nuclear weapons exist — thanks to the policy of nuclear deterrence — there is no policy which can provide the certainty of avoiding nuclear war.

It is necessary, however, to distinguish between different kinds of risk. The risk that is inherent and unavoidable in a policy of mutual nuclear deterrence is an eventual holocaust. The inherent risk for a country or alliance which unconditionally refuses to resort to weapons of mass destruction is nuclear blackmail followed by political defeat or occupation, or possibly a limited nuclear attack which the opponent might launch to show they were not bluffing. This is not to say nuclear blackmail is a necessary or likely outcome of unilateral nuclear disarmament or of a decision not to acquire nuclear weapons, but simply to acknowledge that the danger is there. But equal frankness on the part of the proponents of nuclear deterrence would lead them to acknowledge that their policy involves not only the risk of an eventual holocaust but a willingness to participate in the unleashing of it.

Of course, if Britain and the rest of Western Europe moved away from reliance on nuclear weapons while the superpowers retained theirs, a nuclear holocaust would still be possible, and indeed the opponents of British nuclear disarmament argue that the change of policy might disturb a delicate stability and trigger off nuclear war. But while no policy is free of risk, the evidence for thinking that British nuclear disarmament would lead to nuclear war is not convincing; indeed given the erosion of deterrence that we looked at in the last section, there is a strong case for saying that nuclear war is only likely to be avoided if there are radical shifts in present policy.

No-one can in fact predict the future with sufficient certainty to be able to say that nuclear deterrence, and only nuclear deterrence, will keep the peace, and that any departure from it is likely to set off the catastrophe it is intended to prevent. Such an argument amounts to a form of intellectual blackmail, for its intention is to paralyse strategic thinking outside the orthodox and official framework. Moreover, while none of us can guarantee that any given policy will prevent a nuclear war from occurring, there is an additional burden of proof on those who claim that in order to prevent it they must support a policy of threatening genocide. Only complete certainty that the threat of nuclear war will prevent its outbreak, a degree of certainty that in fact is never possible in the complex world of international relations, could begin to justify preparations for such an enormity.

The record needs also to be put straight about the political objectives of nuclear deterrence. It is not now, and never has been, confined to preventing nuclear war. In the immediate post-war period up to 1949, the USA had a monopoly of nuclear weapons and nuclear war could have occurred only if it had decided to use them. But with British and general Western approval it did threaten to use them if this was necessary to halt a major Soviet conventional attack, and still today NATO policy is that it will use nuclear weapons first if necessary to halt a Soviet advance. The 1958 British Defence White Paper was explicit on the issue.

> "It must be well understood that if Russia were to launch a major attack, even with conventional weapons only, the West would have to hit back with strategic weapons. In fact, the strategy of NATO is based on the frank recognition that a full-scale Soviet attack could not be repelled without resort to a massive nuclear bombardment of the sources of power in Russia."[26]

This doctrine has been somewhat modified by the policy of flexible response, but the plan to use nuclear weapons first if this is necessary to halt a conventional Soviet attack remains. Clearly preventing Soviet military victory and occupation are the primary and essential political objectives for which all along it has been considered right to threaten or wage nuclear war.

Of course, the intention is to deter attack. But it has to be assumed that the threat to wage nuclear war is considered to be commensurate with the disaster it is intended to prevent. The crux of the moral debate is whether the political objective of preventing a possible Soviet occupation would justify waging a nuclear war. The answer from commonsense, from the guidelines of Just War theory, and from the whole ethical tradition of which it is a part, is that it would not.

It is sometimes argued that for a 'morality of consequences', threats as such are of secondary importance, even where there is a conditional willingness to carry them out; it is the outcome being aimed at that is decisive, in this case deterrence.

Of course consequences do have to be considered as fully as we can in deciding whether any particular course of action is justified, and indeed much of Just War theory hinges on considerations of probable consequences. But because consequences cannot be predicted with certainty, some courses of action must be rejected as inherently negating humanity. There is a general consensus, for instance, that torture must be rejected unconditionally, though it is perfectly possible to construct scenarios, and perhaps to point to historical instances, where it might seem to be justified. Nuclear warfare threatens humanity on an incomparably greater scale, and if there is a limit to be set anywhere, then here at least it imposes itself with an inescapable finality.

A pure morality of consequences is untenable because it assumes that human beings really do have the capacity to foresee the total consequences of their actions. In fact even the willingness to engage in certain kinds of action may have significant, if not always immediately apparent, consequences; thus preparations to wage nuclear war may over time produce a climate of opinion in which the use of these weapons is rendered acceptable. Often too the cumulative effect of decisions taken on an *ad-hoc* basis in response to particular circumstances gradually corrupts our thinking about what is permissible. We have only to look back to the shocked reaction in 1936 to the bombing of the Spanish town of Guernica during the civil war to see how far we have collectively travelled since then in the direction of accepting the destruction of centres of population as a necessary and tolerable part of modern war.

We should also remember the importance of individuals who have stood out against apparently irresistible trends. During the Nazi period in Germany there were courageous individuals who refused to co-operate in policies they regarded as evil, and who in many cases suffered torture and death as a result. In terms of a pure morality of consequences, theirs could be seen as a futile sacrifice, for there were plenty of others to do the work they refused. Yet who can doubt that something essentially human would have been lost if that kind of integrity disappeared or ceased to be valued? Who can doubt also that its disappearance would have bleak consequences in the long term?

The threat to use nuclear weapons must mean their possible use, however firmly one may hope that the deterrent effect will prevent war; those who advocate nuclear deterrence have to face up to this. To say (as some have done) that to threaten nuclear war is permissible, but that actually to wage it would be immoral, is an irresponsible evasion.

The implication of this line of defence is that ultimately the threat to wage nuclear war is a bluff. But there are plenty of indications that it is not a bluff — such as the dispatching of US nuclear bombers on their way to strike targets in the Soviet Union when false alarms have been raised. (No doubt there have been parallel incidents on the other side.) Moreover, once you institutionalise a threat in the way the nuclear threat has been institutionalised, it cannot be a bluff as far as the majority of those directly involved in its possible implementation are concerned, nor indeed for the majority of the population.

For the commanders of the Polaris submarines and their crews, and for all those involved in the structure of military and political control, with the possible exception of those at the very top with whom the final decision rests, there can be no bluff. They must be trained in the conviction that the threat is meant and that their duty is to implement it if the order should be given. The majority of the population too must be convinced that the threat is real and intended, and therefore become a party to that intention. Those who support nuclear deterrence but with the mental reservation that they would not support waging a nuclear war are engaging in a fateful exercise in self deception. The end, if it comes, will come too swiftly to allow anyone except the few people at the top to alter the course that has been set. For the rest of the population the only opportunity they can ever have of expressing their opposition to waging nuclear war is by opposing the preparations to wage it, i.e. the whole policy of nuclear deterrence.[27]

No one denies that the greatest care has to be taken in calculating the consequences of policy decisions, or in the way one goes about dismantling the deterrent system, but the absolute commitment to do so must be there. No doubt both unilateral initiatives and international negotiations will be involved in this process; the essential point is that one way or another it *must* be done.

IV. Complementing disarmament

The 1981 Defence White Paper pins its hopes for moving away from reliance on the nuclear deterrent on arms control and other negotiated agreements. However, the most striking thing about the record of disarmament negotiations throughout this century is the meagreness of the results. Discussion of multilateral disarmament at the First and Second Hague Peace Conferences, in 1889 and 1907 respectively, was abortive, though these conferences were productive in other ways. After the catastrophic experience of World War I, many committees and conferences were set up to negotiate disarmament, mainly under the auspices of the League of Nations, but the only significant multilateral disarmament agreements of the inter-war years were the naval treaties concluded in Washington (1922) and London (1930). Since World War II there has been a continuous stream of negotiations about disarmament, mainly under UN auspices at Geneva. But only one agreement has been concluded which involves a significant measure of actual disarmament — the 1972 Biological Weapons Convention, which entered into force in 1975.

Negotiations on more limited measures of arms control have been somewhat more successful than those for disarmament. Significant measures have been agreed and implemented, including the 1963 Partial Test Ban Treaty, the 1968 Non-Proliferation Treaty, and the 1972 SALT-I Accords. However these and similar agreements can be criticised on many grounds, and they have plainly been an inadequate brake on the momentum of the arms race.[28]

There is another tradition of multilateral negotiation and agreement about arms. The 'laws of war' seek among other things to regulate the way in which arms are used in wartime. This is somewhat distinct from arms control, which deals above all with the possession, deployment and testing of weapons in peacetime. Significant restraints on armed conflict are provided for in the many agreements on the laws of war, ranging from the 1907 Hague Convention IV on Land Warfare to the 1925 Geneva Protocol on Chemical and Biological Weapons and, most recently, the 1981 UN Convention on Specific Inhumane Weapons.[29] This approach is very modest in its aims, but it has something to contribute to the limitation of war, and it is likely to be compatible with the kinds of alternative defence policies being considered in this report. Indeed such policies might enlarge the scope for further agreements on the laws of war — for example for a possible agreement banning the first use of nuclear weapons.

The continuous failure of all negotiations for more ambitious and comprehensive disarmament has not been accidental. It is attributable, to a considerable degree, to the lack of will and sincerity on the part of the powers involved, and to quite a lot of cynical manipulation.[30] However, there are also genuine difficulties. There is the problem of balancing weapons and force levels when the weapons systems themselves are often not directly comparable, and when states of different sizes and populations see their defence needs so differently. There is the problem of inspection and control; some nuclear delivery systems for instance are relatively easy to inspect by satellite photographs and other means, but nuclear weapons as such are more difficult. In 1962, a United Kingdom paper prepared in connection with the Geneva disarmament negotiations indicated that it might be possible for a state to conceal from an inspection organisation up to 20 per cent of its nuclear weapon stocks.[31] There is also the question of what sanctions could be taken against a state that was infringing agreements, and the still more fundamental problem of how conflicts within and between states are to be managed after disarmament.

None of these problems is a good reason for abandoning the quest for comprehensive disarmament. Some way simply has to be found to halt the dangerous escalation of armaments and the massive diversion of resources which in effect is killing millions of people even before a shot is fired. What it does suggest is that the multilateralist approach to disarmament by itself is insufficient.

A purely multilateralist approach can lead to three negative sets of consequences. First, some governments claim they are arming in order to achieve or maintain a place in disarmament negotiations, or in order to enable them to bargain effectively in such negotiations — for example by building a weapons system as a 'bargaining chip'. Second, parties to disarmament negotiations frequently put all the blame for failure on other parties; thus the negotiations themselves become a part of political warfare, and the lack of progress in them is used as a pretext for acquiring new weaponry. Third, negotiations tend to focus on numerical equivalence with the result that states may become obsessively concerned with the maintenance of an exact balance of weaponry with a potential adversary, even where this has little military significance. In short, the notion of multilateral disarmament can operate as a cover for the arms race.

The main alternative approach to disarmament has been the unilateralist one. This does not imply a rejection of multilateral negotiations, but means simply that unilateral initiatives are seen as an essential ingredient in the process of halting the arms race. The unilateralist approach also permits popular movements to make concrete and unconditional demands of their own governments and to reject the response that nothing can be done until agreement is reached with the other side. Unilateralist movements may in addition force major powers to take the question of disarmament more seriously and to enter into more serious negotiations. Thus the nuclear disarmament movement in Europe which has experienced such a remarkable resurgence since the turn of the decade can claim some credit for the fact that in 1982 the superpowers are again negotiating about both strategic and theatre nuclear weapons.

While strongly in favour of reaching multilateral agreements wherever possible, the Commission adopts the unilateralist approach that Britain should unconditionally renounce nuclear weapons and ensure the removal of nuclear bases from British territory. It takes the view that unilateral initiatives of this kind can play a constructive part in furthering multilateral negotiations; thus the British renunciation of an independent deterrent would actually remove one of the obstacles in the negotiations between the superpowers on the reduction of strategic forces, since the Soviet Union argues that British nuclear forces should be included in the negotiations and the United States does not accept this. The opposite approach of 'negotiation from strength' has in practice tended to reinforce the arms race.

However, unilateral nuclear disarmament by Britain necessarily implies modifications in present defence strategy, or possibly the adoption of a radically different approach to security, and it is on these alternatives that the Commission's work has mainly focused. Alternative defence strategies should also be of interest to those who believe that disarmament is possible only by multilateral agreement. Firstly, measures of disarmament, even where they are agreed multi-laterally, imply shifts in defence policy, and if states can feel that the strategies they adopt provide a reasonable measure of security, disarmament agreements are more likely to be implemented. Secondly, the unilateral adoption by a number of states of strategies with a defensive emphasis could improve the prospects for reaching multilateral agreements.

Perhaps then the exploration of alternatives can become a common endeavour of all those genuinely interested in the question of disarmament and security.

Notes to Chapter 1

1. J. Perry Robinson, 'Chemical Weapons and Europe', *Survival*, XXIV (January/February 1982), and SIPRI, *The Problem of Chemical and Biological Warfare: A Study of the Historical, Technical, Military, Legal and Political Aspects of CBW, and Possible Disarmament Measures*, 6 vols. (Stockholm: Almqvist & Wiksell, 1971).
2. See M. Gowing, *Independence and Deterrence: Britain and Atomic Energy, 1945–1952*, 2 vols. (London: Macmillan, 1974), Vol. 1: *Policy Making*, pp. 179–85.
3. See L. Freedman, *Britain and Nuclear Weapons* (London: Macmillan, for the Royal Institute of International Affairs, 1980), especially pp. 48 and 52. The decision to go ahead with the Chevaline programme was taken, Freedman says, by a small group within the Cabinet — Harold Wilson, Denis Healey, Roy Jenkins, James Callaghan and Roy Mason (Prime Minister, Chancellor and Home, Foreign and Defence Secretaries respectively). Parliament was officially informed of the programme in January 1980 by the then Conservative Defence Secretary, Francis Pym.
4. See the report of the Independent Commission on Disarmament and Security Issues Under the Chairmanship of Olof Palme, *Common Security: A Programme for Disarmament* (London: Pan, 1982) pp. 161–67.
5. See 'East Timor's Secret Suffering', *The Pacifist*, 18, 9 (July 1980), 11–12.
6. The case in favour of relying on the nuclear deterrent, including the British deterrent, was forcefully expounded by Professor Laurence Martin in the 1981 Reith Lectures, republished in *The Listener* from November to December 1981.

Michael Quinlan, deputy under-secretary of state at the Ministry of Defence, also presents a strong argument in favour of the nuclear deterrent in 'Preventing War', *The Tablet*, 18 June, 1981, and Freedman in *Britain and Nuclear Weapons*[3] presents a short history of the British deterrent and a summary of the arguments. Other recent books with a more critical perspective on the British deterrent are R. Neild, *How to Make Your Mind Up About the Bomb* (London: Andre Deutsch, 1981); J. McMahan, *British Nuclear Weapons: For and Against* (London: Junction, 1981); J. Cox, *Overkill: The Story of Modern Weapons* (Harmondsworth: Penguin, 1981); and P. Rogers, M. Dando and P. van den Dungen, *As Lambs to the Slaughter* (London: Arrow in association with ECOROPA, 1981).

7. See P. Rogers, 'A Guide to Nuclear Weapons 1982-83' *Peace Studies Papers No. 9* (Bradford: Bradford University School of Peace Studies, 1982 and London: Housmans, 1982).

8. Statement on the Defence Estimates, 1981, Cmnd. 8212-1, pp. 11-12.

9. A point made by Lawrence Freedman in *Britain and Nuclear Weapons*,[3] in a discussion of the second centre argument (pp. 127-134).

10. For a fuller discussion of this and other points related to the arguments in favour of Britain retaining nuclear weapons, see McMahan, *British Nuclear Weapons: For and Against*,[6] esp. pp. 14-39. The Commission owes special thanks to Mr McMahan, who sent us an advance copy of his book which was very helpful to us in our deliberations; however, we have taken a different view on a few crucial issues.

11. Mr John Nott, speaking on the London Weekend Television programme 'Weekend World', 28 February, 1982. See the report in *The Guardian*, 1 March, 1982 by I. Aitken, 'Nott sees Trident in Post-NATO Role'.

12. Because of the risk of nuclear blackmail, McMahan in *British Nuclear Weapons: For and Against*[6] argues in favour of retaining the American 'nuclear umbrella', and of permitting some US nuclear bases in this country, in particular the submarine base at Holy Loch in Scotland. See his discussion of 'the Problem of Nuclear Blackmail', pp. 40-47.

13. Cited by McMahan,[6] p. 25.

14. Duncan Campbell, *New Statesman*, 31 October, 1980. We should note also that in a war or extreme emergency there are plans to station in Britain additional NATO aircraft which are at present based in the United States or mainland Europe. In April 1980, Air Vice-Marshall Hine, Assistant Chief of the Air Staff, told the House of Commons Defence Select Committee that up to 40% of NATO's combined air forces, including reinforcements from the USA, would be based in Britain in times of military tension. (*The Guardian*, 16 April 1980). As things now stand, many of these would be armed with nuclear weapons.

15. Cited by Neild, *How to Make Your Mind Up about the Bomb*,[6] p. 104. The communiqué was jointly issued on 9 January, 1952 by Churchill and Truman after talks at the White House, 7-8 January. See *Keesings Contemporary Archives*, VIII (1950-1952), 11945-47.

16. See H. Kissinger, *Years of Upheaval* (London: Weidenfeld & Nicolson and Michael Joseph, 1982), pp. 545-591.

17. Cited by M. Mandelbaum, *The Nuclear Question: The United States and Nuclear Weapons, 1946-1976* (Cambridge: Cambridge University Press, 1979), p. 51.

18. The Defence White Papers use the term 'theatre' nuclear weapons to cover both the short range tactical nuclear weapons, such as nuclear artillery, for use on the battlefield and the medium- and long-range systems for use in the European

theatre of operations. We have followed the practice of distinguishing between the short-range 'battlefield' weapons and 'theatre' weapons, though of course the categories are not hard and fast, and some systems, like the Pershing IA missile deployed by NATO, could be regarded as either battlefield or theatre weapons.

19. Field Marshal Lord Carver, *A Policy for Peace* (London: Faber & Faber, 1982), especially in the chapter 'A Policy for Continuation'. McNamara's views are expressed in an article written jointly with three other influential American figures, McGeorge Bundy, Special Assistant to the President for National Security Affairs from 1961 to 1966, George Kennan, former US Ambassador to the Soviet Union, and Gerard Smith, Chief of the US Delegation to the Strategic Arms Limitations Talks from 1969 to 1972. The article entitled 'Nuclear Weapons and the Atlantic Alliance' appeared in *Foreign Affairs*, 60, 4 (Spring 1982), pp. 753–68.

20. See *The Financial Times*, 22 October, 1981, which quotes President Reagan's statement: "I could see where you could have the exchange of tactical weapons against troops in the field without bringing either one of the major powers to pushing the button", and a subsequent statement in which he branded as "outright deception" any suggestion that the USA could consider fighting a nuclear war at Europe's expense. For the controversy between Haig and Weinberger over whether or not there was a NATO contingency plan to fire a demonstration nuclear shot to warn the Soviet Union against pressing a conventional attack on Western Europe, see *The Sunday Times*, 8 November, 1981.

Controversy over US nuclear war-fighting plans was resurrected in the summer of 1982 when the *New York Times* published a defence guidance statement drawn up by the Pentagon which envisaged a nuclear war lasting for up to six months, at the end of which "American nuclear forces must prevail and be able to force the Soviet Union to seek earliest termination of hostilities on terms favourable to the United States". (Cited in *The Guardian*, 19 August, 1982 in an editorial entitled "The Six Month Delusion"). In the subsequent furore, the US Defense Secretary, Mr Weinberger, took the unusual step of addressing explanatory letters to the editors of newspapers in 15 NATO countries. For the text of this letter see *The Guardian Weekly*, Vol. 127, No. 10, 5 September 1982, p. 9.

21. There is also a controversy over the motive for the US bombing of Hiroshima and Nagasaki, namely whether it was really aimed at avoiding a costly land war against Japanese forces deployed in depth or was chiefly intended as a warning to the Soviet Union not to try to extend its sphere of influence. The discussion, though important, is not central here; in future wars too, considerations extraneous to the immediate conflict could affect the decision of a nuclear power whether or not to use its nuclear weapons.

22. For an excellent discussion of the notion and implications of the just war, see M. Walzer, *Just and Unjust Wars: A Moral Argument with Historical Illustrations* (Harmondsworth: Penguin, 1980).

23. See the report published by the Office of Technology Assessment of the US Congress entitled *The Effects of Nuclear War* (London: Croom Helm, 1980). The report examines four possible levels of nuclear attack: (1) the detonation of a single weapon; (2) an attack limited to 10 strategic nuclear delivery vehicles; (3) an attack confined to missile silos, bomber bases and missile submarine bases, and (4) a very large attack against a range of military and economic targets. Even in (3), the 'counter-force' attack, the report found that the US deaths

could reach 20 million and Soviet deaths more than 10 million. Effective fall-out sheltering, they state, could save many lives under favourable conditions, "but even in the best imaginable case more than a million would die in either the United States or the USSR from a counter-force attack''. (pp. 7-8). In case (4), US deaths in the first 30 days would range from 35 to 77 per cent of the population (i.e. from 70 million to 160 million dead), and Soviet deaths from 20 to 40 per cent; many millions more might die later (p.8).

See also the special issue of *Ambio* entitled "Nuclear War: The Aftermath' (Vol. XI, Number 2-3, 1982), which examines both the scenario of a major nuclear war between the superpowers, and of a 'limited' nuclear war in East and West Germany.

24. For an authoritative discussion of this issue, see Ball, 'Can Nuclear War Be Controlled?', *Adelphi Paper*, 169 (Autumn 1981).

25. Statement on the Defence Estimates 1981, p. 14.

26. British Government White Paper on Defence 1958, cited by Stein, 'Introductory: The Defence of the West', in W. Stein, ed., *Nuclear Weapons and Christian Conscience* (London: Merlin Press, 1961, reprinted 1981), p. 31.

27. This point is forcefully argued by Rev. Roger Ruston in *Nuclear Deterrence — Right or Wrong?* (London: The Commission for International Justice and Peace, 1981), in the chapter entitled 'Moral Arguments'. See also the discussion of the moral argument in *The Church and the Bomb: The Report of the Working Party under the Chairmanship of the Bishop of Salisbury* (London: Hodder & Stoughton, 1982). McMahan in *British Nuclear Weapons: For and Against*,[6] pp. 119-25, argues in favour of a morality of consequences on the basis of which he is able to accept the idea of Britain and Western Europe continuing to rely on the US deterrent to prevent Soviet nuclear attack or blackmail, and of Britain continuing to have US nuclear bases on its territory.

28. Professor Laurence Martin in the first of his 1981 Reith Lectures questions whether there really is a nuclear arms race, and cites as evidence the declining proportion of GNP devoted to defence over the last 20 years by the USA and Britain. But this is only one form of measurement. In terms of the number and destructiveness of weapons deployed, especially in the deployment of a whole range of nuclear weapons, there has undoubtedly been a competitive escalation. (See *The Listener*, 12 November, 1981, p. 564 for Professor Martin's argument on this point). Moreover in one of the subsequent lectures Professor Martin himself argues in favour of the NATO long-range theatre modernisation programme (i.e., the deployment of cruise and Pershing II missiles) on the grounds that the Soviet Union has stolen a lead with respect to theatre nuclear forces: "It has been a great mistake, I believe, if an understandable one, for NATO to seize on the SS20 as a convenient excuse to justify refurbishing NATO's own battlefield and theatre nuclear weapons when, as we can see, the problem is part of the overall decay of NATO's relative capability at this and other levels of warfare." (*The Listener*, 26 November, 1981).

29. For texts of the currently applicable agreements, and lists of states parties, see A. Roberts and R. Guelff, eds., *Documents on the Laws of War* (Oxford: Oxford University Press, 1982).

30. See for example A. Myrdal, *The Game of Disarmament: How the United States and Russia Run the Arms Race* (New York: Pantheon, 1976, and Nottingham: Spokesman, 1980).

31. For details of this 1962 paper see Sir Michael Wright, *Disarm or Verify: An Explanation of the Central Difficulties and of National Policies* (London: Chatto & Windus, 1964), pp. 80-82 and 247-51.

Chapter 2
What threats should a defence policy meet?

I. Assessing threats

Before deciding on a new defence policy, we must think about the threats it is designed to meet. Assessing threats presents several problems. One is that the nature of our defence and foreign policy partly determines who our friends and enemies are. At present the USA is an ally and the Soviet Union a potential opponent. Moreover, we are locked into a military confrontation which means that we are directly threatened by Soviet nuclear weapons, just as the USSR is threatened by the US and British nuclear arsenal. If Britain went non-nuclear and left NATO, we would be less directly threatened by Soviet nuclear strategy, but we might also need to ask whether the USA posed any kind of military threat.

A second problem in assessing threats is that domestic changes within countries may create new causes for aggression. For example Germany, which had not been a threat to peace under the Weimar Republic, became an aggressive power under Hitler. Alterations of military alliances may also open up opportunities for aggression, and so bring about a change in intentions. When discussing whether there really is a threat of Soviet expansion, one of the difficulties is that, while the Soviet government probably has no intention of trying to invade Western Europe at present, the temptation to do so might be greater if the USA withdrew its troops and European countries were not credibly defended.

Therefore assessment of present threats does not conclusively prove or disprove the need for some form of defence. While a strong belief that there is no real threat to our security would clearly strengthen a pragmatic argument for minimal defence, or even pacifism, to base policy on conviction of total security would be to build on sand rather than rock. The future — even the near future — is impossible to predict, and a country without enemies today may find itself faced with serious dangers tomorrow.

The fundamental case for an alternative defence policy does not therefore rest on a belief that a non-nuclear Britain would face few risks, but on a moral, political and strategic rejection of nuclear policies. In particular, the case for non-nuclear defence does not rest on an optimistic view of the Soviet Union. Advocates of nuclear build-up tend to stress the aggressive designs of the USSR, and advocates of nuclear disarmament often query this interpretation, but it is perfectly possible to favour nuclear deterrence while being sceptical of the Soviet threat, or to insist on the necessity of nuclear disarmament while fearing Soviet political intentions.

A final decision on the best policy available does not depend solely on likely threats. It depends also on judgements how best to promote world stability, and whether a particular defence stance will help or hinder urgent measures of disarmament; it depends on what forms of co-operation are possible with other countries; and it depends on the political traditions, economic resources and strategic possibilities of this country, and on balancing the costs of defence against other social priorities.

After allowing for all the other factors which should influence a defence policy, and accepting that assessments of threats are provisional and may be revised, it remains true that no strategy of defence can be adopted without deciding what we are trying to defend and what sorts of attack we fear. Decision on likely threats does not dictate the final policy — there may be several ways of meeting the same threat — but it does determine defence priorities.

This chapter concentrates primarily on the most central political issue, whether we should be concerned about a Soviet threat, but begins by looking at a wider international context.

II. *Possible sources of threat*

Conflicts within Europe

In the past, the main opponents of Britain have been other European powers. War between West European countries would now be conceivable only were there to be a resurgence of fascism. While there is cause for concern in view of the economic recession and signs of growing right-wing violence, the rise of an aggressive fascism which could disturb the peace between European states seems unlikely. The last decade has seen long-established dictatorships in Portugal and Spain giving way to democracy, and the Greek colonels being replaced by a parliamentary regime. Even if the still fragile democracies in these countries were disrupted by military or right-wing dictatorships, it is more likely they would be concerned with internal issues (as before) than with actively promoting European fascism. Those countries most vulnerable to a *coup d'état* are also less likely to have the resources to contemplate a policy of aggression likely to lead to a European war, though there might be local conflicts, as between Greece and Turkey.

The two major European powers which could individually (or in alliance with others) threaten the peace of Western Europe are, as in the past, France and Germany. Twenty years ago it would have been reasonable to worry about the dangerous impact of the Algerian war on France, but today its internal politics seem stable, and French military policies, though creating problems for nuclear disarmament in Europe, are not directly threatening to its neighbours. West German ambitions have in the past been viewed with alarm by many sectors of European opinion, and actual reunification of Germany could still arouse historic fears in West as well as East European countries. But Brandt's Ostpolitik has renounced previous German territorial claims, and German economic success reduces the likelihood of a serious resurgence of extreme right-wing movements. A swing to the right in German national politics could intensify the East–West confrontation, but it seems improbable that even a militant right-wing government in West Germany would directly threaten Western Europe.

It is conceivable that Britain might come into conflict with some of its European partners over economic resources, such as oil, gas or fishing rights; and there might even be some form of limited military action, as in the Cod War with Iceland. Disputes at this level could, however, be resolved by diplomacy.

Outside Europe

In the Middle East, Latin America and Asia the most immediate threat is indirect: that civil or local wars will involve the great powers and escalate into a world war. Nuclear war seems more likely to be started by events in the Middle East than in Europe itself. The long-term threat to world peace springs from the extreme and growing poverty of many areas of the world, since poverty may intensify local political instability and the risks of local wars spreading. Scarcity of valuable economic resources, such as oil and various minerals, many of which are located in less developed areas, could lead to war if the West is prepared to use force to secure access to these resources.

Supplies may be cut off because of local government policy or war, but there is no direct *military* threat by oil-producing or Third World countries to Britain: there will be military confrontation only if we initiate it. The danger of world war depends on great-power involvement, either through a struggle between the superpowers for the resources, or through one power seeking to deny them to the other. US fear that the mineral-rich Soviet Union will use force to stop oil or minerals reaching the West is dramatised in the scenario of the Soviet Union closing the Persian Gulf. Therefore the most direct threat to our safety arises from superpower involvement in the world's trouble spots, and possible preemption or miscalculation by either side.

The USA

The superpowers may pose a much more direct threat to our security and sovereignty by making strategic or political demands upon us. If we start by looking at the USA, it is necessary to distinguish between a transition stage, when we are moving towards an alternative non-nuclear strategy, and the longer-term future. Possibly the USA might try to prevent Britain adopting a defence and foreign policy which might be construed as anti-US, and during a transition stage US intervention is much more probable than Soviet pressure. It is hard to imagine that even a hawkish US Administration would try to retain its bases and surveillance facilities by direct use of force, but economic and political measures of destabilisation are conceivable, especially if we intended to leave NATO. Once the process of transition has been completed, US political intervention seems improbable, but it is possible that in the longer term the United States would still exert pressure to recover use of strategic facilities. Open use of military force is likely only in the event of a European war, when the USA might well seize territory from a non-aligned Britain in order to pre-empt the Soviet Union. (See also Chapter 8, Section II on possible US reactions.)

The USSR

The belief that there is a Soviet threat to Western Europe has been the basis of British defence policy since the late 1940s, supported by the popular fear of Soviet aggression.

Western fears of the Soviet Union have been shaped by the history of Soviet political and military action since 1939, and by perceptions of Soviet military superiority. Western interpretations of Soviet goals also depend on theories about the nature of the Soviet state and its global aims. These factors are examined below.

III. The USSR: the historical record

Fears of Soviet intentions still rest to a considerable extent on the record of Soviet expansion under Stalin. He was ruthless in extending Soviet frontiers in Europe during the Second World War — incorporating parts of Poland, Romania and the three Baltic states into the USSR and liquidating all potential opposition — and imposing Stalinist control over Eastern Europe in the period 1947–53. Western belief that Stalin planned to impose his brand of communist domination upon the whole of Europe, which led to the creation of NATO, was at the time understandable.

In retrospect there are grounds for questioning whether the USSR was pursuing a deliberate policy of global expansion. Stalin's policy can be understood, first, as the restoration of the old Russian frontiers lost in the period 1917–19, second, as creating a buffer zone of satellites to ensure that no future war would be fought on Soviet territory, and, third, as assisting the Soviet post-war economy by exploitation of Eastern Europe. None of these motives justifies Stalin's measures, but in the late 1940s the USSR was acting with caution, and from a position of weakness rather than strength. Soviet troops had, after all, liberated Eastern Europe and entered Eastern Germany as a legitimate occupation army in 1945, and Churchill and Roosevelt had agreed at Yalta and Potsdam that Eastern Europe was a Soviet sphere of influence. Stalin, possibly motivated by prudence, respected the agreement that Greece 'belonged' to the West and failed to back up the Greek communist guerrillas.

Outside Europe Stalin faced a predominance of US influence and Western colonial power. Soviet encouragement for North Korea to attack the South in 1950 can be seen as an attempt to consolidate the power of a communist regime in a peripheral area, rather than as part of a policy of active aggression. Korea had been divided between the occupying powers, the USSR and USA, at the end of the war, and US refusal to recognise the autonomous People's Republic Government created by the internal resistance had ensured the ideological and military division of the country. However, withdrawal of US troops and several public statements by leading Americans, including Secretary of State Acheson's famous speech in January 1950 on US security in the Pacific, which omitted any mention of South Korea as part of the US defensive perimeter, gave grounds for assuming that the USA would tolerate reunification of Korea under the North Korean communists.[1]

Western thinking at the height of the Cold War was characterised by stereotypes about Soviet aggressive designs, but the reverse image of a Soviet Union acting defensively in response to the USA is also oversimplified. Stalin may well have aspired to encompass all of Europe in the Soviet sphere by political means; it is debatable how seriously he was prepared to envisage doing so by force of arms.[2]

Whatever conclusions we reach about Stalin's ambitions, since his death a totalitarian regime dominated by the arbitrary will of a supreme dictator has been replaced by a regime which, despite its autocratic and illiberal character, is characterised by stable institutions and rational decision-making procedures.[3] Internationally, a monolithic communist movement dominated by Moscow for its own ends has broken up into competing ideological groupings.

Current alarm about Soviet aims stems largely from Soviet moves in the 1970s. These are sometimes interpreted as the systematic extension of Soviet military power from the Horn of Africa and Angola towards South Africa; to Yemen and the Middle East; and, through the invasion of Afghanistan, an advance towards the Persian Gulf. This view assumes a global masterplan by the Soviet Union, whereas the evidence points to the importance of much more specific political factors, for example the fact that some of the liberation movements against Portuguese colonialism and apartheid have (lacking support in the West) turned to the Soviet Union for aid. This Cold War view not only oversimplifies Soviet intentions, but also exaggerates the degree of Soviet power, because it tends to see the world solely as a theatre for great power conflict and ignores the independent and complex reality of the countries they seek to include in their spheres.

It is, however, true that there has been a shift in Soviet policy during the 1970s. The most obvious example is the invasion of Afghanistan, the first time since World War II that the Soviet Union has directly invaded a country outside its recognised sphere of influence. It can be argued that the Soviet Union had assumed since 1978 when a pro-Soviet communist regime came to power in Kabul, that Afghanistan was within its sphere, but if the Soviet government feels entitled to invade any country which has been sympathetic to Moscow, the implications are very disturbing.

Nevertheless, there are good reasons to doubt whether the invasion was the first step in a deliberate plan to dominate the Persian

Gulf. Afghanistan borders on Moslem areas of the Soviet Union, and at a time when Iran was already in turmoil, the Soviet leaders were certainly anxious to avoid further unrest on their borders. In addition Soviet advisers and troops had already been committed to Afghanistan, so there were pressures on the leadership not to withdraw. The progressive embroilment of the USSR in the affairs of Kabul from 1978 has parallels with the disastrous commitment of the USA to South Vietnam, in which political involvement led to military escalation.[4] The occupation of Afghanistan is therefore, in the view of most informed commentators, a response to local political pressures, not a deliberate step as part of a grand design.

The use of Soviet and Cuban troops in Africa is a new departure. Taken in conjunction with the pattern of wider naval deployment, and the establishing of a military base in South Yemen, it appears that the Soviet Union intends to assert itself as a global power. Whether or not this Soviet approach is seen as any more sinister than the USA's global military presence and naval deployment depends on how one assesses the nature of both superpowers.[5]

If the deductions which can be drawn from the historical record are not wholly conclusive, the same applies to deductions from Soviet military strength. There has been well publicised official anxiety about the size of Soviet conventional forces, and about the Soviet nuclear build-up in the 1970s. Debates about force levels are bedevilled by problems about the presentation of statistics and by the variety of criteria which can be applied to assessing the conventional or strategic nuclear balance. The central issue is not, however, whether the USSR has in fact overtaken the USA, but what can be deduced from the facts of military hardware. The West does not perceive its own nuclear arsenal as evidence of aggressive intent against the USSR. It is plausible that the Soviet Union was alarmed by US nuclear superiority in the 1950s and 1960s, and interprets its own missile force as a reasonable defence against US temptation to launch a first strike.

Brezhnev's explicit public claim that the aim of the Soviet Union is nuclear parity with the West, not superiority, may have been propaganda, but, given a number of good reasons for the Soviet Union to welcome such restrictions on the nuclear arms race, it should be weighed seriously.[6]

In practice, pursuit of parity promotes a nuclear arms race, and the Soviet Union can be criticised by the disarmament movement for accepting the military logic of nuclear build-up at the risk of world peace, but this does not prove any aggressive design.

IV. What is the nature of the Soviet state?

We cannot prove from the 'facts' what the intentions of the Soviet Union are. To interpret the facts we need to construct a model of the Soviet state and to test it in turn against the evidence. The most important theories about the nature of the Soviet regime and its military/political aims are:

(1) The USSR is a Marxist–Leninist regime committed to its original goal of world wide communist revolution;

(2) the Soviet state is uniquely militaristic and so aspires to world domination;

(3) the Soviet Union has inherited the mantle of Russian national-ism and is aggressively imperialistic in its policies;

(4) the Soviet Union is internally a rather conservative regime, seeking recognition as a greater power on the international stage, and liable to behave much like other great powers;

(5) internal weakness in the USSR may result in adventures abroad;

(6) the USSR's internal structure is not directly relevant, but its external policies have been shaped by awareness of economic and military weakness in relation to the West and a profound desire for military security based on memories of World War II.

All these theories assume a unity and coherence of purpose seldom displayed by states in the real world, and a further theory could be put forward which emphasises the plurality of institutions and interests affecting policy-making, despite the key role of the Party Politburo, and allows more room for policy shifts, political opportun-ism and bureaucratic muddle. In extreme form this approach might suggest that Soviet foreign policy is based purely on *ad hoc* reaction to events, but it is put forward here simply as a modification of the other models, which are assessed below.

(1) Promotion of world communist revolution

The theory that the USSR is a communist regime still committed to promote communism in the rest of the world by subversion or military force is put forward by some experts as well as in political speeches.[7] Debate about this proposition tends to be confusing, because it is not clear what assumptions are being made. Clearly, since Lenin's death, Soviet leaders have not been idealistically committed to rapid creation of Marx's vision of communism at home and abroad, and the more distant the revolution of 1917, the less the genuine revolutionary zeal. Even those who assume the USSR has revolutionary goals abroad tend to argue that the lip service paid by Soviet leaders to Marxism at home sounds increasingly ritualistic. The Brezhnev leadership after all prudently postponed the achieving of 'communism' (which means an economic system based on 'from each according to his ability, to each according to his needs' and the withering away of the state) to the indefinite future.[8]

Neither has the USSR's 'commitment' to create a communist world meant principled support for communist parties in other countries on a basis of comradely solidarity. The USSR under Stalin, and since Stalin, has not given support to movements simply because they are communist; it has backed Third World governments to the detriment of local communist parties, for example in Egypt where the USSR ordered the communist party to dissolve itself and join Nasser's party, and much more recently in Iraq, where the Soviet Union countenanced execution of Iraqi communists.[9] The opportunism with which in 1977 the USSR abandoned its military support for Somalia, and switched to backing Somalia's more powerful enemy Ethiopia, underlines the tendency of the Soviet government to pursue great-power interest rather than to champion revolutionary governments.

But perhaps the USSR's commitment to create a communist world does not require pure revolutionary faith or solidarity, and ideological goals can be pursued opportunistically, as Lenin himself claimed. Soviet foreign policy has always distinguished between preserving the interests of the Soviet state and promoting revolution elsewhere, and the interests of the Soviet Union have always come first, because the security of the Soviet state is the first necessity for the success of world communism.[10] However, increasing disarray inside the world communist movement — the ideological competition with China, the growth of Euro-Communism and the unwillingness of many Marxist regimes to be tied too closely to the USSR — seriously undermines Soviet claims to lead the movement, and suggests there may be even sharper divergence between Soviet national interest and those of Marxist revolutionary parties than in the past. Moreover, the appeal to Lenin may explain the apparent cynicism of much Soviet foreign policy, but leaves it unclear how far there is any genuine ideological commitment influencing immediate decisions in defence and foreign policy.

Soviet leaders do still operate in a context which is shaped by their ideological heritage:[11] they are expected to support anti-colonialist and socialist movements in the Third World, they cannot easily abandon links with other communist parties, their legitimacy at home and abroad is based on a claim to represent the revolution against capitalism and imperialism and their language is publicly framed in ideological terms. Their thinking and their strategy are therefore coloured by ideological assumptions — for example the predominant Soviet interpretation of 'peaceful coexistence', which sees it as quite compatible with continuing political struggle against pro-Western regimes, differs from a Western understanding of detente, which assumes it means respect for the world status quo. But the ideological colouring of the Soviet approach tells us very little about the USSR's identifiable goals in the next ten to twenty years.

One way of interpreting Soviet ideological motivation is to deny that the Soviet leaders care about Marxism for its own sake, but to claim that they have totally identified the victory of socialism with Soviet great-power domination. Marxist-Leninist ideology then provides a convenient rationalisation of 'real' Soviet interests, and the Soviet party system an efficient method of political control within satellite states. It then becomes necessary to explain why the Soviet Union should be impelled to impose its own style of communism wherever possible.

(2) Military dominance in policy-making

There are two theories that can be invoked to explain why the USSR might be motivated to seek military domination and hegemony over the rest of the world: that the Soviet Union is an inherently militaristic and highly militarised state;[12] and that the Soviet regime has inherited the imperial Russian ambitions of the Tsars.[13] The two are often combined, with reference to the militarism of Tsarist Russia, but they are really distinct; belief in Soviet militarism does not require an appeal to history.

What is meant by saying the Soviet state is militaristic? It implies firstly the dominance of the military over political, social and economic life and over social values, and second that this military dominance at home results in military aggression abroad.[14] The arguments used to support the view that the USSR is militaristic may point to the power of the 'military–industrial complex' in the Soviet Union, the priority accorded to defence needs and the percentage of the gross national product spent on defence, the prestige accorded to the armed forces and the emphasis on military education among the young. There is undoubtedly some force in these arguments.

Though it is debatable in what sense there is a 'military–industrial complex', the military are clearly powerful.[15] The armed forces are, for example, well represented on the CPSU Central Committee, and since 1973 the Defence Minister has sat on the Politburo. Many observers see an increase in military power under Brezhnev, who conciliated military interests (unlike Khruschev, who battled to cut conventional forces and inveighed against the 'steel eaters') and took on himself the military title of Marshal.[16] Defence requirements are given economic and technological priority, though statements about the high percentage of gross national product (GNP) spent on defence are misleading, partly because of the difficulty of acquiring reliable statistics on the Soviet economy, and partly because spending a high percentage of GNP may mean inefficient use of resources as much as a vast armoury.[17] The militarisation of Soviet society is reflected in the maintenance of conscription, the military training of secondary school children, and general propaganda to promote admiration for the armed forces.[18] Desire to promote an internal and external image of Soviet military power is symbolised by the May Day Parades with their display of missiles and tanks. It is less clear that these facts prove the dominance of the military in decision-making.

If, as some experts argue, there is a conflict of aims and values between the party and the military, this clearly limits military power;[19] if on the other hand the alternative argument is accepted — that the party has identified its goals with a martial patriotism and, under Brezhnev, given the military their head in defence spending — then the military have a considerable leverage but remain the servant of the party.[20] They undoubtedly influence military decisions, but may not dictate the whole course of foreign policy. There are two reasons why their decision-making power may be limited: first, that they are primarily concerned with specialist defence issues and with matters such as the security, prestige and pay of the officer corps;[21] second, that the military themselves are divided into conflicting special interest groups, not only on budget allocation but on major policy decisions such as the invasion of Czechoslovakia.[22] Moreover, even if the military did dominate foreign and defence policy-making, it would not necessarily be in their interest to promote consistently aggressive policies. They might at least as plausibly use their influence to ensure from the Soviet standpoint strong military defences and an avoidance of any repetition of 1941.[23]

(3) Historic imperialist tradition

Various commentators on the Soviet Union have stressed the extent to which the Soviet regime has been shaped by the traditions of Tsarism, and Stalin's deliberate fostering of Russian nationalism in internal politics, and his ambitions to regain historic Russian frontiers for the Soviet state, add plausibility to this thesis. However, although Soviet attitudes and claims to great-power status may be influenced by Russian nationalist ideology, the fact that the Tsarist empire expanded in the 19th century does not prove that expansion is an inevitable result of Russian nationalist ambition today. Indeed, contemporary Russian nationalism may also prompt strong nationalist reactions from the other diverse nationalities of the USSR. Demographic trends, which show that Russians will soon be under 50% of the total Soviet population, and political trends which indicate an intensification of semi-official and dissident non-Russian nationalism, both suggest that Russian nationalism may be on the defensive inside the USSR.[24]

(4)   Great-power status

Estimates of the influence of Russian nationalism on Soviet policy tend to merge into a rather different thesis about the Soviet Union: that the regime seeks international recognition as a global power. This interpretation stresses that the Soviet Union is still reacting against its weakness and sense of vulnerability in relation to the West in the period 1918–39, its comparative military inferiority to the US until the 1970s, and a sense of exclusion from the international community. Hence the insistent assertion of a right to great-power status and equality with the USA, and of the ability to claim this status. Gromyko said at the Twenty-fourth Party Congress in 1971 that: "Today, there is no question of any significance which can be decided without the Soviet Union or in opposition to her."[25] He was asserting an aspiration rather than a fact — for example, the USA excluded the USSR from the Camp David negotiations on the Middle East — but Soviet policy is designed to make this aspiration a reality.

Commentators who agree about the Soviet Union's global aspirations are less united in their assessment of how the USSR wishes to use great-power status.[26] Will it have a genuine stake in creating a stable international order or is it anxious to challenge the USA for predominance — will the Soviet anxiety for great-power status make for caution or adventurism? Whatever the present intentions of

Soviet policy-makers, a prediction that the Soviet Union increasingly wants to prove its great-power status cannot be wholly reassuring. The record of other great powers and what is entailed in being a great power, for example the claim to undisputed dominance in spheres of influence, has never boded well for the sovereignty and independence of smaller nations, or for the human rights of peoples caught up in great power politics.

(5) Military adventurism to divert from internal problems

It has also been argued that economic weakness and potential political unrest may encourage Soviet leaders to indulge in adventures abroad, to stimulate patriotic loyalty and divert attention from internal problems, just as the Argentine junta invaded the Falkland Islands at a time of economic and financial crisis.

The Soviet Union is indeed facing major economic problems. Despite its economic growth since World War II and technological achievements, the USSR now faces a low economic growth rate, continuing inferiority to the West in areas like computers and oil-drilling equipment, doubts about the future supply of previously abundant oil,[27] and a repeated shortfall in grain supplies.

A falling birthrate in Russian and other European areas of the USSR means a reduction in the future supply of skilled industrial labour in those areas where industry is now concentrated. The higher birth rate and growing population of the Central Asian republics of the USSR suggests future economic and political difficulties in these so far subordinate areas, especially as their population may be affected by the growth of Islamic nationalism. Population trends also have military significance, since the non-Russian nationalities may be less highly trained (it is thought that Central Asian troops are largely used as auxiliaries) and may also be less politically reliable. If the Soviet government has to impose longer terms of conscription among Russians, this may exacerbate other economic and political problems.

The thesis that this weakness will encourage military action abroad is less convincing. There is no evidence of the Soviet press treating military action in Afghanistan in a way to promote jingoism.[28] Moreover, further diversion of resources to military ends is likely to intensify economic difficulties inside the Soviet Union, and there are signs that the Soviet leaders are anxious to avoid shortages of food and consumer goods which might lead to strikes or riots.[29] Foreign adventures also increase the hazards of Soviet citizens being exposed to disturbing political influences. Though it is hard to assess the evidence, it seems reasonably clear that Soviet troops did become disaffected in Czechoslovakia in 1968, and potential disaffection may have been a factor in the removal of the original predominantly Central Asian divisions from Afghanistan.[30] Therefore it is questionable whether domestic weakness will result in recklessness abroad, especially since Soviet foreign policy has been characterised by caution rather than risk-taking.

(6) Defensive military strength

The final model stresses the defensive nature of Soviet military and foreign policy. This view appeals to Soviet history: the traumatic experience of the surprise attack by Hitler in 1941, the death of 20 million Soviet citizens in World War II and the devastation suffered. As a result, there is a deep desire for peace among the Soviet people, and the Soviet leaders seem to share a genuine anxiety to avoid world war. This approach also stresses the reality of Soviet fears of China, with which there have been military clashes over a boundary dispute as recently as 1969.[31]

This interpretation of Soviet perceptions and behaviour concurs with the impressions of many visitors to the Soviet Union and makes a good deal of sense.[32] But popular desire for peace inside the Soviet Union cannot be translated easily into direct pressure on Soviet leaders, and the leaders' concern with security does not automatically mean they are committed to disarmament. So far, while making far reaching proposals for disarmament, they have pursued a policy of maintaining military strength. Soviet fear is also a major reason for the Soviet Union maintaining its defensive perimeter in Eastern Europe.[33]

Accepting this interpretation would mean dismissing the spectre of Soviet communism poised to attack Western Europe, and taking very seriously the Soviet fears of an alliance between the USA and China, and of being faced with a new version of 'capitalist encirclement' and the danger of a war on two fronts. This leads directly into the general theory about the reciprocal nature of arms races, which does not require any particular view of the Soviet regime, but which implies that any state that feels threatened will do its utmost to avoid being left in a position of severe military inferiority.[34]

In conclusion, theories of the USSR today which claim that the nature of the Soviet system results in an inevitable drive towards world domination are not convincing, and are not supported by the available evidence. Soviet statements and Soviet actions, however, give grounds for believing that the USSR aims to be a global power on a par with the US; they also support the theory that it is deeply concerned about its security and the threat of war. Although it is sensible to assume that in foreign and defence policy the Soviet Union is in many ways liable to act like other states, the secretiveness inherent in the Soviet system, the centralised and dictatorial nature of Party rule, and the absence of channels for organised opposition or popular pressure, may strengthen a tendency to ruthless action and military solutions. Future policy will be influenced by international developments, but will also depend on political conflicts within the party or the military elite, on the relative leverage of various institutional groups, on whether economic or political reforms are undertaken, and on the nature of the post-Brezhnev leadership. None of these can be confidently predicted.

We can, however, examine whether the present condition of the Soviet Union is conducive to military expansion or to arms limitation and accommodation with the West. Economically, it is clearly in the interests of the Soviet Union to reduce the burden of military expenditure. The Soviet gross national product is lower than that of the USA and the proportion of it spent on defence is higher. Moreover, the military sector absorbs technology and skills which could usefully be re-directed to more economically beneficial ends — it is much clearer in a centrally planned economy that resources being used for armaments are being diverted from peaceful productive purposes than it is in the USA, where arms production may provide employment and in the short term boost the economy. Soviet statements show that they see that high expenditure on arms is damaging to Soviet prosperity.[35]

V. *Would changes in Western defence policy affect Soviet behaviour?*

Before concluding this discussion of a possible Soviet threat to Europe, it is important to raise specifically the question of how European defence policy relates to potential Soviet threats. In particular it is important to consider how US withdrawal from Europe, or the abandonment of nuclear weapons in European defence policy, might affect the Soviet behaviour. Even if the Soviet Union had no plan of European conquest in the late 1940s, if the West had not formed a military alliance and if the military risks had seemed negligible, Stalin might possibly have been tempted to seize West Germany.[36] The question which arises is whether the Soviet Union might experience similar temptations in the future if it believed it had a decisive military advantage. The leadership of the Soviet Union has of course changed; but although a reversion to Stalinism in internal politics is unlikely, it cannot be guaranteed that a future Politburo would abstain from an adventuristic policy as a world power. We must therefore assess Soviet interests in Europe.

The position today is very different from the position in 1950. Soviet experience in Eastern Europe has demonstrated the long-term difficulties of trying to impose Soviet style regimes on unwilling countries by force of arms. Pressures for political reform undermine the legitimacy of the Soviet style of government, and are in danger of spreading to the Soviet Union itself; satellite states do not provide wholly reliable military allies. Whereas in the early years Soviet economic relationships with Eastern Europe benefitted its own economy, by now the USSR is to some extent underwriting East European economies with relatively cheap supplies of oil and gas, and deferring repayment of Polish debts.

Soviet relations with Western Europe have altered as well. Soviet attitudes to the EEC have changed from regarding it as a political threat to conceding the economic advantages of relations between East European countries and the EEC.[37] In addition, there has been a major shift in Soviet attitudes to West Germany. At the 1966 CPSU Congress Brezhnev commented: ''Today West German imperialism is the United States' chief ally in Europe in aggravating world tensions.''[38] But as a result of the success of Brandt's Ostpolitik and the signing of the Helsinki Agreement recognising Europe's present frontiers, the USSR now has good diplomatic relations with West Germany, and Soviet (and Polish) fears about the potential threat of a revanchist Germany have been quietened.

It is clear that a Soviet attack upon and military occupation of one or several West European countries would increase its military and administrative burdens, probably add to its political problems in controlling satellite states, and result in a disruption of relations with Western Europe, or, in a more extreme scenario, in the destruction of the existing West European economy, all of which would exacerbate economic and political problems inside the USSR and Eastern Europe. Conversely, the Soviet Union may now have political and economic incentives to relax its grip on Eastern Europe and security considerations based on fear of West Germany may also have been modified. Therefore some forms of disengagement and demilitarisation in Central Europe may now be more acceptable to the USSR than in the past.

Nevertheless, disarmament and defence policies in Western Europe and in Britain should not be made too dependent on an optimistic assessment of Soviet intentions or of rational Soviet choices. Leaders of great states may be assailed by a lust for power which overrides caution. Thus US withdrawal from Europe could mean that Soviet leaders might be tempted to overlook long-term costs in order to make short-term gains or to enhance their own personal power, if the military costs of an attack seemed low. So even if the likelihood of a Soviet attack seemed minimal, despite the changed situation which could exist after a US withdrawal, the construction of some form of credible non-nuclear defence, pending moves towards effective disarmament in Europe, clearly remains essential.

VI. *Types of Soviet threat to Western Europe*

Threats which might endanger Britain fall into two categories: those which arise out of a crisis affecting Western Europe and those which are directed solely against us. We are more likely to be drawn into war as a result of Soviet military intervention in Greece or an outbreak of war on the West German border, than to be the primary target for Soviet military action. Thus it might be argued that the more closely we identify our interests with those of Western Europe in military terms, the more vulnerable we are. On the other hand, in the unlikely event of Soviet aggression against Western Europe, a non-aligned Britain would also be vulnerable to forms of attack or military pressure.

The danger of a nuclear pre-emptive attack in Europe

It is generally agreed that at present the most likely reason for war in Europe is miscalculation as a result of conflict in some other part of the world. In that case a nuclear pre-emptive strike seems much more likely if nuclear weapons are deployed in Europe; if there were no danger of a nuclear strike, the USSR would have no reason for pre-emption.

A blitzkrieg attack to conquer Western Europe
Unlikely as this is, it is probably still the main popular fear, and is

invoked implicitly or explicitly in many political speeches stressing Soviet aggressiveness. A deliberate attempt to occupy all of Western Europe would be economically and politically irrational, would be exceedingly risky in terms of US and Chinese reactions, and would be an extremely costly way of seeking global status. These considerations would still apply to a non-nuclear and disengaged Europe, even if the threat of direct US retaliation were somewhat reduced. Many strategic theorists share this scepticism about the likelihood of the USSR attempting all-out conquest and occupation of Western Europe. Some of them have tentatively suggested possible limited alternatives, covered below.

Limited attacks on Europe

Possible scenarios for a limited Soviet attack are:

(1) rapid seizure of a city or piece of territory with political or strategic importance in the hope of presenting the West with a *fait accompli* — Berlin or northern Norway have been suggested;

(2) Soviet intervention in a civil war or local war in order to extend its sphere on the pretext of being invited in by one side — sending Soviet troops to safeguard the unity of Yugoslavia or intervention in a war between Greece and Turkey, for example; and

(3) a spill-over from a conflict in Eastern Europe — for example, if the Soviet Union did invade Poland — resulting from the Soviet Union's desire to neutralise 'the source of infection', or to pursue retreating freedom-fighters or refugees.[39]

The first two presuppose a fundamental aggressive intent on the part of the Soviet Union and an opportunistic policy of military encroachment. They also presuppose a Soviet penchant for risk-taking. The underlying assumptions are therefore dubious, although for geographical reasons a take-over of Berlin is the most credible suggestion. As the USSR has made no such attempt since 1949, and when given the opportunity of the 1974 war between Greece and Turkey appears to have tried to limit, not exacerbate, the conflict,[40] these scenarios are improbable. The case of Yugoslavia is somewhat different, and the Yugoslavs themselves do take seriously the danger of Soviet attack, especially since 1968. But Yugoslavia has in fact successfully remained independent of Moscow for 34 years.

If the possibility of these scenarios is considered in a different military context, for example a nuclear-free Western Europe and no alliance with the USA, then the risks of nuclear escalation would clearly be low, but the strategic or political advantages to the Soviet Union still highly debatable. We cannot totally rule out a pattern of piecemeal encroachment based on seizing *ad hoc* advantage. However, as argued in the previous section, such a policy may not be in the Soviet interest for political and economic reasons.

The third scenario, of a Soviet military attack on the West as a spill-over from a crisis in Eastern Europe, seems improbable if the purpose were to attack the 'source of infection' for movements in the East. Whatever they may say, Soviet leaders are not likely to believe that the Czechoslovak Reform Movement or Solidarity were primarily inspired from the West, and even if they did, to invade while fighting in Eastern Europe would make no military or political sense. In a much longer-term perspective, if the Soviet Union were the only major military power in Europe, if unrest continued in Eastern Europe and if the option of greater liberalisation was rejected, the Soviet Union might believe that various forms of pressure, including military action, against the West European countries was necessary to neutralise the influence of independent countries on East European aspirations. This kind of strategy cannot be excluded, but is unlikely to involve the Soviet Union starting a European war while suppressing an East European revolt.

Rebellion in Eastern Europe is more likely to lead directly to war through western intervention, if political pressure leads to some kind of military aid to Eastern Europe. In this context, refugees fleeing over the border, or trying to do so, might encourage limited western military activity on the border; or prolonged and bitter fighting in Central Europe might draw in western troops. So the possibility of war by miscalculation, or as a result of western military action, arising out of an East European crisis, is real; but a deliberate Soviet attack in these circumstances much less plausible.

Forms of direct military pressure

An alternative scenario is that the Soviet Union might use military superiority in an area, together with military harassment, for example of shipping, to extract specific strategic or political concessions such as the use of bases and facilities, or political neutrality. Norway is suggested as a possible target for this kind of pressure. Since in the context of NATO such action would be less hazardous than an overt attack, it is more likely than the types of limited military action discussed above. This kind of pressure cannot be excluded if some West European countries became non-aligned or formed some kind of European non-nuclear alliance, though whether it would be in the interest of the Soviet Union to indulge in this kind of direct military pressure is doubtful. In the short term any Soviet action which discouraged a process of nuclear disarmament in Europe would be wholly counter-productive, since this process would clearly be welcomed by the USSR; in the longer term the nature of the strategic and political situation in the whole of Europe and developments inside the Soviet Union would determine the rationality or irrationality of such action.

Direct military pressure to achieve use of strategic facilities is, however, one of the more plausible scenarios for a Soviet threat to Britain. It is possible that the USSR might be interested in placing nuclear bases here, though questionable whether it would risk putting nuclear weapons into a potentially hostile country, as it seems to avoid putting long- and medium-range missiles into Eastern Europe. Naval bases in Britain, whether for nuclear or conventional purposes, would be more attractive, especially given Soviet problems about winter access from its northern ports and its increased naval deployment. The Soviet Union might possibly therefore use some form of harassment to acquire use of naval facilities.

In a time of crisis the Soviet government might conceivably risk direct seizure of a key port if this seemed possible without a major military confrontation. Short of a crisis, the Soviet Union seems more likely to use indirect, rather than overt, military pressure, and to seek more limited concessions, such as the use of dockyards for refitting, which it has sought in the past from Yugoslavia.

Indirect military pressure

Because many strategic theorists have been sceptical of the likelihood of the Soviet Union attempting to occupy Western Europe or of pursuing the more limited forms of attack or harassment which can be imagined, the main threat often cited is that of indirect military pressure; the term 'Finlandisation' is often used in this context. Whatever the term used, what is at issue is the presumed willingness of a militarily weaker country to accommodate its foreign and defence policy, and to a lesser extent its domestic policy, to the interests of a stronger military power.[41] It might also mean certain concessions in foreign policy, without any loss of internal control. The threat involved is largely implicit, and when it becomes explicit it may take the form of political and economic pressures, rather than overt military threats.

The term Finlandisation tends to be used in a way that oversimplifies and exaggerates the degree of control exercised by the Soviet
Union over Finland. Though Finland is obliged to observe a neutrality which in some respects leans towards the Soviet Union, and limits
its criticism of the Soviet Union, it undoubtedly retains independent
democratic institutions, and its economic links with the USSR
benefit Finland and do not prevent it from trading freely with the rest
of the world. The military agreement between Finland and the
USSR only requires Finland to defend its own territory in the event
of attack and Soviet troops can intervene only by mutual agreement.[42] A comparison with Panama's relationship to the United
States (which until 1977 gave the USA total military control over the
Canal Zone and which still reserves some military rights to the USA
when Panama attains full control of the Canal in the year 2000) puts
Finland's position into better perspective. As a country small in
population bordering on a powerful neighbour, and occupying a
position of strategic importance to it, Finland enjoys a reasonable
degree of autonomy.

The historic, geographical and economic factors which impose
some limitations on Finland's ability to take an anti-Soviet stand do
not apply to Western European countries, either individually or as an
entity. If US commitment to Europe were abandoned, would Soviet
military dominance on the one hand, and lack of nerve on the part of
West European governments on the other, automatically result in
concessions to the USSR? One crucial element — both in Finland
and in a putative attempt to control Western Europe — is obviously
the political will to remain independent. Political will cannot be
guaranteed, and depends on internal political factors, but its lack
cannot simply be ascribed to military pressures.

VII. Involvement in a world war

The greatest danger that confronts Britain, and indeed Western
Europe as a whole, in the foreseeable future is not of deliberate Soviet
aggression, but involvement in a general war between the great
powers, which might well start through miscalculation.

If nuclear war broke out, Britain would run less risk of a direct
nuclear attack if all nuclear bases had been removed. But some
missiles might hit us by accident, or the targeting policies of one or
both the great powers might include (in an all-out exchange) striking
non-nuclear countries in order to 'deny' them to the enemy. Limited

nuclear strikes might also be used to neutralise conventional military bases and ports, especially if we were still part of NATO. At best there would be considerable radioactive fall-out from a nuclear war in Europe.

The greatest risk of a conventional attack on Britain would also occur in a general war. Both the Soviet Union and the United States might try to control Britain for strategic purposes during a European war, if we had adopted neutrality. If, on the other hand, a non-nuclear Britain remained part of NATO, the surveillance and early-warning systems, and our role as a staging post for US troops, would clearly mean that we would remain a Soviet target.

So one of the priorities of a new defence policy must be to encourage measures to reduce the risk of a general war being waged in Europe.

VIII. Summary of the argument

Assessment of the threats is partly related to choice of defence and foreign policy and must be provisional, but nevertheless a coherent strategy requires clarity about the threats we need to guard against.

In the past we have been at war with other European powers, but today that is not credible, unless there were a major revival of fascism, which seems unlikely. We might be in dispute with other European countries over resources, but this should not lead to serious military action. There is a danger that local conflicts in the Third World will involve the great powers, or that the USA and the USSR will in the future come into conflict over Third World resources. Although Britain might be denied access to vital supplies by a Third World country, this would not be a *military* threat. Our security is threatened primarily by possible great-power confrontation. The USA might try to intervene (by non-military means) if we adopted a non-aligned policy, but once the transition stage was completed, a US threat to Britain is improbable, though there might be pressure for a renewal of strategic facilities. If there were a European war, the USA might pre-emptively seize parts of Britain for strategic purposes.

The central question which requires detailed discussion is whether there really is a Soviet threat. This chapter has examined the historical record in the Stalinist period and the more recent developments in the 1970s, and looked at the argument that Soviet military power indicates aggressive intent. The historical or military 'facts' cannot prove conclusively what Soviet goals are, though they may indicate tendencies.

Six theories about the nature of the Soviet state were briefly assessed as a means of finding a framework in which to assess the facts. Two realistic theories are that the Soviet Union is seeking great-power status on a par with the USA, and that its strategy is still shaped by fear of external aggression. Neither theory is wholly re-assuring: great-power ambitions can result in ruthlessness, and a defensive fear can result in a commitment to military power. But neither supports the idea that the Soviet Union is bent on global conquest, whether for ideological or nationalist reasons.

If the USA pulled out of Europe it is possible the Soviet Union would see fewer risks in military aggression, but the political and economic circumstances of the USSR make it doubtful whether aggression would be in its interest. Western countries should not, however, *rely* on Soviet goodwill, and a credible defence needs to be maintained.

A number of scenarios of possible Soviet military action, ranging from a blitzkrieg attack to overrun the West to more limited seizure of territory, military harassment and indirect use of military power, have been considered. Most of these scenarios seem unlikely, though a war arising out of East European unrest is possible if the West tried to intervene, and a Soviet seizure of Berlin could occur.

If the Soviet Union were to pose any direct threat to Britain, it is most likely to seek *strategic* gains, in particular naval facilities. In a war or at a time of crisis, the Soviet Union might try to seize ports directly, otherwise indirect pressure seems more likely than overt harassment of shipping or a military build-up in our waters.

IX. Conclusions

To sum up, the Commission concludes that the main threats to British security are the following:

(1) involvement in a nuclear war between the great powers;

(2) involvement in a conventional war in Europe — either directly through membership of NATO or a European Alliance, or as a possible strategic target if Britain was non-aligned;

(3) that great-power pressure, falling short of direct military attack, might be exerted to ensure use of strategic facilities in Britain in time of peace, most probably by the USA to keep facilities it already has, but possibly by the USSR.

The threat of Soviet military action to include Britain in its sphere of influence, or to impose a Soviet-style communism upon it, is a very much more remote possibility. There were some differences among Commission members in their detailed assessment of the Soviet regime and its intentions, but they agreed that a politically motivated attack could not be discounted altogether.

Notes to Chapter 2

1. On Korea see: D. F. Fleming, *The Cold War and Its Origins, 1917–1960* (London: Allen & Unwin, 1961), Vol. 2: 1950–1960. pp. 589–95; also Soon Sung Cho, *Korea in World Politics, 1940–1950* (Berkeley: University of California Press, 1967).

2. Debate about the origins of the Cold War is now a major historical topic, with the revisionist school (Gabriel Kolko, David Horowitz) challenging earlier more anti-Soviet interpretations. There are good grounds for doubting simple versions of Soviet aggressive designs, but it is also important to take account of evidence which gives weight to Stalin's expansionist ambitions, for example, evidence produced by the Czechoslovak emigré Karel Kaplan, on the basis of his access in 1968 to Czechoslovak Party Central Committee files, recording a meeting between Stalin and Defence Ministers from most European states in 1951, at which Stalin apparently spoke of the need to drive the USA out of Western Europe before it consolidated its military presence, and envisaged doing so before 1955. Kaplan brought out his files in 1977 and the information so far available depends on his own articles and talks with journalists — see *The Times*, 6 May 1977 and *Le Monde*, 20 May 1977. There is also a brief reference drawing on Kaplan's information in Nikolai Tolstoy, *Stalin's Secret War* (London: Cape, 1981). It is difficult to assess the full significance of this evidence until there has been a more detailed analysis and interpretation of the 'Kaplan Papers'.

3. This is a simplified summary of a large question. In the series of *Encounter* articles, which started with George Kennan's reassessment of Soviet policy 30 years after his article formulating the Containment Policy ('Mr K Reconsiders: A Current Assessment of Soviet American Relations', *Encounter*, 50, 3 (March 1978), 7–13), Kennan contrasts the USSR under Brezhnev "an authoritarian state" headed by a "moderate, in fact conservative man", with the "totalitarian monstrosity" created by Stalin's "combination of paranoia with cruelty and political mastery". This view is attacked by Richard Pipes ('Mr K. Revises', *Encounter*, 50, 4 (April 1978) 18–21), who denies that " 'changes' of any magnitude have occurred in the Soviet Union since 1953". Most authorities on the internal politics of the Soviet Union agree that there have been major changes — an end to terror and the dominance of the secret police over the party and the society, and to absurd ideological distortions of academic and scientific thought (e.g. Lysenko). While the Brezhnev regime was less liberal than the Khruschev period, it probably involved greater institutional stability and more cautious and consistent policies at home and abroad. See for example: J. F. Hough and M. Fainsod, *How the Soviet Union is Governed* (Cambridge: Harvard University Press, 1979); M. McAuley, *Politics and the Soviet Union* (Harmondsworth: Penguin, 1977); A. Brown and M. Kaser, eds., *The Soviet*

Union Since the Fall of Khrushchev (London: Macmillan, 1979).

4. There are various interpretations of Afghanistan. See Fifth Report from the Foreign Affairs Committee, House of Commons, 1979—80, 'Afghanistan: the Soviet Invasion and its Consequences for British Policy', HMSO, 1980, for a range of views. The Committee said in its conclusions: ''The Committee heard no evidence that the invasion of Afghanistan was part of a Soviet grand strategy to extend its influence to the Gulf and threaten Western oil supplies'', while noting that the USSR was militarily capable of undertaking such an invasion (p. xxx). For accounts which lay stress on the complex regional factors affecting Soviet decisions, see S. S. Harrison, 'Dateline Afghanistan: Exit through Finland?', *Foreign Policy*, 41 (Winter 1980—81), 163-87; D. Murarka, 'The Russian Intervention: A Moscow Analysis', *Round Table*, 282 (April 1981), 122-39; and R. Medvedev, 'The Afghan Crisis', *New Left Review*, 121 (May/June 1980), 91-96.

5. For a summary of Soviet policy in Africa, see J. F. Gutteridge, 'Africa', in K. London, ed., *The Soviet Union and World Politics* (London: Croom Helm, 1980), and W. E. Griffith, 'Soviet Power and Policies in the Third World: The Case of Africa', in C. Bertram, ed., *Prospects of Soviet Power in the 1980s* (London: Macmillan, 1980). Commentators tend to suggest that the main aim of the Soviet Union is to consolidate its presence in Africa as part of its global strategy. They also stress the complexity of African politics and the dangers of over-simplification.

6. Brezhnev repeated this claim in his speech to the Twenty-sixth Congress of the CPSU: ''We have not sought, and we do not now seek, military superiority over the other side. That is not our policy. But neither will we permit the building up of such superiority over us.'' Report of the CC of the CPSU to the XXVI Congress of the CPSU (Moscow: Novosti, 1981), p. 39.

7. It is put forward by Richard Pipes, who links it however to a thesis stressing Soviet militarism and the historic nature of the Russian state. See: R. Pipes, 'Militarism and the Soviet State', *Daedalus*, 109, 4 (Fall 1980), 1-12, and R. Pipes, 'Soviet Global Strategy', *Commentary*, April, 1980, pp. 31-39.

8. Seweryn Bialer notes the incongruity between the dominant Western image of Soviet domestic politics and the image of ideological commitment in Soviet external policy. See his essay 'Soviet Foreign Policy: Sources, Perceptions and Trends', in S. Bialer, ed., *The Domestic Context of Soviet Foreign Policy* (London: Croom Helm, 1981), p. 421

   For the Brezhnev ideological formulation of the stage reached by the Soviet state, see A. B. Evans, 'Developed Socialism in Soviet Ideology', *Soviet Studies*, XXIX, 3 (July 1977), 409-28.

9. See G. Golan, 'The Middle East' in London, *The Soviet Union and World Politics*.[9]

10. See H. Adomeit, 'Ideology in the Soviet View of International Affairs', in Bertram *Prospects of Soviet Power in the 1980s*.[5]

11. Bialer in *The Domestic Context of Soviet Foreign Policy*,[8] pp. 422-25, makes a useful distinction between ''pure'' ideology which he thinks no longer motivates Soviet leaders, and ''practical'' ideology as a constellation of influences which does.

12. See for example Julian Amery's submission to the House of Commons Select Committee on Foreign Affairs Report on Afghanistan, and Pipes, 'Militarism and the Soviet State'.[7]

13. This is in slightly different variants a widely held view. Bialer lays some stress on the role of Russian nationalism. See also A. Ulam, 'Russian Nationalism', in Bialer, *The Domestic Context of Soviet Foreign Policy*.[8]

14. For other interpretations and a useful discussion of the question of how far Soviet society is militarised, see D. Holloway, 'War, Militarism and the Soviet State', reprinted in E. P. Thompson and D. Smith, eds., *Protest and Survive* (Harmondsworth: Penguin, 1980).

15. For a brief discussion of the theoretical issues surrounding the concept of a "military industrial complex" see Holloway, 'War, Militarism and the Soviet State',[14], pp. 157–60. See also V. V. Aspaturian, 'The Soviet Military Context:— Does it Exist?' and W. T. Lee, 'The "Politico-Military Industrial Complex" of the USSR', *Journal of International Affairs*, 26, 1 (1972), 1–28 and 73–86.

16. For an account of Khruschev's political battles, see M. Tatu, *Power in the Kremlin. From Khruschev's Decline to Collective Leadership*, trans. H. Katel (Baltimore: Johns Hopkins University Press, 1966). For general political assessment of the Brezhnev years see Brown, *The Soviet Union since the Fall of Khruschev*.[3]

17. Soviet and Western figures on Soviet growth rates differ and there are problems about the criteria to be used. There are also problems about identifying Soviet defence spending, some of which is hidden. See for example H. S. Levine, 'Economic Development, Technological Transfer and Foreign Policy', and M. Bornstein, 'Economic Growth and Foreign Policy', in Bialer, *The Domestic Context of Soviet Foreign Policy*.[8] But when the CIA revised in 1976 its estimate for the proportion of Soviet GNP spent on defence from 6–8% to 11–13%, the point was not that the USSR was acquiring greater military strength than previously thought, but spending more to acquire it.

18. This process has been documented by W. E. Odom, 'The "Militarization" of Soviet Society', *Problems of Communism*, XXV (September/October 1976), 34–51. It is also referred to proudly in Soviet military writings. For example, Marshal Grechko, 'On Guard over Peace and Socialism', in *Selected Soviet Military Writing* 1970–75 (Washington, DC: US Air Force, 1976?), pp. 20–21.

19. See R. Kolkowicz, *The Soviet Military and the Communist Party* (Princeton: Princeton University Press, 1967).

20. See D. Holloway, 'Military Power and Political Purpose in Soviet Policy', *Daedalus*, 109, 4 (Fall 1980), 13–30, who suggests that despite some tensions in the relationship between the High Command and Party leadership, "the principle of Party supremacy has never seriously been challenged" (p. 25). See also D. Holloway, 'Decision Making in Soviet Defence Policies', in Bertram, *Prospects of Soviet Power in the 1980s.*[5]

21. These considerations are adduced by T. J. Colton, *Commissars, Commanders and Civilian Authority* (Cambridge: Harvard University Press, 1979), who argues that the interests of the Soviet military and the CPSU intermesh, and that the Soviet military has abstained from active political intervention.

22. See J. Valente, *Soviet Intervention in Czechoslovakia, 1968* (Baltimore: John Hopkins University Press, 1979), who documents splits within the military on the advisability of invading Czechoslovakia.

23. There is an additional argument put forward by Pipes and others that the fundamentally aggressive designs of the Soviet military are manifested by the fact that Soviet strategic doctrine envisages a first strike with nuclear weapons. Other Soviet experts believe that this is a misreading of Soviet thinking. See Holloway, 'Military Power and Political Purpose in Soviet Policy'.[20] See also J. Erickson, 'The Soviet Military System: Doctrine, Technology and Style' in J. Erickson and E. J. Feuchtwanger, eds., *Soviet Military Power and Performance* (London: Macmillan, 1979)

24. See J. Azrael, ed., *Soviet Nationality Policy and Practices* (New York: Praeger, 1978), also J. Azrael, 'The "Nationality Problem" in the USSR: Domestic Pressures and Foreign Policy Constraints' in Bialer, *The Domestic Context of Soviet Foreign Policy*.[8]

25 Quoted by R. Levgold, 'The Concept of Power and Security in Soviet History' in Bertram, *Prospects of Soviet Power in the 1980s*.[5]

26 For a variety of approaches see R. Levgold, 'The Concept of Power and Security in Soviet History' and P. Windsor, 'The Soviet Union in the International System of the 1980s' in Bertram, *Prospects of Soviet Power in the 1980s*;[5] and Vernon V. Aspaturian, 'Soviet Global Power and the Correlation of Forces', *Problems of Communism*, XXIX (May/June 1980) 1–18

27. How far the USSR will in the future become more dependent on oil and other imports from the third world is an issue on which there are conflicting Western estimates — especially on the topical problem of oil. The USSR will have increasing difficulty in providing oil to Eastern Europe and using oil exports for hard foreign currency earnings as well as meeting its domestic demand, but how far there is likely to be a crisis in Soviet oil production by the 1990s depends not only on (uncertain) estimates about how much oil may potentially be available, but also on such factors as the efficiency of Soviet techniques in discovering it and extracting it, the amount of future Soviet investments in oil production, the effectiveness with which it can develop alternative energy supplies (coal and natural gas) and international developments affecting the price and availability of oil. The CIA has in fact revised its 1977 estimate that the USSR would be *importing* oil by 1985 and predicted in 1981 that by the mid 1980s the USSR would still be exporting oil (*The Economist*, 23–29 May 1981).

28. Soviet statements have stressed that the Afghan government asked for Soviet intervention, and that Soviet troops would be withdrawn once "imperialist intervention" ended. See A. L. Monks, *The Soviet Intervention in Afghanistan* (Washington DC: American Enterprise Institute Studies in Defense Policy Research, 1981).

29. This is cited as a constraint on the Soviet leadership by A. H. Brown, 'Policy Making in the Soviet Union', *Soviet Studies*, XXIII, 1 (July 1971), 120–48.

30. Withdrawal of Soviet troops from Czechoslovakia and Afghanistan is not in itself evidence of disaffection, since it can be ascribed to normal Soviet military practice of troop replacement. But many Czechs have claimed that troops were punished for signs of dissent. In the case of Afghanistan, some evidence from defectors in Pakistan is cited by Alexandre Benningsen, 'Soviet Muslims and the World of Islam', *Problems of Communism*, XXIX (March/April 1980), 38–51.

31. The reality of Soviet fears of China is generally acknowledged and appears to be common to different sectors of Soviet society. H. Smith, *The Russians* (London: Sphere, 1976), p. 411 comments: "on no other issue did private opinion seem to coincide more closely with the official line than in the deepseated fear and mistrust of the Chinese." See also G. F. Kennan, *The Cloud of Danger: Some Current Problems of American Foreign Policy* (London: Hutchinson, 1978), pp. 192–93.

32. See also H. Smith, *The Russians*,[31] chapter XXII on the impact of the Second World War. See also statement of US Ambassador Averell Harriman, 20 April 1977, extract in P. Rogers, M. Dando and P. van den Dungen, *As Lambs to the Slaughter* (London: Arrow, 1981), p. 245.

33. Z. Mlynar, *Night Frost in Prague* (London: Hurst, 1980), pp. 239–40, gives an account of Brezhnev's explanation to the Czechoslovak leaders of the Soviet

invasion: that the Soviet Union bought East European territory at great sacrifice in World War II, and that the borders of the socialist camp guarantee USSR security.

34. The most eloquent recent statement of the ''reciprocal logic'' at work in both blocs is E. P. Thompson, *Beyond the Cold War* (London: Merlin Press, 1982).

35. See Bornstein, 'Economic Growth and Foreign Policy'.[17] Essays by H. Machowski and G. Sokoloff in Bertram, *Prospects of Soviet Power in the 1980s*,[5] also deal with economic resources and problems.

36. This is argued by M. Howard, 'Social Change and the Defense of the West', *Washington Quarterly*, 2, 4 (Autumn 1979).

37. J. Laloy, 'Western Europe in Soviet Perspective', in Bertram, *Prospects of Soviet Power in the 1980s*,[5] pp. 44–45.

38. Cited by W. Hyland, 'Soviet Security Concerns in the 1980s', in Bertram, *Prospects of Soviet Power in the 1980s*,[5] p. 95. He quotes Brezhnev's contrasting statement in 1978: ''Today, however, the relations between the USSR and the FRG — without shutting our eyes to the negative moments — have become an important element of stability in Europe . . . ''

39. These scenarios are usefully summarised by R. J. Vincent, 'Military Power and Political Influence: The Soviet Union and Western Europe', *Adelphi Paper*, 119 (1975).

40. Vincent[39] (p. 14) footnotes a caveat about the Greece/Turkey example in the light of 1974. The Soviet Union switched diplomatic support from Turkey to Greece after the fall of the military junta in Greece on 24 July, asserted the need to restore independence, unity and territorial integrity of Cyprus, and was active in the UN Security Council in July and August 1974. See Wolfgang Berner *et al.*, *The Soviet Union 1974-5*, (London: Hurst, 1976) pp. 234-37.

41. Vincent[39] (p. 16) does produce a model of ''Finlandised'' Europe: (1) considerable deference to Soviet interests in policy-making; (2) a ''Russian party'' in domestic politics; (3) a neutrality tilted towards Moscow; (4) Soviet pressure making independence conditional but not normal; and (5) Soviet suzerainty embodied in the public law of Europe and recognised *de facto* by other powers accepting Europe in the Soviet sphere. This model can with slight adaptation fit individual countries.

42. On Finland see: D.G. Kirkby, *Finland in the Twentieth Century* (London: Hurst, 1979) M. Jakobson, 'Substance and Appearance: Finland', *Foreign Affairs*, 58, 5 (Summer 1980), 1034-44, and F. Singleton, 'The Myth of Finlandisation', *International Affairs*, 57, 2 (Spring 1981) 270-85. The Commission is indebted to Jennifer Macias for a research paper on Finland.

Chapter 3
Britain, NATO and Europe

I. Options for Europe

The most important question for Britain without the Bomb is whether to remain in NATO. Some countries which ban nuclear bases and have renounced producing their own nuclear weapons, like Norway and Canada, are still members of NATO, but this raises problems about the consistency of their non-nuclear stance. In Britain, supporters of nuclear disarmament are divided over this crucial issue.

The aim of peace in Europe eventually requires an end to the rigid division between East and West and a dissolution of the two opposed military blocs. If these developments also meant a reduction in Soviet and US influence over their respective allies, Europe would gain greater political independence as well as greater security, although in the foreseeable future it seems utopian to envisage an Eastern Europe wholly independent of the USSR. The most urgent priority is to de-nuclearise Europe and promote other forms of arms limitation which will reduce tension and lessen the destructiveness of the weapons deployed.

The problem in thinking about the future of Europe is that focusing solely on defence seems to imply an acceptance of Europe's division, yet any immediate emphasis on diplomatic and political settlements is unrealistic. First it is necessary to create new strategic and political conditions in which both sides might negotiate seriously. Whether the goal of promoting a context in which both military blocs could be dissolved is more likely to be achieved by a number of countries working through NATO, or by some form of action which will jolt the present structures, is one of the issues to be resolved.

This chapter explores the arguments for and against a non-nuclear Britain staying in NATO, explains the Commission's proposals on this question, and discusses the implications of the two main alternatives to NATO: a European Defence Association and a non-aligned Britain.

II. The orthodox case for NATO

NATO was founded in order to combat the perceived threat of Soviet aggression, and the primary argument for maintaining the Alliance is still that a co-ordinated West European defence effort is necessary to discourage Soviet ambitions. In addition, US military support and the presence of US troops in Europe are seen as essential elements in Western defence strategy.

A second argument central to the case for NATO is that Western Europe shares political and economic interests with the USA, and that it is to our advantage to foster these links. The existence of NATO can also be seen as a means for Western Europe to influence US policy — including its policy on nuclear weapons and arms control.

A third, less obvious, reason often given for supporting NATO is that Europe, which has been the main theatre for two devastating world wars this century, might generate new national conflicts if the present power blocs are dismantled. The present European status quo is therefore said to promote stability and security.

Whether Britain should stay in NATO depends of course partly on a general assessment of NATO's role, but the decision must also be influenced by more specific calculations of national interest and national obligation. Britain is bound to Europe by cultural, political and economic ties and it can be argued that it should demonstrate this solidarity through common defence arrangements. A secondary consideration is that Britain may be legally obliged to keep the British Army of the Rhine in West Germany, but it is doubtful whether this is really binding.[1]

There is also a purely military case that the most realistic defence policy for Britain requires us to hold the line on the East German border, because if we had to face a Soviet-controlled Europe across the Channel, at that stage the chances of an effective defence would be minimal.

The additional arguments for Britain staying in NATO stress the possibly dangerous consequences of withdrawal; these are considered below in the section on the tactical reasons for staying in NATO.

III. The peace movement case against NATO

Opponents of the Alliance often reverse the assumptions underlying the orthodox case. NATO, it is suggested, through its policies and its very existence, has encouraged an exaggerated fear of the

Soviet Union, prompted the Soviet Union to build up its conventional forces in Central Europe, and is primarily responsible for the
amassing of battlefield nuclear weapons. As a result, war with the
Soviet Union is more likely to be caused than prevented by NATO.

The price for US military support in Europe is US dominance in
NATO and pressure on European governments to accept US
policies. At the same time it can be questioned whether Western
Europe has to rely on US military support to create a credible
defence, if one looks at the population, economic resources and
present military establishments of European NATO members.

The fact that NATO links Europe to the USA can be seen not as an
argument in favour of the Alliance, but as one of the gravest objections to it, because it aligns Western Europe with Washington in the
rivalry between the superpowers, and with US policies in other parts
of the world like Vietnam or Latin America. The likelihood of
Europe being drawn into war as a result of US involvement in a crisis
elsewhere — for example the Middle East — is another urgent
argument against the NATO link. When the world has been on the
brink of a world war — Cuba in 1962 or briefly over the Middle East
in 1973 — Washington has in the heat of crisis scarcely found time to
inform, much less consult, its NATO allies; so greater vulnerability
is not offset by greater direct influence at times of greatest danger.[2]
The leverage European countries do have on long-term US policy
may not compensate for the ability of the US to override their
interests.

Critics of NATO reject the claim that great-power control of
Europe has averted war. Independent political developments in
Western Europe since 1945 have made Europe internally stable, and
residual national rivalries in Eastern Europe are hardly likely to
result in a major war unless the great powers are drawn in. Indeed
Eastern Europe is a much greater source of instability while Europe is
divided into blocs, since the Soviet Union cannot prevent the
periodic rise of popular movements demanding democratic reform,
and Western governments are under pressure to give more than
rhetorical support in a crisis.[3]

For nuclear disarmament movements, however, the overriding
objection to NATO is its nuclear strategy — in particular the fact that
NATO is prepared to use nuclear weapons first in a conventional war
and, if it is deemed necessary, to engage in all-out nuclear war.

The specific arguments cited earlier for British membership of
NATO — the need to show political solidarity with Western Europe,
and the military advantages of a joint defence — could be equally met

by some form of European defence association. Nor does political solidarity necessarily have to be expressed in military terms, and not everyone in Britain wishes to tie us closely to Europe. On the military level it can even be argued that Britain would be in greater danger as part of an Alliance than as an independent, non-aligned, state.

From the political perspective held by most members of the Commission, the balance of the argument so far favours withdrawal from NATO. But before coming to a firm conclusion it is necessary to consider the consequences of leaving NATO, and the possibilities of altering the nature of NATO itself to overcome some of the present objections to it.

IV. The tactical arguments for staying in NATO

The first and most important argument against British withdrawal, which carries weight both with supporters of NATO and some of its peace movement critics, is that British withdrawal could have repercussions which would reduce the prospects of peace in Europe. One common objection is that the political and military role of West Germany would be increased and that this would heighten tension by alarming the Soviet Union. This objection probably exaggerates present Soviet fears in view of the cautious Soviet–German rapprochement over the last decade. But if NATO re-organised itself on a US–German axis, public anxieties in both these countries, and the need to mobilise political support for a stepping up of their own military preparations, could damage the international climate. In addition, the USA might put greater pressure on other countries to accept US bases.

Another possible consequence of British withdrawal is the break-up of NATO. We have argued in chapter 2 against the orthodox fear that this would automatically lead to indirect Soviet domination of Europe; the spectre of a Soviet–German rapprochement to the detriment of the rest of Europe is probably based on dubious historical analogies.[4] But there are other dangers. A German government, bitter at desertion by its allies, might turn to a Franco–German military pact based on the *force de frappe*, or decide to become an independent nuclear power. An isolationist USA turned into a nuclear 'fortress Americana' could thwart all possibilities of arms control or nuclear disarmament. Such counter-productive results are only possibilities, and should not be seen as certainties. They are however risks to be weighed.

A secondary, but serious, argument against British withdrawal from NATO is that of national self-interest. A British unilateralist government which demanded withdrawal of US bases might in any case face some diplomatic or economic sanctions. Withdrawal from NATO could exacerbate US hostility and might simultaneously alienate our European partners — which could greatly strengthen the force of any US sanctions. Withdrawal from NATO also seems at present more likely than British nuclear disarmament as such to promote very bitter opposition from some political and military groups within Britain, and to make more probable US intervention in our political life.

The reasons for staying in NATO are not, however, purely negative. There are a number of positive grounds for believing that a Britain without nuclear weapons could promote disarmament and disengagement more effectively by staying in the Alliance. There is a general diplomatic case for working from within existing bodies. And this tactic gains greater relevance from the present strength of popular peace movements in Europe, which already puts pressure on the various governments to move in a non-nuclear direction. The European movements are in fact divided in their attitudes to NATO, but anti-NATO groups might give provisional support to attempts to change NATO policies. The more recent growth of popular concern about nuclear weapons in the USA has also impelled a reluctant Administration to make at least formal concessions on negotiations, and oppositional forces in US politics could assist European demands for changes in NATO strategy. The perceptible shift in some orthodox military circles in Britain and the USA in favour of raising the nuclear threshold also increases the likelihood of some serious re-thinking of NATO policy, though the establishment critics of present nuclear strategy are hardly likely to go as far as the peace movements think necessary. By 'raising the nuclear threshold' we mean here devising a NATO strategy which does not require early use of battle-field nuclear weapons. The September 1982 speech by General Rogers, Supreme Allied Commander of NATO, suggesting that NATO could unilaterally raise the nuclear threshold and make some reductions in the NATO stockpile of battlefield nuclear weapons by greater reliance on modern reconnaissance techniques and guided conventional weapons, indicates the possibilities for change, but also the limits to radical action inherent in this new military thinking.[5]

The majority of the Commission concluded that these tactical arguments for staying in NATO must be given great weight, especially when linked to the case for political solidarity with

Europe. The most crucial consideration, then, is whether a non-nuclear Britain could consistently stay in what is at present a predominantly nuclear alliance.

V. *Does unilateral nuclear disarmament require withdrawal from NATO?*

One obvious possibility in relation to NATO would be for Britain to follow the example of Canada and Norway, who do not allow nuclear weapons on their territory but remain full members of the Alliance. Norway refuses to have nuclear bases, but does allow deployment of nuclear weapons in time of war, and has participated in the Nuclear Planning Group. Canada has since 1969 very gradually phased out carrying US nuclear weapons on its aircraft, and denuclearised its contingent of 3,000 troops in Germany, but has not openly opposed NATO's nuclear policies.[6] In practical political terms, however, it is doubtful if Britain can be compared to either Norway or Canada, since British unilateralism would have a more significant effect on US and NATO strategic dispositions; the more important question is whether such an approach is consistent with a commitment to nuclear disarmament.

The answer to this question depends partly on the reasons for going non-nuclear. If British unilateralism were based only on limited objections to a British Bomb (doubt that it can be a credible deterrent against the Soviet Union, desire to discourage proliferation, etc.), but did not involve rejecting the general theory of nuclear deterrence, then it would be consistent to rely on the USA and to stay in NATO. And again if the reasons for refusing to have US nuclear bases arise only from anxiety about British safety and sovereignty, it would be reasonable to stay in NATO but to oppose NATO's present policy on 'theatre' nuclear weapons and argue for a 'minimal' deterrence stance by the USA. If, however, this unilateralism is also based on a more fundamental rejection of nuclear weapons strategy — the view held by the Commission — the *prima facie* case for withdrawing from NATO is compelling, whatever the strengths of the tactical reasons for staying in.

The Commission is acutely aware of this dilemma. In view of the clear necessity of moving towards a complete rejection of nuclear deterrence, but also of the important advantages at this time of working for nuclear disarmament from within NATO, the

Commission explored the possibility of creating a nuclear-free Europe in NATO.

This choice takes account of the fact that if Britain were to make its willingness to remain a member of NATO *conditional* on the Alliance taking specific steps to disengage itself from reliance on nuclear strategy, it could have a coherent policy on nuclear weapons, and at the same time seek to have a constructive influence on NATO.

VI. Conditions for a nuclear-free NATO

A policy of staying in NATO conditional on progress towards a non-nuclear strategy in Europe would require a clear progamme for Britain to propose to its partners. This would involve four main steps.

(1) The acceptance by NATO of a no-first-use of nuclear weapons policy

This would signal clearly NATO's intention to raise the nuclear threshold and to abandon its present willingness to resort rapidly to nuclear weapons against a conventional attack. There is a military case for such a move so as to increase the credibility of NATO's strategy, and to reduce pressure on the Soviet Union to use nuclear weapons pre-emptively.

There are also politcal advantages. The Soviet Union should welcome such a move, which it has itself advocated in the past and NATO has rebuffed. Recently the USSR pledged itself unconditionally to no-first-use in a message to the UN 1982 Special Session on Disarmament.[7] A mutual pledge might ease the way to further agreements.

The most obvious doubt about a formal no-first-use pledge is whether it would really be binding on either side once war broke out. So in order to give credibility to such a pledge, NATO would have to reassess publicly its conventional military strategy, which is at present tied to possible nuclear escalation. A reassessment may mean some increase in conventional forces — this is open to debate — but it could also lead to more fundamental changes in strategy and deployment. NATO would have to convince both the Soviet Union and its own people that it was committed to a non-nuclear stance, and therefore its planning and its war games would have to be based on a new conventional strategy. (For a discussion of alternative defence strategies for NATO, see Chapter 5).

(2) A phased but total withdrawal of all battlefield nuclear weapons

These weapons create the greatest risk that a conventional war might escalate rapidly to the nuclear level, since they are essentially war-fighting weapons, and tend to blur the distinction between nuclear and conventional weapons; the neutron or enhanced-radiation bomb, intended as an anti-tank weapon, graphically illustrates this point. If the Soviet Union would agree to abandon its own battlefield nuclear weapons in response to a NATO initiative, the gain would be considerable. Since the Soviet Union introduced such weapons after the West had done so, it is possible they would reciprocate, although at present possible use of battlefield nuclear weapons does appear to be an integral part of Warsaw Pact planning.[8] It should be noted that verifying the removal of such weapons is technically very difficult, so there are both technical and political reasons why it would be unrealistic for the West to insist on detailed inspection should agreement on joint withdrawal otherwise appear to be possible. The Palme Commission's suggestion that troops on both sides in an agreed non-nuclear zone should not be equipped with protection against fall-out would provide an obvious sign of non-nuclear intent.[9] If NATO gave up all battlefield nuclear weapons unilaterally, which it might have to do in order to pursue a serious commitment to de-nuclearise, it would have to face the military implications of this choice (see Chapter 1)

(3) Removal of all US 'theatre' nuclear weapons

If cruise and Pershing II missiles are, despite strong opposition, based in Britain and Europe, removing them would be a priority for a British government committed to a non-nuclear strategy. However, the total removal of all US nuclear bombers, and of sea-based missiles allocated to the European theatre, is a more far-reaching goal which can appropriately be seen as the third stage of de-nuclearisation. It is a more radical demand than that for the removal of battlefield nuclear weapons, and some strategic thinkers who are increasingly sceptical about reliance on battlefield nuclear weapons would not endorse the further step of removing theatre nuclear weapons unless this could be achieved by agreement with the USSR. A coherent policy of de-nuclearisation must, however, include willingness to act unilaterally.

There are strong arguments for insisting on the removal of theatre nuclear weapons. First, one reason for their deployment is that they can be used for striking military targets as part of NATO strategy and are therefore seen as war-fighting weapons. In this sense they resemble battlefield nuclear weapons and in fact the dividing line between the two is not clear-cut. Second, removal of theatre nuclear weapons is necessary to minimise the risk that Europe will be a target for a pre-emptive Soviet nuclear strike in the event of war. Third, withdrawal of the theatre nuclear weapons would create a genuine nuclear-free zone in Western Europe and so would be a decisive step away from the present confrontation; this would not be achieved by the removal of battlefield nuclear weapons alone.

Priority should be given to removing land-based weapons, since these have a more clear-cut role in NATO strategy. In political terms it is easier to mobilise pressure for the removal of land-based systems, it is easier to ensure they really have been removed, and it would probably be easier to secure US agreement at this level. However, a total renunciation of the use of nuclear weapons in a European war would in addition require European countries to withdraw base facilities from US ships carrying nuclear weapons. Such sea-based nuclear forces can be seen as part of the general US deterrent force and not simply as weapons assigned to the European theatre, so this final step would raise directly the issue of whether European NATO countries should decouple their strategy explicitly from the US nuclear deterrent.

(4) Decoupling NATO strategy from the US nuclear deterrent

Even if all nuclear weapons and bases were removed from Europe, so long as the US is a nuclear power, the European NATO countries can in a sense not avoid being associated with some form of strategic deterrence. This is the most difficult element in a policy of de-nuclearising NATO strategy.

Unless the USA and the USSR achieve agreement on measures of joint nuclear disarmament, or unless the Soviet Union has shown a willingness to reduce its own nuclear arsenal, West European countries may be very reluctant to take this step. It is, however, an essential element in creating a genuinely non-nuclear strategy, and a decision to maintain the US nuclear umbrella would make it very difficult to refuse the United States any nuclear bases or facilities.

The first element in decoupling NATO strategy from the US nuclear force would be for the West European members to declare publicly that they did not wish the USA in any circumstances to use nuclear weapons in response to Soviet *conventional* attack, even in the event of a Soviet victory. Strictly speaking this policy is contained in a no-first-use commitment, but there is a big gap between renunciation of early use of nuclear weapons (which is how a no-first-use commitment may be implicitly interpreted) and an explicit request to a nuclear ally not to use them on one's behalf even in the last resort.

The second and really crucial issue — the nub of the problem of decoupling Europe from the US nuclear force — is whether or not Europe should ask the USA to be prepared to threaten retaliation for any Soviet *nuclear* attack on Europe, thereby aiming also to prevent Soviet nuclear escalation or blackmail.

There is a strategic case, in addition to the argument from principle, for seeking to avoid even this limited reliance on the US nuclear deterrent. The case against any form of nuclear deterrence includes the impossibility of securing permanently stable deterrence, and a conviction that a nuclear holocaust would be worse than any other conceivable disaster. Any form of US nuclear commitment to Europe would mean that a war in Europe could escalate into a global nuclear conflagration.

There is also reason to doubt whether the USA would undertake to threaten reprisals on behalf of a Europe which refused to have nuclear bases on its territory, and whether such an undertaking, if it were given, would be believed either by the Europeans or by the USSR. If there is some doubt *now* about US willingness to risk devastation on behalf of Europe, that doubt would be much greater once all US nuclear weapons had been removed.

Thus simply in terms of political realism it may be preferable for a non-nuclear Europe in NATO to rely on political and economic factors to deter the nuclear bombing of non-nuclear countries, and to seek to decouple US nuclear weapons from NATO strategy in Europe. There is in addition the clinching moral argument that one should avoid any reliance on nuclear weapons since this must entail sanctioning their use under some circumstances.

The third issue is what kind of guarantee European countries could reasonably expect from the USA about decoupling its nuclear forces from European defence. Europe could not ultimately prevent US nuclear threats or nuclear retaliation, and as long as the USA maintains over 200,000 troops in Europe, it may hesitate to undertake in advance never to use its nuclear weapons in a European war; moreover there are limits to what European states can stipulate about the defence policy of the USA itself. If the USA, as is quite possible, responds to European pressure for de-nuclearisation by withdrawing its forces from Europe, then even if it retains links with NATO, there would in practice be some decoupling of Europe from the US nuclear deterrent. Nevertheless, the situation needs to be made clear and the European members of NATO could therefore seek a public US acceptance that its nuclear force has no place in *Alliance* strategy.

VII.　*How strong is the case for a nuclear-free Europe in NATO?*

In the previous section we suggested conditions under which a non-nuclear Britain could stay in NATO. It is now necessary to look at the desirabilty of such a policy.

The obvious case for de-nuclearising NATO is that this would retain the present political and military advantages of a joint alliance, would remove the major dangers of its existing nuclear strategy, and would hold out some hope of greater security in Europe and of promoting other measures of disarmament.

The main objections to the idea in principle are: first, that however far Europe goes in trying to decouple from US nuclear strategy, a total dissociation cannot be guaranteed; second, that Europe would still be tied to US global policy as the price for keeping US troops in Europe; and third, that the very reduction of the risks of nuclear war may increase to some extent the risks of a conventional war occurring.

A rather different kind of objection is that reconstructing NATO as a conventional defensive alliance might help to perpetuate present political and military divisions, especially if it results in a conventional military build-up. But it would still be open to NATO to avoid what could be construed as an aggressive posture by switching its strategy to one more clearly defensive.

The other problems which arise concern the practicality of the idea. There are three obvious difficulties: Would NATO if necessary adopt this strategy unilaterally? How would a nuclear France fit into the picture? Would the USA tolerate a nuclear-free Europe?

It does appear at the time of writing that the Soviet Union would welcome a nuclear-free Europe and might be prepared to make some concessions on deployment of missiles inside European Russia; however, such an outcome cannot be counted on, any more than one can count on success in other East–West negotiations. So to achieve a nuclear-free Europe in NATO could require unilateral action, and the likelihood of this depends to a large extent on the future development of anti-nuclear movements in Western Europe.

The second problem is that France seems deeply committed to a nuclear strategy. This too might be altered by popular opposition to the French Bomb; otherwise it is debatable whether French governments would be amenable to NATO pressure. If an agreement were being negotiated for the whole of Europe, France might find it invidious to refuse all co-operation, but if negotiations failed to create a nuclear-free Europe, a French government might well prove intransigent. A nuclear-free Europe in NATO could only seek to isolate France by renouncing the degree of military co-operation that now exists, and by severing all connections between France and NATO

How far US reactions would constitute a difficulty may depend on the nature of the Administration involved in such negotiations. There are good reasons why it would be in the US interest to strengthen the conventional defence of Europe and reduce the danger of being drawn into nuclear war as a result of the escalation of a European conflict; indeed some US governments have said as much. The extent of US nuclear commitment is historically due to European unwillingness to increase conventional forces and to European pressure for a visible commitment of the US nuclear forces to the defence of Europe. But the public stance of the Reagan Administration indicates that it would totally oppose such a plan.

Despite the problems associated with a policy of de-nuclearising NATO strategy, such a policy would have considerable advantages for a unilateralist British government. It would not involve any sharp break with the USA or our European allies, so would reduce the danger of counter-productive US or German reactions and the risk of sanctions against us, and it does hold out positive hopes for moving Europe away from the brink of nuclear war. The proposals would, moreover, certainly receive support from some sections of European opinion. If, however, this plan for removing nuclear weapons from Europe ran into insurmountable obstacles, European countries committed to a non-nuclear strategy, or Britain alone, could fall back on other approaches to non-nuclear defence.

The majority of the Commission concluded that a nuclear-free NATO should be worked for as a first choice. While many of the arguments in favour of this approach would apply equally to a non-nuclear European defence association, there are three reasons for giving priority to conditional NATO membership. The first is that NATO actually exists, and the idea of a European association is purely hypothetical, so that staying in NATO is a more immediately realistic policy. The second is that there are clearly advantages (as well as drawbacks) to association with the USA, and to attempting as allies to influence US policy. The third is that there appear on examination to be considerable problems with the idea of a European defence association which are discussed below.

A minority of the Commission remained unpersuaded by the idea of conditional NATO membership, both on grounds of principle and because they judged that tactically the case for British withdrawal was stronger than the case for staying in. The main reasons are referred to in the section on non-alignment.

VIII. How should Britain contribute to a non-nuclear strategy?

If a unilateralist Britain did stay in NATO, on condition that it moved towards a non-nuclear policy, it would still be necessary to make decisons about the form of our military contribution to the Alliance. This would depend on two main factors: British assessments of national interest in terms of the economic costs and relative dangers of various forms of military co-operation; and British policy preferences for the type of strategy to be adopted by a non-nuclear Europe in NATO. But it must be assumed that a British government committed to staying in NATO provided it adopted a non-nuclear strategy would be willing (within reasonable economic limits) to make the type of contribution most appropriate to a jointly agreed strategy.

The timing and phasing of British nuclear disarmament could be affected by whether or not it was considered necessary to co-ordinate steps with other European countries in NATO. In our view it would be essential for Britain to take immediate steps to abandon its own independent deterrent, and to dismantle the systems involved as quickly as possible, as sign of its determination to pursue a non-nuclear path.

But the withdrawal of 'battlefield' nuclear weapons deployed with British forces in Europe under a dual-key arrangement with the USA could well be phased out at the same time as other NATO battlefield nuclear weapons (which we suggest in Chapter 8 ought to be within three to four years of the election of a British unilateralist government). The alternative would be for Britain to withdraw battlefield nuclear weapons straightaway from its forces in Europe, thereby creating in the short term a nuclear gap in the areas where the British Army of the Rhine is deployed. The effect of this would be to underline the incompatibility of Britain's non-nuclear stance with NATO's nuclear strategy. On balance, however, a policy of co-ordinating British moves in this respect with those of other NATO countries seems preferable.

Britain's major contribution to NATO's nuclear strategy is to accept US nuclear bases, nuclear weapon dumps, airborne nuclear command centres, and various early-warning, surveillance and monitoring facilities. British refusal to co-operate directly in nuclear weapons policies would require the removal of all specifically nuclear bases. Decisions about the early-warning, monitoring and surveillance systems, which may be relevant to both nuclear and conventional strategy (for example, submarine tracking stations), would be more difficult. Britain could, however, insist on taking over all US facilities and operating those relevant to conventional warfare on NATO's behalf.

The central question to be considered here is what contribution Britain should make towards NATO's capacity for conventional military defence. We could go on providing our present conventional contribution to NATO, minus the nuclear element, or actually increase that contribution in order to enhance NATO's conventional deterrence. Alternatively, we could instead opt for partial or total withdrawal of ground or air forces in West Germany, while still offering naval and other forms of support to NATO; or we could withdraw all our forces from the NATO Command, but still offer landing facilities for US troops, and co-operation in early-warning and surveillance activities. There could obviously be problems about substantially reducing commitments and at the same time setting conditions for continued British membership, though some changes which might result in greater specialisation in national contributions to NATO could be acceptable. It has, for example, quite often been argued that Britain could contribute most effectively by concentrating on its naval role and withdrawing forces from Germany, though this may also carry with it the danger that the more specialised the British contribution became, the more difficult it would be ever to withdraw from NATO. What forces we should make available is also dependent on the form of alternative NATO defence we wish to see in Europe.

IX. *Alternatives to NATO*

Supporters of nuclear disarmament who oppose NATO have to decide whether they wish to promote some kind of alternative political and defence association or whether they favour a purely independent British foreign and defence policy. Similarly if the attempt to create a non-nuclear NATO was unsuccessful, fall-back options would have to be considered.

The most obvious alternative to NATO, which has been canvassed by some sections of political opinion in Britain, is a purely West European conventional defence association.

A non-nuclear European defence association

The case for a European defence association is that Europe would no longer be linked in any way to US nuclear strategy, and that a Western Europe independent of both great powers is a desirable political ideal. Other considerations are that Western European countries might find it easier to agree a new defence strategy without the USA, and the new association could be a relatively egalitarian body, unlike NATO where the USA inevitably tends to dominate. Europe arguably has different defence interests from the USA.

A unilateralist British government might see considerable advantages in such a policy. It would safeguard our links and commitments to Europe, ensure us support against any US hostility, and give us substantial defence advantages by maintaining a multinational defence in Central Europe. It is a policy which would also gain some support from the pro-European section of British political opinion, and would ensure our links to European anti-nuclear movements.

Despite the potential attractions of a European defence organisation, there are substantial disadvantages to be weighed. Many of the possible objections to a non-nuclear Europe in NATO might be applied to a purely European body. It might be urged that the military task of providing a credible conventional defence against the Soviet Union would be even more formidable without the USA, and could entail a very substantial military and economic burden for the European countries involved, which they might be unwilling or unable to sustain. Consideration of the population and economic resources of Western Europe in relation to the USSR and Eastern Europe suggests that a substantial West European defence effort should not in principle be impossible, but may not, especially in a period of recession, be politically practical.[10]

The political objections to any projected build-up of conventional forces in Central Europe and to the strengthening of political and military divisions by promoting a new defence arrangement in Western Europe, apply with greater force to a new organisation than they do to NATO. In the latter case a conventional defence strategy may, as suggested, be seen as an interim process leading to eventual dissolution of an organisation already in a state of flux. But if Western European nations consciously set out to create and legitimize a new form of defence association, it would be much harder (having mobilised political forces behind the new idea) to go on to modify or abandon it later. Military organisations, like others, develop their own vested interests and forces of inertia which tend to inhibit radical reappraisal of their aims and methods, and to perpetuate assumptions from the past. This happened to NATO, but the strength of opposition to making Europe a theatre for nuclear war has led to intellectual and political reassessment. A European defence body, though intended to reduce the risk of nuclear war, and to fill an apparent gap in the present West European defences, would be in danger of creating new rigidities and blocking further progress towards an undivided Europe.

In addition the idea of a European defence association carries with it all sorts of political and military overtones from past projects. It could be associated with a desire to create a Europe that was not simply independent of the USA and the USSR but was a great power in its own right. The 'European nationalism', associated with some projections of the possible political and military future of the EEC, is opposed to many people's views of the kind of international system conducive to world peace, and is inherently controversial. The position of France becomes much more central in a projected European defence association — it would be hard to have a credible European organisation without France — and the French commitment to a nuclear policy becomes even more difficult in this context. France might well offer its *force de frappe* to a projected European defence body (this possibility is part of the official rationale for keeping the French Bomb) which would be totally at odds with the whole concept of a non-nuclear European defence body, though attractive to some political groups.

However, if a European defence association was created for the specific purpose of avoiding any reliance on nuclear weapons, this could be written into the founding document of the new body and would at least diminish the chances of its developing into a nuclear alliance. Moreover, by rejecting nuclear weapons the European states would in a sense be renouncing the ambition of becoming collectively a major power, and the association could scarcely be seen as a genuine threat to the Soviet Union and Eastern Europe if it remained non-nuclear and sought no more than to maintain sufficient forces to deal with a possible Soviet conventional attack.

A further possibility would be to reject the idea of creating an integrated European force with a unified command structure, and to envisage an association based on much looser military co-operation, relying primarily on the national defence of each member state, but guaranteeing certain kinds of practical assistance and solidarity in the event of an attack. This sort of loose association, as opposed to a unified military force, might rely on in-depth territorial defence, would have less threatening overtones, be less likely to perpetuate Cold War divisions, and would be less associated with pan-European ambitions.

Nevertheless, once such a plan had been projected, it might tend to become more centralised, and might still arouse some of the fears surrounding a European force. Also, such a loose association, depending largely on promises of help in the event of war, might fail to reassure those European countries with memories of being overrun by Hitler's troops with such ease in May and June 1940, and certainly British guarantees of aid might be viewed with some scepticism unless British forces were irrevocably committed to mainland Europe. It could therefore be argued that a loose mutual defence pact has none of the solid military advantages which could accrue to a unified European force, and does not wholly avoid the political disadvantages of such a proposal.

The balance of these arguments about a European defence association throws doubt on the desirability of deliberately breaking up NATO in order to form such a body — especially as NATO is in existence and a European defence association is at present purely speculative. But if the attempt to de-nuclearise NATO was obstructed by the USA, and there was strong European support for a non-nuclear defence organisation, this could clearly not be ruled out as an option. In this context, especially if concern for a nuclear-free Europe was linked to a desire to promote further measures of arms limitation, it might avoid some of the more undesirable political connotations set out above.

The political implications of a European defence association might depend not only on whether it had an integrated military command structure, but on the type of defence strategy adopted. It would not be essential to concentrate on high-technology conventional forces of the type now deployed by NATO. Three broad alternative strategies would be open to a new European defence organisation.

The first possibility would be to emphasise in-depth territorial defence, using less well trained troops and cheaper technology, but deploying these forces to maximise the difficulties of taking over an entire country. Territorial defence is central to present Swiss strategy, and its goal is to create a strong deterrent to attack while not posing an apparently military threat to others (see Chapter 5).

The second possible course would be to make preparations for guerrilla warfare central to defence strategy as a deterrent to occupation. Vietnam and Afghanistan have demonstrated the potential of guerrilla methods against major military powers, and a European alliance could provide for guerrilla tactics to be used in occupied areas to harass invading troops in the rear (see Chapter 6).

Guerrilla warfare as a long-term strategy involves reliance on political as well as military factors, and in the context of the highly industrialised and densely populated countries of Western Europe, there is thirdly a case for switching the emphasis decisively towards moral, political and economic factors by adopting nonviolent methods of resistance (see Chapter 7).

If preparations for nonviolent civil resistance were given a central place within defence planning, or simply a recognised role, it would be important to make advance plans for European cooperation. The idea of this kind of defence is taken rather more seriously by some political groups in Europe than it has been so far in Britain. Governments in the Netherlands, Denmark and Sweden have sponsored research into its potential; it has been researched in academic institutions and peace movements in a number of countries, and has been discussed by the Green Party in West Germany as a possible alternative defence policy.

An emphasis on territorial defence, guerrilla warfare or civil resistance, or some combination of these strategies, would underline the purely defensive nature of a European association, would facilitate measures of conventional as well as nuclear disarmament in Europe, and would therefore tend to minimise the possibility of dangerous connotations of a European defence body. As things stand, the likelihood of a European association giving primary emphasis to these more radical strategies in preference to strengthened conventional forces is probably not very high, but it is something that could be canvassed for and might gain wider acceptance if the peace movements continue to grow.

X. British non-alignment

So far we have discussed ambitious policies Britain might try to promote in conjunction with other countries. The only policy which is totally within the control of a British government is to leave NATO and opt for non-alignment, and the clarity of this option is itself an attraction.

There is a strong case in principle for this option, as it is a way for Britain to dissociate itself unambiguously from US nuclear policy. It would also distance Britain from US foreign and military policies in the world as a whole and enable us to become more independent of Cold War rivalries. These points do apply also to a European association, but that option may simply not be available and the practical choice that Britain could face might be whether to remain in NATO or leave it. The possible repercussions within NATO and Europe of a British decision to leave the Alliance do therefore merit special attention.

At the tactical level, leaving NATO could be seen as a more effective way of influencing political developments in Europe than staying in. There may be very substantial difficulties in achieving major policy changes through NATO in view of US military and political dominance. So if the aim is to stimulate pressure for radical change by mobilising European peace movements, an unambiguous and dramatic move by Britain might be more effective than attempting to work from within the Alliance. At government level, British withdrawal would force reappraisal of the political and military situation in Europe, and could in favourable circumstances encourage the superpowers to reconsider their policies on disarmament and disengagement.

Finally, there is a good case in terms of national self-interest for Britain to leave NATO, in order to reduce the risk of being a principle target in a nuclear war, and to enhance British independence in foreign policy. The term 'non-alignment' implies here British withdrawal from all military alliances and pursuit of an independent defence policy. It also implies political independence from the great powers and a refusal to take sides in the Cold War, though in practice non-aligned countries usually have political and ideological preferences, arising out of their internal politics, which make them somewhat more favourable to one side. The most obvious model for Britain to follow is the Swedish form of neutralism. Whether Britain would attempt to interpret the requirements of neutralism as rigidly as Sweden — for example, committing itself to a general ideal of independence and self-sufficiency, relying largely on arms manufactured domestically, and abstaining from full membership of any international organisation liable to compromise national independence such as the EEC — is open to debate.

What is entailed in the concept of 'non-alignment', as opposed to the concept of 'neutralism', is well illustrated by Sweden's present foreign policy stance in comparison with its traditional interpretation of neutrality.[11] Pure neutrality implies an isolationist view of the world, and an attempt to avoid involvement in either military or political conflicts between other states. This form of neutralism is open to criticism on strategic grounds, since it is debatable how far any state, particularly a small one, can secure itself against possible great-power attack, and in the nuclear age the ability to ensure non-involvement in war has become impossible. It is also open to criticism on political and moral grounds as a refusal to take responsibility for helping to tackle world problems or to stand by important principles. Both forms of criticism are questionable. Neutrality may be much safer than involvement in alliances, especially in a world where alliances include nuclear powers, and for countries which have no reason to feel themselves under direct threat. Political neutrality is also preferable to the other extreme of unconditional endorsement of simplistic and biased interpretations of 'right' and 'wrong' which can arise out of alliance politics.

There is, however, some force in the argument that neutrality is not enough, and that countries fortunate enough to be able to avoid direct involvement in military alliances have some moral responsibility to try to end conflicts elsewhere and to act to promote conditions of peace. Hence the concept of non-alignment has been developed to denote countries which are neutral in the military and ideological conflict between the USA and the USSR, but also try to act as a positive force for peace.

Sweden itself has over the last 20 years stressed that non-involvement in alliances can be combined with a positive foreign policy role; this involves active mediation, attempts to initiate disarmament agreements or to break the deadlock in disarmament negotiations, a prominent part in UN peacekeeping, and general support for the independence of small countries, for the right to national liberation and for the rights of developing nations. This foreign policy has had repercussions on Swedish defence policy. Armed neutrality may imply heavy investment in armaments rather than setting an example in disarmament, and in the late 1950s Sweden seriously considered adding tactical atomic weapons to its arsenal. At the time the decision not to develop atomic weapons was taken on military grounds. Since then Sweden has become committed to non-proliferation of nuclear weapons and is politically bound to remain non-nuclear.

If non-alignment is understood in this positive sense, one of the most obvious objections which might be made against a neutralist Britain — that neutralism encourages an isolationist outlook on the world — is met. A non-nuclear and non-aligned Britain clearly could contribute to conflict resolution and to disarmament negotiations, and would have taken the initial steps towards a reconsideration of its role in the North–South conflict as well as the East–West division of the world. How effectively in practice a neutral Britain would also espouse positive non-alignment depends partly on internal political factors and partly on how skilfully British foreign policy operated within the organisations available. Could the EEC be used to press for non-aligned policies or would continued British membership of the EEC be incompatible with a non-aligned stance? There are two potential arguments about the foreign policy implications of the EEC, which are analysed in the next section. One is the argument put forward in the 1960s, when British membership was first canvassed, that the EEC's goals and its military implications would make it impossible for a Britain which had withdrawn from NATO to be a member; the other, which might be put forward today, is that, if there is a prospect for Europe as a whole adopting a non-aligned position, then the EEC might be a forum for expressing a non-aligned foreign policy. (The economic debate about EEC membership, or internal political considerations, are of course outside the scope of the Commission.)

XI. Implications of EEC membership for a non-nuclear Britain

Clearly membership of the EEC would pose no problems for a Britain which remained part of NATO or which took part in some kind of European defence association. The issue which is necessary to resolve here is whether EEC membership would conflict with a decision to become non-aligned. There appeared in the 1960s to be cogent reasons for saying it would. At this stage enthusiastic exponents of the EEC looked forward to a process of increasing political unification into a federation of EEC states which would then be a new great power on the world stage. It was a logical corollary of this vision to assume a European federation would be well armed and might acquire its own European Bomb. Even in the early 1970s, the Conservative government under Mr Heath explicitly considered how the British nuclear forces might be integrated into Europe, and as noted earlier this is still one argument used for the French *force de frappe*. The political and military projection clearly suggested a permanent political and military division of Europe and a definition of European culture and interests which excluded East European states altogether.

The dangerous implications of this picture of the EEC for disarmament and disengagement were underlined by the intense Soviet hostility to the EEC. It was also possible in the early 1960s to look on the seven European states organised in the looser economic association of EFTA (European Free Trade Area) as an alternative to the EEC.

A great deal has changed since the 1960s.[12] The experience of the EEC to date does not suggest that a federation of European states is on the agenda in the foreseeable future; individual states press their national interests vigorously through the Council of Ministers and flout EEC regulations when they feel discriminated against, and the strength of nationalist sentiments and hostilities has if anything been increased as a result of various economic conflicts. Moreover the EEC is still growing in size, with the recent accession of Greece, and the projected membership of Spain and Portugal, which reduces the prospect of integration in the foreseeable future.

Proposals for European great power and military status also appear to have lapsed from the agenda, but there are still pressures from within the European Community for greater collaboration on defence, particularly at the level of defence planning. The British government has since 1979 pressed for further defence co-operation in the EEC and closer links with NATO.[13] Although co-operation in military procurement may be seen as a logical extension of trying to develop common EEC policies in, for example, the aircraft industry, and although the growing overlap between EEC and NATO membership creates pressure for co-ordination between the two bodies, the national obstacles to political integration apply equally strongly to military integration. Eire, as a non-aligned state, has already acted to block British moves towards links with NATO, and a future non-aligned Britain could, by reversing its present policies, greatly reinforce resistance to making the EEC an arm of NATO.

The Soviet Union has, as noted earlier, modified its previous hostility to the EEC, and both the USSR and Eastern Europe have developed economic ties with the Community. Therefore it is doubtful whether EEC membership is necessarily incompatible with non-alignment. Although the existing European neutrals, apart from Eire, have always assumed that full EEC membership would compromise their neutrality, all have some form of association with the EEC.

One further consideration is that if Britain withdrew from NATO, and was vulnerable to intense US hostility on this score, to break off all ties with the EEC at the same time could further antagonise many European countries, and leave Britain politically isolated and open to a range of economic sanctions from both the USA and the EEC. Conversely, a British government which stayed in NATO, at least for a transition period, would be better placed to assess independently the economic and political case for staying in the EEC, or coming out.

XII. Forms of limited NATO membership

If membership of NATO is rejected as a long-term policy for political reasons, Britain could consider transitional membership for a period of several years. It would be possible in principle to set some minimum conditions for staying in beyond the statutory year's notice — for example a no-first-use of nuclear weapons commitment — but in practice it would be diplomatically awkward to make conditions if we intended to leave within a few years. Transitional membership could instead be a means of gradually phasing out our contribution to NATO, and so easing the difficulties caused by British withdrawal, and reducing possible hostility from our NATO allies. If, however, the phasing out process were too extended, the impact of a decisive change in policy might be lost.

A final choice, just short of total withdrawal and non-alignment, would be to leave the integrated military command structure, but to stay in the NATO Alliance. Whether Britain would be more influential in securing progress towards disarmament or disengagement in Europe by retaining this residual link with NATO, or by adopting a fully non-aligned policy, is a tactical judgement. It would be impossible to make this kind of limited political membership conditional on any policy changes, and no member of the Commission wished to argue strongly for it as a compromise position.

XIII. Summary of the argument

This chapter began by looking at the orthodox case for NATO: that a joint European and American defence effort is needed to deter the Soviet Union, the desirability of close links with the USA, and the role of NATO in creating stability in Europe. From a British standpoint, political obligations to Western Europe, and the military advantages of a forward-based European defence, are important reasons for staying in NATO.

The peace movement case against NATO is grounded in the fundamental objections to NATO's nuclear strategy. It also argues that the existence of NATO increases tension and the likelihood of war, that it is dangerous and undesirable to be so closely linked to US global policies, and that the division of Europe is destabilising.

There are, however, strong tactical reasons for staying in NATO, if membership can be made compatible with a British non-nuclear commitment. British withdrawal could have dangerous repercussions on West German and US military policies which would reduce the prospect for future disarmament. A Britain leaving NATO would be especially vulnerable to sanctions from its former allies. A more positive reason is that political developments in Europe and the United States suggest that a non-nuclear Britain in NATO might be able to contribute significantly to wider nuclear disarmament.

A non-nuclear Britain could not consistently remain in NATO if the Alliance continued to be committed to its present nuclear strategy, but conditional British membership would be possible provided NATO freed itself from reliance on nuclear weapons. The four steps which are required to fulfil the process of de-nuclearisation are: (1) acceptance by NATO of a no-first-use of nuclear weapons policy; (2) withdrawal of all battlefield nuclear weapons; (3) removal of all US intermediate-range, 'theatre', nuclear weapons, including sea-based missiles; (4) decoupling NATO strategy from the US nuclear deterrent by renouncing any reliance on US nuclear weapons, whether as a last resort in a conventional war or in the context of a Soviet nuclear ultimatum or nuclear attack. The terms on which Britain could retain conditional membership are discussed in Chapter 8.

One alternative to NATO is a European defence association which would dissociate Europe wholly from US nuclear strategy and from its world policies, while retaining the advantages of a joint European conventional defence. But there is the danger that a European defence association might give rise to a new continental nationalism with its own nuclear weapons, and that it might perpetuate the East–West division in new and unpredictable forms. The wisdom of mobilising political energies behind an attempt to create such an alliance is therefore dubious — especially as there are substantial problems in developing a purely European conventional strategy. Nevertheless, the idea of a European association might gather support, and have to be seriously considered, if NATO broke up.

The possibly counter-productive implications of a massive conventional defence effort would of course be greatly reduced if a European association moved towards less orthodox strategies of territorial defence, guerrilla warfare or civil resistance which would have a clearly defensive emphasis.

The other alternative for a unilateralist Britain is non-alignment, an option that has the attraction that it does not depend on the agreement of other countries for it to be adopted. It is attractive to those who oppose NATO on political grounds, and wish for a total break with US nuclear strategy but who for other reasons do not support the idea of a European defence association or who think that it is unlikely to come into existence. Non-alignment may also be seen as tactically the most promising way of making other countries consider a new settlement in Europe, and of strengthening pressure for disarmament. The most obvious model for a non-aligned foreign and defence policy is Sweden, although Britain would not necessarily have to observe strict neutrality — for example in avoiding membership of the EEC.

XIV. Conclusions

The Commission does not on the whole accept the orthodox political case for NATO, and sees a dissolution of both NATO and the Warsaw Pact as the desired goal. It also accepts the argument that a non-nuclear Britain cannot stay in NATO while its strategy remains committed to nuclear weapons.

A majority of the Commission did, however, attach considerable importance to the tactical arguments for retaining NATO membership. They also believe that pressure through NATO to move towards a non-nuclear strategy holds out the possibility of a major advance towards general nuclear disarmament. They agreed that this approach was on balance preferable to trying to create a European defence association, although this would be a possible fallback option if the USA opposed attempts to de-nuclearise NATO.

A minority of the Commission remained unpersuaded by the arguments for retaining conditional NATO membership and believe both on grounds of principle and political tactics that Britain should leave NATO and pursue an independent, non-aligned policy.

Although members of the Commission differed about the best strategy to promote a nuclear-free Europe, they agreed that Britain should clearly dissociate itself from any reliance on nuclear strategies.

The Commission hopes that cruise and Pershing II missiles, and the neutron bomb, will never be deployed in Europe, but if they were to be deployed their removal would be a top priority to signal the commitment to move towards a nuclear-free Europe.

Notes to Chapter 3

1. The precursor to NATO was the Brussels Treaty signed in March 1948 between the UK, France and the Benelux countries creating a defensive alliance; when this treaty was revised in Paris in 1954 it committed Britain to keep 'four divisions and the Second Tactical Air Force' on mainland Europe. The legally binding nature of this document is however undermined by Article VI which allows signatories to plead that financial pressures or emergencies elsewhere require troop reductions. These clauses have been used to enable Britain to reduce the 77,000 men in BAOR in 1954 to 55,000 today. It has also been assumed that, if foreign exchange pressures and military logic dictated Britain should switch its contribution to NATO to a greater naval effort and concentration on defence of the 'northern flank', the revised Brussels Treaty would be no obstacle. It is in any case clearly possible for a Britain determined to leave NATO to renounce its Brussels Treaty obligations at the same time. See L. Freedman, 'British Foreign Policy to 1985', *International Affairs*, 54 (January 1978) 44. See also *The Times*, 18 May 1981, Henry Stanhope, 'Threat of Tory Revolt on £1,000m cuts in defence': "Although the Foreign and Commonwealth Office believe that Britain could easily get round the terms of the Brussels Treaty — under which troops are maintained in Germany — this is not thought to be the time to do so."
2. On Cuba see F. A. Beer, *Integration and Disintegration in NATO* (Colombus, Ohio: Ohio State University Press, 1969), p. 24: "The American decision to institute a military blockade of Cuba was taken almost completely without Allied consultation." See also A. J. Pierre, *Nuclear Politics* (London: Oxford University Press, 1972), p. 224: "Britain was informed but not consulted as her principal ally took rapid decisions involving the serious risk of nuclear war while acting essentially alone." On the 1973 Middle East crisis, see Editorial in *The Spectator*, 3 November 1973, p. 563: "What the United States did last week by putting the Strategic Air Command bases in this country on war alert was to demonstrate its readiness to go to the brink of war, and if necessary beyond, without consultation with the Prime Minister."
3. A strong case can be made that the Soviet invasion of Czechoslovakia in 1968 was largely motivated by strategic concerns, which greatly increased Soviet sensitivity to ideological and political deviation. Soviet military wishes relating to stationing of troops, manoeuvres and command structures were among the issues on which the Czechoslovaks were reluctant to make concessions to the USSR. See K. Dawisha, 'Soviet Security and the Role of the Military: the 1968 Czechoslovak Crisis', *British Journal of Political Science*, 10, Part 3 (July 1980), 341–63.
4. There may be fear that if NATO broke up, Germany and the USSR would ally themselves, as they did between the wars at Rapallo and later in the Molotov–Ribbentrop Pact. The democratic nature of the present German government and its close association with Western Europe suggest, however, that these historic parallels may be misleading, if a German-Soviet rapprochement is regarded as sinister.

5. *The Guardian* 29 September 1982. General Rogers also indicated his hope that agreement could be reached between NATO and the Warsaw Pact for the removal of battlefield nuclear weapons.

6. Norway, like Denmark, is a country with a history of neutrality which influenced its position in NATO from the outset: both refused to have foreign troops or nuclear bases on their soil — though in time of war the qualification about troops and deployment of nuclear weapons would be waived — and both contribute to NATO by mounting within their means a strong national conventional defence. R. Sohlberg, 'Analysis of Ground Force Structure on NATO's Northern Flank', *Rand Report*, N–1315–MRAL (February 1980), p. 4, comments on Norway and Denmark: "During the postwar period both countries adopted the policy of neither permitting foreign troops to be stationed on their soil in peacetime nor nuclear facilities to be established. However, preparations may be made in peacetime for receiving foreign troops in case of crisis." J. Grepstad, 'Norway's Ongoing Struggle', *European Nuclear Disarmament Bulletin*, 3 (1980), 14, underlines, however, Norway's involvement in nuclear policy: (1) as a rotating member of NATO's Nuclear Planning Group it has supported all public NATO decisions on nuclear strategy; (2) it provides navigation and communication stations which are explicitly linked to the US Fleet Ballistic Missile programme; and (3) use of nuclear weapons on and from Norwegian territory is allowed in wartime, and staff exercises are held which simulate transfer and use of nuclear weapons. Canada's position is somewhat more comparable to Britain, since until 1969 Canadian troops were deployed in Germany with missiles with nuclear warheads, and Canadian aircraft were equipped to carry nuclear weapons. Canada also consciously reversed its policy on nuclear weapons, as Britain would do if we went unilateralist. But there are now only 3,000 Canadian troops stationed in Germany, compared with Britain's 55,000, so Canada's de-nuclearisation of its contingent does not leave the same kind of gap in NATO's nuclear battle order as a British decision to do the same would cause; similarly the Canadian decision gradually to phase out carrying US nuclear weapons on its aircraft has not jolted American nuclear deployment in the way a withdrawal of all US nuclear bases in Britain would. Canada is also much more removed from Europe both geographically and politically. On Canada's non-nuclear policy see: C. Hitchens, 'Canada's Nuclear Departure', *New Statesman*, 13 June 1980, p. 888.

7. The Warsaw Pact Political Consultative Committee has publicly proposed to NATO countries a number of times that participants in the Helsinki European Conference should pledge themselves not to use nuclear weapons first. And on 15 June 1982 Soviet Foreign Minister Andrei Gromyko announced a no-first-use commitment which was to take effect that very day. (*The Times*, 16 June 1982). Robert McNamara, McGeorge Bundy, George Kennan and Gerard Smith have proposed that the West should make a no-first-use declaration, as part of a package proposing a build-up of conventional forces and a possible return to conscription in the US. See McGeorge Bundy *et al.*, 'Nuclear Weapons and the Atlantic Alliance', *Foreign Affairs*, 60, 4 (Spring 1982), 753–68.

8. See for example J. Hemseley, 'The Soviet Ground Forces', in J. Erickson and E. J. Feuchtwanger, eds, *Soviet Military Power and Performance* (London: Macmillan, 1979), p. 47: "Soviet military doctrine is based on the development of a dual capability — i.e. for both nuclear and conventional warfare. It seems most probable at the moment that they would be prepared to commence with conventional operations in the event of a war in Europe; however their tactics and

equipments are such that they retain the option of going nuclear at any stage.''

9. See *Common Security: A Programme for Disarmament. The Report of the Independent Commission on Disarmament and Security Issues under the Chairmanship of Olof Palme*, (London: Pan Books, 1982), p. XVIII.

10. See R. L. Sivard, *World Military and Social Expenditures 1982* (Leesburg, Virginia: World Priorities, 1982), p. 27, which shows the total population of NATO Europe as 325,151,000 as compared to the Warsaw Pact population (including the Soviet Union) of 372,183,000; the GNP of NATO Europe is shown in million US$ as 2,562,261, and the GNP of the Warsaw Pact as 1,538,160. The statistics relate to 1979; France is counted on the NATO side but not Spain, which was not in the Alliance at that time.

11. Sweden's evolving policy of 'non-alignment' is summarised by A. Roberts in *Nations in Arms* (London: Chatto & Windus, 1976), pp. 79–83.

12. The Gaullist policies pursued by France did much to torpedo the aspirations of Jean Monet for rapid moves towards European federation. The great difficulties experienced in moving towards some form of monetary union also throw doubt on the likelihood of political union.

13. F. Gregory, 'The European Community and Defence', *ADIU Report*, 3, 5 (September/October 1981), 5–9, discusses pressures inside the EEC for common defence procurement and for an EEC role in defence. It also appears that European governments put pressure on Canada by making it clear in the mid 1970s "that a contractual link with the European Economic Community was partially dependent upon Canada increasing her NATO contribution". R.B. Byers, 'Canadian Defence: The ASW Dilemma', *Survival*, XVIII (July/August 1976), p. 155.

Chapter 4
British non-nuclear defence: the military options

I. Introduction

There are two reasons why it is necessary to consider a purely British defence despite the fact that the Commission tends to favour, on balance, conditional membership of NATO. First, if the conditions were rejected by the USA or by West European states, and if no alternative option could be agreed, a Britain committed to a total non-nuclear stance would have no choice but to adopt an independent defence as a non-aligned state. Second, we need to examine all the possible options for non-nuclear defence of Britain. Despite some military disadvantages in separating the defence of Britain from that of mainland Europe, an independent Britain relying on conventional defence would be less likely to suffer a direct nuclear attack than if it were a member of even a 'non-nuclear' NATO.

This chapter concentrates on choices in planning a military defence of Britain alone, as opposed to those strategies which focus on a common defence of Central Europe. It considers, therefore, policies we could adopt if Britain had become non-aligned, like Sweden, or had opted for an independent defence posture while retaining political links with Western Europe. Very similar policies would also be relevant if Britain were a member of a loosely linked West European defensive alliance (or of a transformed NATO without an integrated military command structure) which relied largely on each member maintaining a strong national defence.

The two types of defence to be considered here are a conventional frontier-based military strategy and the less orthodox in-depth 'territorial defence', which demands less sophisticated weapons technology and usually relies on reserves who have had army training as conscripts, or on local militias. Territorial defence is often associated with the tactics of partisan, or guerrilla, warfare, and this chapter discusses briefly the connection between maintaining military resistance after an enemy has occupied large parts of one's territory and the use of partisan tactics in the occupied areas. Pure reliance on guerrilla resistance is examined in Chapter 6. Because this chapter focuses on forms of military defence, it does not explore the possibility of adopting nonviolent civil resistance as a total alternative strategy of deterrence and defence, or as a major strand of defence policy. The possible roles of civil resistance are examined in Chapter 7.

II. Models for independent non nuclear defence

The first step in clarifying principles for an independent military defence for Britain is to look at the policies adopted by countries not reliant on nuclear weapons or on military alliances. Three European neutrals — Sweden, Switzerland and Yugoslavia — provide relevant case studies. Despite their similarities, these countries also present three distinct types of defence policy.

Sweden

Sweden has a tradition of armed neutrality which depends on having enough military strength to deter a military attack; it has succeeded in keeping out of war for over 160 years, though some concessions were made to Germany in World War II. The main threat is now seen not as a full scale military occupation but the seizure of areas of strategic importance by either side during a major European war.

Sweden has a system of universal conscription for periods ranging from $7\frac{1}{2}$ to 15 months, reinforced by compulsory refresher courses. Half the air force, over half the navy and four fifths of the peacetime army are conscripts. Out of a population of 8.3 million there are 64,500 in the armed forces, 47,100 conscripts and 17,400 regulars, all of whom are officers or NCOs. The total strength of the armed forces after mobilisation over 72 hours would be approximately 800,000. In addition there is a Coast Guard service. Excluding civil and economic defence, Sweden spends a total of about US $3,431 million a year, approximately $412 per person, on military defence, which is about 3.1 per cent of GNP.[2]

Sweden could be attacked by air or sea as well as by land, and has invested heavily in its air force, which has about 420 combat aircraft, made up of fighter squadrons, fighter–ground attack aircraft and reconnaissance planes, plus anti-aircraft missiles. In keeping with its defensive stance Sweden has no long-range bombers. The Swedish navy is less substantial than its air force, but has 12 submarines, 2 destroyers, 35 fast attack craft, and fairly numerous minelayers, minesweepers and coastal patrol boats. Its main function is coastal defence.

The Swedish army is organised to put up a substantial frontier defence, although since 1967 the Swedish government has laid much greater emphasis on 'inner defence' or defence in depth. This decision reflected budgetary constraints, since defence in depth implies producing large numbers of technically simpler weapons rather than highly expensive sophisticated weapons systems; the concept of a citizen army also had ideological attractions. But Swedish defence policy still lays stress on the requirements of mobility and efficient armaments: the war establishment of the army includes five armoured brigades. The role of small local units, which could be used to maintain a stubborn resistance and could resort to guerrilla tactics is subsidiary, except as part of the coastal defence preparations. As the population is heavily concentrated in the South, and large areas in the North are virtually uninhabited, four brigades are assigned specifically to the Norrland.

The Swedish concept of 'total defence' includes not only military preparations but a civil defence programme, which aims to provide deep shelters for the whole population, and economic defence measures to meet the problems of disruption of supply, for example stockpiling food, fuel and various strategic materials. There is also a rather shadowy category of 'psychological defence' which is concerned with questions of morale and propaganda, and a generalised provision for civil resistance as an auxiliary form of resistance, together with a more explicit emphasis on guerrilla tactics to complement in-depth defence.

Switzerland

Switzerland, like Sweden, has relied on armed neutrality to avoid attack, and has managed to maintain this neutrality through a number of European wars involving its immediate neighbours, including both World Wars. Switzerland has a long tradition of relying on a citizen army and places less reliance on high technology weaponry than Sweden. Swiss military planners, like the Swedes, see the main threat arising out of a European war. Swiss strategy is based on the principle of exacting a 'high entry price' from invaders. The goal is not ultimately to prevent an enemy from achieving military success, which is seen as unrealistic, but to convince a possible aggressor that Switzerland is ready and able to make his military victory unreasonably costly.[3]

Swiss military service involves only 17 weeks basic training of recruits, but requires refresher courses of 3 weeks a year for 8 years out of 12 up to the age of 32 and 2 weeks once every 3 years to the age of 42. Out of a population of 6.4 million there are only 1,500 regular troops, but within 48 hours total mobilised strength should be 625,000 men. Once all brigades are deployed in a chessboard pattern throughout Swiss territory, there is a greater troop density than anywhere else in Europe. Switzerland spends approximately US $1,780 million on defence annually, about $281 per person and 1.8 per cent of GNP. In addition Switzerland has a major civil defence programme, including fall-out shelters in private houses, and an economic defence programme of stockpiling to avert the shortages which might arise in wartime for a country heavily dependent on external trade.

Swiss strategy is purely defensive. As a landlocked country, the main emphasis is naturally on the army. There is a fairly substantial air force of 334 combat aircraft, but according to General Frank Seethaler, 'it operates always in co-operation with ground forces'.[4]

The strategy of the armed forces comes much closer than in Sweden to being a pure form of in-depth territorial defence, though with an element still of frontier defence. The aim is to give up as little of Swiss national territory as possible. Defence strategy relies primarily on dispersing static infantry units to hold key positions — dispersion also greatly reduces the advantages to the enemy of using tactical nuclear weapons. The static units are supplemented by mechanised mobile units designed to carry out counter-attacks; these are equipped with tanks. If hard pressed, Swiss defences may centre on the fortified areas of the Alpine 'redoubt' (at St Gottard, St Maurice and Sargans) and aim to hold the North–South passes and tunnels. Three mountain infantry divisions are specially assigned to the redoubt, though its strategic importance is limited if the attack comes from the East. Transport links would be destroyed to hold up a mechanised thrust into Swiss territory, and the mountainous terrain and areas of forest lend themselves to the obstruction and harassment of an advancing enemy. Similarly, at the political level, the tradition of the citizen soldier with a rifle at home lends itself to a strategy of defence in depth.

Switzerland provides a classic example of a citizen army committed to territorial defence. But defence policy has shied away from the further step of advocating tactics of guerrilla harassment, which official military writings tend to suggest cannot be planned in advance. A 1969 report by a Commission on Strategic Questions urged that ''even the occupation of the entire country must not signify the end of resistance'',[5] and passive resistance to an occupying power is specifically envisaged, though in rather general terms, and seen as complementary to possible armed resistance.[6]

Weakness of the Swiss system may arise partly from the degree to which it is rooted in tradition, since this leads to conservatism in thinking and strategy (the cavalry was not abolished until 1972), and since political movements to change Swiss society may also challenge a conservative defence policy.[7] At a more technical level, the cost of domestic arms production and the fact that there are large numbers of men under arms, necessarily means the Swiss army is likely to be operating with inferior equipment.[8]

Yugoslavia

Yugoslavia differs from the traditional neutrals. Its political stance evolved specifically in the context of the Cold War between East and West, after Tito broke with Stalin in 1948 and was expelled from the Soviet camp. Yugoslavia is much more nervous of Soviet attack, especially since the invasion of Czechoslovakia in 1968. Therefore its strategy aims to deter a great power attack, not simply ward off military intervention in the context of a wider war. As a result, since 1968 the Yugoslavs have laid a great deal of stress on in-depth defence, drawing on local territorial defence forces to supplement the Yugoslav People's Army.[9] The Yugoslavs have delegated some of the responsibility for mobilising and organising territorial defence units to local bodies — the republics, communes and even large enterprises. Unlike the Swiss, the Yugoslavs very explicitly plan for indefinite partisan resistance if the country is occupied, and have organised sections of the army, as well as the territorial defence forces, to transform themselves into guerrilla fighters. This commitment to partisan resistance makes sense in light of the impressive record of the Communist-led Yugoslav partisans in World War II and in view of the need to maximise deterrence to an occupation.

There is compulsory military service of 15 months in Yugoslavia for all men. Total armed forces are 250,500 (154,000 of them conscripts) out of a population of 22.7 million. After initial training 20% of conscripts are assigned to the Yugoslav People's Army Reserves of 500,000 and the rest are assigned to the Territorial Defence Force. All citizens, women as well as men, receive some basic military training at school and afterwards, and women are included in Territorial Defence units. The maximum size of the Territorial Defence Force is 3 million. In addition there is a Civil Defence Force, organised parallel to Territorial Defence units, of 2 million when mobilised. Civil defence has a vital role in trying to protect and aid the civilian population in the course of what is envisaged as a probably very destructive war. Yugoslavia spends an estimated US $2,870 millions, on military defence annually, about $126 per head, and approximately 4.6 per cent of GNP.

Yugoslav military planners envisage two possible scenarios. One is a limited military attack by an East European state, with indirect Soviet support.[10] In this case the Yugoslavs expect to mount a successful frontier defence. The army has air backing from an air force with 400 combat aircraft, comprising 12 fighter–ground attack squadrons and 9 interceptor squadrons, plus reconnaissance and transport planes. The Yugoslav navy includes 9 submarines, 1 frigate and 3 corvettes, but its main strength is in fast attack craft, patrol craft, minesweeping and minelaying vessels, and its main role is defence of Yugoslavia's long coastline. The second scenario assumes a full-scale Soviet attack, including airborne landings to capture key cities, which the Yugoslavs could not halt unaided. The strategy here is for the regular army to hold the attack during mobilisation; it is claimed that half the territorial defence force could be mobilised within 6 hours and the rest within 24 hours. The army would then retreat from border regions, but continue to wage an active defence in depth with heavy armour as long as possible. In occupied areas the army would transform itself into a more lightly armed body waging partisan warfare alongside territorial defence units.[11]

The deterrent effect of Yugoslavia's preparations depends on the credibility of the Yugoslav commitment never to surrender. This commitment was underlined by the 1969 National Defence Law which made capitulation or surrender of territory punishable as an act of treason,[12] but its real credibility depends on perceptions of Yugoslav willingness and determination to resist at all costs, on awareness of the warlike traditions of the Yugoslav peoples, and on the lessons of recent history. So the Yugoslav model of defence will not necessarily be transferable to different circumstances.

Applicability to Britain

How far, if at all, is any of these three models of defence applicable to Britain? If comparison is made in strategic terms, a non-aligned

British position appears most comparable with that of Sweden. We are not as vulnerable to the Soviet Union as Yugoslavia, and a Soviet attack directed against us as a primary target seems extremely improbable, but we could become strategically important to both sides in the event of a war in Europe. British terrain is much less favourable to an in-depth territorial defence than Switzerland or parts of Yugoslavia, but Britain has the considerable advantage that it is an island, and does not have to plan to meet an overland blitzkrieg attack, and can lay stress on frontier defence. In this respect also Britain is most comparable to Sweden.

Both Sweden and Switzerland assume that the Soviet Union would only use a small proportion of its forces against them. This assessment is an extension of their belief that a Soviet threat exists primarily in the context of a broader European war, and in this sense their strategy is influenced by the existence of NATO. In addition, both expect that, after a war had broken out and they had been attacked, NATO countries might come to their aid. If British withdrawal from NATO did not disrupt the Alliance, we could probably make similar calculations. If on the other hand British action in leaving NATO, and denying all facilities to the USA, resulted in a dissolution of the the Alliance, then we (and indeed the present European neutrals) would have to plan for a different European environment. Since our political aim in leaving NATO might well be to promote the goal of a Western Europe politically and militarily independent of the USA, we would have to *plan* to be self-reliant. Depending on subsequent developments in Europe after we had taken this unilateral action, we might be able to assume that, as a result of multilateral measures of nuclear or even conventional disarmament, the risk of attack was extremely remote; or we might together with other West European countries be somewhat more vulnerable, if the USA had withdrawn from Europe and there had been no Soviet arms limitation.

Internal factors too make Britain most comparable to Sweden which also has a parliamentary democracy and a welfare state, is economically reliant on imports and exports, and which has laid great emphasis on modern technology. There are major differences in historical tradition, given Britain's recent imperial role and its involvement in two world wars, but a Britain which fully renounced claims to great power status (implied by the British Bomb) and opted for non-alignment might be comparable to Sweden, and might achieve a similar 'transmigration of the martial spirit' undergone by Sweden in the past two centuries after it relinquished any claim to be a major European power.[13]

Potential similarities in British and Swedish defence may be increased by the fact that Swedish defence planners have been influenced by Britain's experience in 1940 and in particular by the Battle of Britain. Two of the significant differences — the absence of conscription in Britain and the much larger population — to some extent cancel each other out. The British armed forces based on voluntary enlistment are about five times as large as the Swedish armed forces (professional and conscript combined) at any one time: 327,600 to 64,500. After mobilising regular reserves and the Territorial Army, Britain's full strength on paper in 1982 was about 609,300 for all services, though the numbers at present actually available at any given moment are rather lower;[14] this compares with Sweden's estimated total strength of 800,000 which it expects to be able to mobilise within 72 hours in an emergency. At present most of Britain's army of 163,100 and army reserves of 139,600 are scheduled in time of war to fight in West Germany, as are some of the Territorial Army, now listed as 70,200 strong, and due to rise to 86,000 by the early 1990s.

By most criteria Britain not only spends a great deal more on defence in absolute terms, but also spends more in relative terms than Sweden.[15] Since British defence costs at present include maintenance of an independent nuclear deterrent, and the foreign exchange costs of the British Army of the Rhine and RAF Germany, plus naval support and reinforcements for NATO, we could, with an independent defence policy, maintain an air force larger than Sweden's — at present the RAF has about 700 combat aircraft to Sweden's 420 — a larger navy and a larger standing army than Sweden, whilst actually achieving some saving in real terms. Sweden does, after mobilisation, deploy more soldiers on the ground, but Swedish territory is almost twice the size of Britain and Sweden is now committed to an in-depth defence which Britain would not necessarily have to emulate. It is often argued that a purely conventional defence would be more expensive than reliance on nuclear weapons, an argument sometimes backed by reference to the high cost of Sweden's forces. While this might apply to a major British contribution to a conventional defence of Europe, combined with a serious defence of Britain itself, it is not true of a conventional defence of Britain alone, unless force levels are set at a considerably higher level than in Sweden. The actual costs of a wholly British conventional defence would naturally depend on the strategy adopted and the type of personnel and equipment required.

III. The context and purpose of British defence

Britain is a predominantly industrial and urban society, with a high population density. It has no modern tradition of 'citizens in arms', either in terms of a local militia system or of conscription (national military service, introduced in World War II, was phased out again after 1957) and has relied instead on a volunteer professional army. As an island it has naturally stressed its naval force, and in the latter part of this century its air force. Because Britain is an advanced industrial country and was until recently a world power, the armed services have been committed to equipping themselves with the latest military technology.

The nature and size of the armed forces, in particular the navy, have been shaped by Britain's past imperial role. The dissolution of the British Empire since World War II, and various government decisions to cut back overseas commitment of British forces, have eroded this global element in British defence planning, but it is still reflected in British naval deployment. Whether Britain should be willing to use armed force to secure its access to raw materials, for example in the Persian Gulf, is one major policy issue to be decided. It was argued in Chapter 1 that we should exclude this option and seek alternative methods. What military provision, if any, Britain should make in the future to cover its remaining overseas commitments (for example in Hong Kong and Belize) is another question of considerable political importance, as the Falkland Islands crisis has demonstrated, and has implications for future force structure. This chapter assumes that Britain will finally divest itself of post-imperial responsibilities, and will abandon its global role.

Since the last war British defence policy has for the first time been closely integrated with the defence of Western Europe, and our commitments under the Brussels Treaty and NATO largely determine the disposition of our army and the strategy assigned to the navy. If, however, a non-nuclear Britain withdrew all its forces from Europe, or withdrew from NATO's integrated military command structure, so becoming either totally independent, or a member of a much looser European defence coalition, then we should have to rethink what would be involved in a defence of this country alone.

This re-evaluation of British defence policy would raise three fundamental questions. First, should we emulate the decision of other neutrals to adopt a policy of 'defensive deterrence', by eschewing potentially offensive weapons and strategic deployment in favour of a stance that appears to be designed solely for defence?

Second, what is the fundamental rationale of a new defence policy: do we for example expect to win a major war or opt for more modest political and military goals? Third, in order to assess the nature, level and deployment of the forces required, it is necessary to itemise the specific threats we expect to have to meet.

The advantages of a defensive deterrence policy are clear: it is conducive to good relations with other countries, removes any excuse for a pre-emptive strike by a potential enemy, and is a defence policy compatible not only with nuclear disarmament but with limitation of various kinds of conventional weapon. At a military level, however, it creates a number of practical problems; if enforced strictly, for example, it prohibits counter-offensive strikes against enemy air-fields, communications or concentrations of troops waiting to invade. Some compromise may be possible. Renouncing long-range missiles and bombers while maintaining some fighter–ground attack aircraft, as Sweden does, is one possibility. Once war has broken out, a policy of defensive deterrence might allow for attacks on, for example, an invasion fleet still in harbour, or sabotage of crucial facilities on the enemy side. The purpose of defensive deterrence is to deter; its characteristic capability is one that does not pose a threat to any other state.

What rationale should underlie British defence policy raises more fundamental problems. Britain could think of its military forces as having primarily a 'policing' role: guarding its territorial waters and enforcing fishing limits, preventing attack on its oil rigs, and being able to prevent minor armed incursions of any sort against parts of its territory.

The next stage up is to regard the armed forces, in addition to their policing role, as having the function of asserting the nation's sovereignty in a symbolic sense at an international diplomatic level. So if one ship, or a small garrison is present in an area, this consti-tutes an assertion of sovereignty, and any attack constitutes a clear act of aggression. Thus the armed forces, in this approach, would not be expected to defeat a *major* attack in the event of war, but to 'up the ante' by putting up sufficient resistance to show beyond doubt that aggression had occurred and thus to mobilise international condem-nation and sanctions. Both a policing role and a symbolic role imply relatively low force levels, though the latter may involve a broader array of weapons and ships or aircraft if the aim is to provide a minimum capability against a serious attack.

If the aim of a defence policy is to go further and to provide a significant deterrent, even to a larger military power, the next stage is to opt for the idea of exacting a 'high entry price', the basis of the defence posture of Sweden, Switzerland and Yugoslavia.

The most ambitious goal would be to aim to *defeat* an attack by any likely aggressor. This goal implies very high levels of military investment and preparedness, and would be unrealistic if the opponent were one of the superpowers. If Britain opted out of all military alliances (or was a member of a loosely co-ordinated defence association based primarily on national defence) it could not expect to match the conventional forces of the USSR or USA. Britain could of course plan to match the other secondary powers, should that ever prove to be militarily necessary, and use its forces to threaten a very high entry price for the USSR or the USA.

Which role Britain should adopt depends partly on the wider international context. The concept of a pure policing role is attractive if serious aggression is unlikely. It might be appropriate if defence policy were being framed as a minimum position compatible with agreed measures of substantial disarmament in Europe, or if the main emphasis of defence was on civil resistance. It is more difficult to justify a mainly symbolic role for defence. In practice there is a good deal of symbolism in all defence policies in projecting an international status and reassuring domestic opinion, but it is hard to argue that a defence posture should be *primarily* symbolic. Nevertheless, a minimal defence, capable of token resistance to major aggression and of fulfilling policing roles, would make sense if the aim were to move deliberately away from reliance on military force and to develop instead the potential of nonviolent methods. It could also be combined with a strategy of guerrilla resistance.

If, on the other hand, there are serious potential threats to British security, and prospects for agreed conventional disarmament seem low, the most realistic military choice appears to be a strategy of exacting a high entry price. Whether this should be through conventional forces, or by a territorial in-depth defence, depends partly on the precise threats envisaged and partly on the inherent advantages and disadvantages of each approach for Britain.

IV. Threats relevant to defence strategy

The threats which a 'high entry price' defence policy might have to meet can be broadly sub-divided into (1) attacks on Britain by either of the superpowers for limited strategic purposes in the course of a European war, or (2) the more remote possibility of a major attack by the Soviet Union with the aim of occupying the country.[16] (If the USA wished to exert control over British policies, it would almost certainly seek this by economic, diplomatic or undercover means, not by overt military action).

The first possibility is that during a European war either side would destroy military bases and facilities, such as ports and airports, in Britain. If the aim were to destroy them totally, this could be done by bombing or missile raids using conventional explosives; or in certain circumstances by chemical or nuclear warheads. The purpose could be to prevent Britain itself from joining in the war, or to render it incapable of military resistance at a later stage, or more probably, if Britain were neutral, the purpose could be to prevent the other side having access to these facilities. Anti-aircraft defences might be suitable for dealing with this type of attack, but, since Britain cannot afford anti-missile defences, its ability to prevent such destruction is probably limited. Civil defence measures to restrict civilian casualties are clearly worth consideration in this kind of scenario. Military installations might also be destroyed or damaged not by long-range missiles but by sabotage teams, which suggests they should be guarded either by units within the armed services or by home defence forces.

The second possibility is that either side might try to seize facilities directly for immediate use and to prevent the other side getting there first. For example, the USA or the USSR might try to seize the Shetlands and Northern Scotland if a battle developed for control of the North Atlantic. Britain could, like Sweden, aim to make the cost of such an attack unacceptably high to either power. A conventional capability to attack aircraft and naval vessels, and to beat off a landing force, would probably be the most effective response, although if it is necessary to meet possible landings from the sea or air at a great many points, use of the Territorial Army or some other volunteer local defence body equipped to hold an area for an initial 24 to 48 hours could also be required. A longer-term commitment to sabotage any military installations seized by an outside power, and to harass an occupying force by guerrilla tactics, could also deter. If the USA and USSR were actually fighting over British territory, although a British government might wish to assert its determination not to cede sovereignty by a symbolic confrontation with both forces, it could not credibly take on both at once. A possible strategy would be to make it clear that, whichever side did seize portions of British territory would then have to face serious military resistance, with the aim of making our territory a less attractive prize.

If the threat envisaged is an actual Soviet occupation, either for long-term strategic advantage, or for political and ideological reasons, one possible scenario is an attack directed solely against Britain. Apart from the political reasons for doubting this scenario, there are also strategic reasons why it is almost incredible. Launching a major invasion force by sea and air against an island about 1000 miles away is intrinsically an unattractive military exercise. Moreover, the Soviet Union has traditionally been a land power not accustomed to exercise imperial rule over far-flung parts of the globe. Despite the much wider naval deployment and development of overseas military bases during the last decade, the USSR has never yet attempted direct military involvement in major hostilities overseas. During and since World War II the Soviet Union has acquired the capability for limited air and sea landings, but Soviet strategy and forces are not at present geared to the possibility of launching an air and sea attack on a country able to mount serious military resistance.[17] Therefore although the USSR has the capacity to muster a vast array of forces against Britain, the difficulties and costs would be unacceptably high, even excluding the possibility of military pressure by other powers against a Soviet Union committed to an act of major aggression. It is even less likely that in a time of general peace the Soviet Union would undertake the lengthy exercise of a blockade of British territorial waters, or the drastic option of threatening mass conventional bombing or a nuclear strike in order to secure submission.

Secondly, the Soviet Union might adopt a strategy of gradual encroachment. If Sweden and Norway had been taken over by Soviet forces, or ceded military facilities to the USSR, an attack on Britain would become a more feasible military exercise, and it would also be somewhat easier to impose a blockade. A convincing British defence stance of exacting a high admission price, including sea and air attacks on a blockading navy, might ensure that the gains from an invasion or a blockade were not worth the probable costs.

If the Soviet Union were planning a full-scale attack on Western Europe, Britain could face not only the threat of attacks on bases or seizure of strategic areas, but the possibility of total occupation. The Soviet Union could adopt either of two approaches to a full-scale attack on Western Europe. The first is one which does not figure largely in present NATO planning, but which appears in principle plausible: that Soviet forces would attack the relatively vulnerable Norway and Denmark first,[18] go on to seize Britain, and only then concentrate on Central Europe. In that case Britain could mount a military resistance in the hope of eventual victory, and even if overrun by Soviet forces, could still harry them by partisan tactics and sabotage.

The other possible approach by the Soviet Union would be to launch a major attack on Central Europe aimed at reaching the Channel. If this succeeded, and assuming the USA remained neutral, Britain would be isolated as in 1940. In these circumstances — given that a considerable number of Soviet troops would be deployed in holding down Western Europe and in preventing unrest in Eastern Europe — although Britain could not prevent an attack its ability to exact a 'high entry price' might make possible negotiation of favourable terms. In this context, however, Britain would most probably have to face military pressures other than the threat of an invasion: for example a blockade, or threatened destruction of its cities by either conventional or nuclear means. In this extreme scenario Britain could possibly mitigate the effects of a blockade by measures of economic defence, and of bombing attacks by civil defence, but without outside support could not avoid a military defeat. Whether a British government should try to settle for a client regime, or should be committed to long-term political resistance, would depend partly on whether there was a commitment to guerrilla or civil resistance as an element in our defence policy, and partly on the situation in the rest of Europe at that stage, since a combined resistance would be much more promising.

Assessment of threats we might conceivably have to face points to the value of looking at all possible elements in a defence strategy. But at this point it is necessary to concentrate on the main military options for British defence.

V. *Frontier-based conventional defence*

The first option is of course to maximise the advantages we have from being an island, and to plan to engage any attacking force by sea or in the air. The importance of a sea barrier has obviously been reduced since the development of bombers and missiles, but if the aim is invasion and not simply destruction, it still has strategic significance.

The problems of an airborne or seaborne invasion do not seem to have altered significantly since World War II. A successful airborne invasion probably depends on having control in the air.[19] It is easier now than in the past to reinforce a front line by airlifting troops (hence the greater reliance of the USA on rapid reinforcement of its

NATO contingents than in the 1950s), and once in control of some territory, it is easy to ferry in ordinary troops to an airbase provided they are safe from attack in the air. But until an opponent's fighter force, and anti-aircraft missiles and artillery have been destroyed, a major parachute drop or helicopter-borne landing cannot make sense.

An invasion by sea may be feasible without overwhelming naval superiority provided the attacking force has sufficient craft to engage an opponent's navy on at least equal terms, but to launch an invasion force liable to serious attrition from naval and air attack before it reached its actual destination would not be rational for a country choosing to start an offensive war. Nor would it make sense to try to land a major invasion force (of say 500,000 men) if while establishing a beach-head they not only had to contend with land-based coastal defences and possible naval attacks, but also were subject to heavy bombardment from the air. In the last war the British did manage to effect a retreat by sea from Dunkirk despite German aerial bombardment, but the D-Day landings were not attempted until the Allies had undisputed command of the air.

If a would-be occupying power preceded an invasion by aerial bombardment, anti-aircraft guns and a surface-to-air missile force could make a conventional bombing attack costly to the enemy, although the ability to deliver bombs by missile from an aircraft at some distance from the target suggests the need for interceptor aircraft as an important element in air defence.

A strong British navy and air force could therefore exact a high price from an attacking force, whether it was aiming at strategic seizure of certain areas during a war, or was intended as a full-scale invasion force. Should a blockade be imposed, British air and naval forces could also inflict considerable damage on Soviet forces, though they could not actually defeat a Soviet blockade by military means without outside assistance.

If a frontier-based defence were adopted, the role of ground forces would be secondary, but the ability to defeat a moderate-sized attacking force would be crucial if our aim was to deter attempts to seize part of our territory for strategic purposes during a war. An efficient ground force could make an all-out invasion look more unattractive if the Soviet Union was hesitating over the advantages of an attack. In view of the differing aims which might lie behind any invasion of British territory, and the possibility of forces landing from the sea or by air at many points, the only real option would be to have a few highly mobile mechanised and armoured divisions, possibly supplemented by some helicopter-borne units, who could be rushed to wherever enemy troops were landing.

In addition to these mobile forces, there would be a case for a more localised static defence around vulnerable points, in case of enemy attempts to seize key facilities, and possibly in some coastal areas. This kind of defence could be organised by units of the regular army (or in certain cases of the marines or the RAF) drawing for reinforcements on regular reserves or on the Territorial Army (TA). Since Soviet military planning includes eight airborne divisions designed to secure airfields, ports and communication centres, measures to defend such facilities seem relevant, and a regular army relying on mobility could be spread too thin or arrive too late.

A strategy for a frontier-based conventional defence is inextricably linked to the nature and level of weapons systems and personnel available, and the resources allocated to defence. The aim of such a defence, if it goes beyond a symbolic role, is to let through as little as possible or, if faced by clearly superior forces, to inflict serious losses on enemy ships and aircraft. These aims would imply a substantial modern navy and air force, so it is necessary to ask whether Britain has the ability to maintain such forces.

There is no doubt that, despite past cuts, Britain still has a relatively large navy and a sophisticated modern air force. Future problems could arise because in the long term it may not be economically feasible to keep up with the latest technology.

In the short term, abandoning the costs of the British nuclear bomb and missile system would release some funds for alternative forms of defence, and withdrawing British troops from Germany (which is assumed in the option of a defence policy for a Britain independent of military alliances) would ease our foreign exchange burden. But in the long run, if Britain's growth rate is minimal and the costs of the most recent conventional weapons technology rise rapidly, it is doubtful whether Britain can continue to be a major second-class naval and air power into the 1990s and beyond. Sweden's partial switch from high technology as the basis of defence to greater emphasis on in-depth defence relying on manpower and much cheaper weapons is instructive.

It has been cogently argued that the most sophisticated trends in arms development are self-defeating, since they involve enormous investment in, for example, multi-purpose aircraft of great complexity and debatable operational efficiency. The term 'gold-plated' technology has been coined to refer to the process of adding ever more but marginal increments to capabilities, usually through the use of very costly advanced electronics. The improved performance, if it is real, is offset by increased unit costs resulting in lower numbers, and by much more demanding maintenance requirements, meaning lower numbers of combat-ready systems. Moreover, the improvement in performance is often not real, especially in the case of multi-purpose equipment which is unable to perform any single role as well as a specialised system. The increased sophistication of equipment often puts greater stress on its operators who must also be trained to higher levels of skill (taking more time and expense). There are high technology systems, for example the Harrier jump jet, which are efficient provided that they are not subject to excessive refinement. But technology now needs to simplify not complicate. It would be possible to develop an effective conventional capability at a simpler technological level, using models designed for one purpose, at lower cost.[20] But this approach might imply acquiring larger numbers of ships or aircraft, and so does not wholly solve the economic problems of mounting a viable conventional defence. Therefore there are economic constraints in planning future conventional force levels for a frontier-based defence.

What would this kind of frontier-based defence mean in terms of personnel and military equipment? One possible starting point is to look at the forces presently assigned to defence of 'the United Kingdom base'. This means not only excluding forces already in Germany, but the reinforcements earmarked for Germany; excluding parts of the navy assigned to a NATO role in the East Atlantic; and excluding the special reinforcements for NATO's northern and southern flanks. According to the 1981 Statement on the Defence Estimates, the forces assigned to UK defence are: a fighter screen of seven squadrons, plus some squadrons of anti-aircraft missiles; surface ships, helicopters and maritime patrol craft to prevent the mining of submarines, and torpedo and missiles attacks on shipping, plus some mining capacity; and on land about 30 per cent of the mobilised strength of the army, including the Territorial Army, i.e. about 100,000 men.[21]

Present planning for the defence of the home base could clearly not be an entirely adequate basis for an independent Britain. It sees defence of Britain taking place primarily on the West German frontier and to a lesser extent on NATO's northern flank in Norway and Denmark, not on the frontiers of the United Kingdom itself. The extremely high likelihood of nuclear attack on Britain in the early stages of a European war under present policies must also influence attitudes to defence of the home base. The scepticism was in fact indicated in the 1981 Defence Estimates, which describe the duties of the home force as:

(1) guarding vital military and civilian installations against sabotage and attack, for which highly trained men are not required;
(2) seeking to destroy any force landed by an enemy;
(3) assisting the civil police.

The main focus of present planning for this country seems therefore to be maintaining internal order and guarding against sabotage, not a serious expectation of conventional attack. Mr Nott's June 1981 Defence Review acknowledged the inadequacies of home defence, and projected an increase in the Territorial Army, and the formation of an additional home guard force. In practice, however, these moves may be seen as filling the gap created by cuts in the regular army, by finding more volunteers.

Therefore, even if planning for the future defence of Britain starts from the present forces allotted to the UK base, and this is as good a starting point as any, it would be necessary to augment and restructure these forces in various ways to provide a credible conventional defence.

It would clearly be rational to improve the air defence of Britain, which has been a low priority. Mr Nott revealed that until recently more was spent on defending the fleet against air attack than on defending Britain itself.[22] Although the 1981 defence decisions did involve an investment in more combat aircraft and surface-to-air missiles (SAMs) for this purpose, a British-centred defence would have to lay greater emphasis on defences against air attack. In the short term the SAM and fighter squadrons now based in Germany might be brought to Britain.

The navy might be augmented for certain important roles, whilst at other levels it should probably be scaled down for a British-centred defence strategy. Our present provision for protecting our fishing rights and offshore oil and gas resources has been criticised, so has our present capacity for coastal defence. Both require patrol craft, air support and counter-mining measures. In order to provide defences against submarines in our coastal waters, there may be a case for improving our own minelaying ability.[23]

Apart from safeguarding our resources and inshore waters, the navy needs to be able to counter submarines operating in our territorial zone. At present this is seen as an extension of anti-submarine activity in the East Atlantic, and anti-submarine carriers equipped with Sea Harriers and helicopters, air defence destroyers and anti-submarine frigates have been allocated to this task. Nuclear-powered attack submarines may also be deployed for this purpose. There is a technical dispute whether submarines can be tracked and countered most effectively by other submarines and land-based aircraft, or by surface ships such as cruisers, destroyers and frigates with anti-submarine warfare (ASW) capability. If the emphasis is on British defence, there could clearly be a role for land-based aircraft, and although Britain is now equipped with ASW carriers, the doubts about their efficiency and their vulnerability to attack suggest that they should be phased out.

The most controversial question concerns what role, if any, there is for a high seas battle fleet of aircraft carriers, cruisers, destroyers and frigates. This issue was raised sharply in 1981 by Mr Nott's Defence Review, which did represent a willingness to scrap aircraft carriers, and a shift from large surface vessels towards greater emphasis on nuclear- and diesel-powered submarines. If future Falklands task forces are ruled out, and the navy is not expected in peacetime to safeguard shipping or our access to economic resources in distant parts of the world, is there any purpose in having destroyers and frigates? These vessels are vulnerable to air attack, as the Falklands war has demonstrated, and tend to be very expensive. Type 22 frigates, for example, cost £125 million each.

There are, however, arguments in favour of retaining some larger vessels. Rough seas in the Eastern Atlantic and North Sea require relatively large craft, even for coastal defence, so this would be a reason for some frigates. In order to maintain British claims to sovereignty we may need some larger ships to intervene in certain cases where our territorial limits are challenged by other warships. If Britain adopted a high entry price policy, we would need a force capable of engaging an enemy fleet, and although this might be assigned largely to land-based aircraft and to submarines, the existence of a force of surface warships might be seen as a clear signal of commitment to a naval defence. There may also be periods of crisis when the government does wish to be able to provide some naval protection to merchant shipping or military supplies — for example in the run-up to a threatened blockade. Finally, if we were not wholly non-aligned, but a member of a loose European defensive alliance, we might need to protect shipping in the Channel and North Sea in time of war.

Both air and naval defences require efficient early-warning and radar systems, which are already part of the home defence system. If we were still loosely allied to some European countries, this would also be an area in which we might well wish to extend technical co-operation. The airborne early-warning system based on the Shackletons is being replaced by the Nimrods, and a British-centred defence would presumably continue to invest in this type of provision.[24]

The numbers required for the armed services would depend, of course, partly on the size of the RAF and navy, but to a considerable extent on how much emphasis is laid on repelling a possible attack on Britain after forces have landed. There is a case for retaining a force of marines, partly for policing purposes, since they would be involved in protection of oil rigs, and partly because they could be used to recapture areas like the Shetlands, should we be invaded for strategic purposes. It is doubtful if we would wish to attempt to maintain the army at 1982 levels, of about 163,000, of whom 9,700 are recruited abroad;[25] a drop in future recruiting can in fact be expected as numbers in the appropriate age group decline. The 1981 Defence Review planned to cut the army to 135,000 trained men by 1986. Whether the army should be kept at the projected 1986 level, be reduced, or slightly increased, again depends partly on whether we think an invasion of this country is at all probable. However, in view of the cost of maintaining a large professional army, practical problems such as providing quarters, and the possible political disadvantages of a sizeable army based at home with little to do except train its members, there is a positive case for cuts.

In principle it might be desirable to rely more heavily on reserves in the unlikely event of an invasion threat. If the regular army has been cut, there will of course soon be a drop in the number of trained regular reservists available. This problem could be partly met by provisions to extend the period of availability of reserves and to update their training. While this would cost money, for example in bonuses to reservists, compensating employers for periods of leave for further training, and providing more equipment, it would be preferable to having an unnecessarily large permanent force. Numbers available in a crisis could also be augmented if incentives were introduced to encourage people to join the Territorial Army, which is already scheduled to increase from 70,000 to 86,000 men by 1986, or by creating an additional home guard force (as envisaged on a small scale in the Defence Review of 1981) to watch over fuel dumps, power stations and communications links. If the total size of the regular army were 100,000 it should be possible to raise the total number of combat troops plus supporting units to 300,000 in an emergency, drawing on both reserves and volunteers. If the Territorial Army were scheduled to play an important role in future home defence, it would be necessary to tackle some of the problems it has faced in the past.[26]

If in planning for a British-based defence the possibility of an invasion is given real weight, we need to give serious consideration to a defence policy which would mobilise a large sector of the population for a determined armed resistance after an invasion force had landed: territorial defence.

VI. In-depth territorial defence

The obvious alternative to a frontier-based conventional defence is an in-depth defence on the Swiss model. These two models should not be visualised too literally. A frontier-based defence must include repelling airborne landings behind the lines, and it is rare for an in-depth strategy to make no provision for frontier defence. In the case of Britain it would be ludicrous not to make serious provision for coastal defence as part of an in-depth strategy, but it would be possible to do so with a limited number of frigates, small patrol craft, minelaying and minesweeping facilities, coastal batteries and reliance on local militias along the coast to meet seaborne landings. This kind of coastal defence would dispense with the expensive submarines and surface fleet implied by a conventional naval defence, and also with the high-technology fighters required for conventional air defence. Anti-aircraft guns and the cheaper kinds of surface-to-air missile would, however, be an obvious element in a militia-based coastal defence and city defence.

Discussion about territorial defence is often confused by the fact that there is some ambiguity about what it really means. In-depth defence can be carried out solely by regular troops and reservists, or can assign a substantial role to volunteer part-time forces like the Territorial Army. Alternatively, it can be carried out by a 'citizen army' based on a system of universal conscription, or give a large role to local citizen militias based on some system of universal part-time military training. In practice most systems use a mix of regular troops (or at least professional officers and NCOs) and conscripts, plus local defence forces and civil defence bodies. The arguments for territorial defence therefore fall into two parts: (1) the strategic, political and economic arguments for this defence concept; and (2) additional and separate arguments about the inherent virtues of a citizen army.

The general strategic case for in-depth defence is that it does not mean surrender as soon as frontier defences are overcome, may be better able to meet the problem of dispersed airborne landings than mobile regular forces, implies troop dispersal and so reduces the likelihood of an enemy using battlefield nuclear weapons, and if convincingly organised is a significant deterrent to an attack or occupation. Its political advantages are that it is a form of defence clearly suitable to countries maintaining independence from alliances, an exclusively defensive form of military organisation and thus conducive to good relations with other countries, and is compatible with forms of international conventional disarmament which might focus on offensive weapons and high technology weapons. In addition the fact that it can be carried out with relatively simple technology underpins political autonomy, since reliance on arms from other countries should be unnecessary, and it is economically attractive because of its relative cheapness. There is good reason therefore to consider it seriously.

The case against in-depth defence is that it has military limitations. Territorial units cannot halt an armoured attack or drive out an invasion force, though they can slow it down, harass it and cause a great deal of damage. It is difficult to conduct an effective defence on the ground if one is under air attack as well, and although an in-depth defence might include the use of anti-aircraft missiles (for example the Blowpipe missile, used in the Falklands, which can be carried by one man, and is being made available to the territorial army,[27] the concept of a prolonged in-depth resistance to advancing troops, who have already seized part of the country, rests on the premise that the invasion force has the military advantage and has control of the air. In these circumstances the commitment to a last-ditch stand for every yard of ground may prove to be a romantic illusion, and demoralised soldiers armed with inferior equipment facing advancing armoured divisions, as well as suffering dive bombing and attacks from the air, may not prove the indomitable defenders projected by the strategy.[28]

A second argument against in-depth defence is that extensive territorial warfare might result in much greater suffering for the civilian population than could be justified. If the morale of the defending forces does remain high as a result of patriotic determination, the resulting loss of life by the civilian population as well as the defence forces, and the likely destruction of economic resources and devastation of cities, towns and villages, means that this kind of in-depth defence is extremely costly.

It follows that countries which include large areas with scattered population and formidable terrain (like the mountain and forest areas of Switzerland) are much better suited to this kind of defence strategy than predominantly urban and densely populated countries. If in-depth defence is convincingly organised, its deterrent value is high, but if it has actually to be implemented it is very costly. Like nuclear deterrence, it therefore suffers (though at a qualitatively different level) from an incongruity between deterrence and actual defence.

The separate arguments for a citizen army or citizen militias are primarily political, though countries with a relatively small population may be obliged to rely largely on conscripts or militias in order to field the numbers required for an in-depth defence. The idea of citizens in arms is part of a political tradition which goes back to the French Revolution, and has roots in the republican political theory which is inspired by the Greek city states. The central idea here is that the privileges of citizenship, which include the right to participate in politics, also confer duties, a central duty being, as in the Swiss tradition, the duty to bear arms to defend the freedom of the republic. The idea of citizens in arms is also espoused by those who fear a professional army as a threat to democracy.

The decentralised nature of an in-depth system, which places great responsibility and initiative on each unit in a situation where command and communications may be impossible, can be seen as intrinsically more democratic than professional armies organised in a more centralised fashion for set-piece battles. Certainly a territorial defence system, if it decentralises responsibility in advance to local government units and even to factories can be compatible with a decentralised and participatory framework of political organisation.

The argument against a citizen army in principle is that any serious system of citizen-based territorial defence must imply widespread military training and this could lead to some disaffected groups or criminals using more sophisticated weapons. It could also lead to some militarisation of society, for example in a high value being placed on military virtues and the military training of youth. The Yugoslav system involves a considerable militarisation of society, invoking the revolutionary myth of the liberation war, appealing to patriotic pride, stressing military duty and holding in contempt alien traditions of conscientious objection or nonviolent resistance. However, universal military training in a society with different traditions might not have the same results — Sweden is not a particularly warlike society. In Britain the creation of a citizen army would mean involving the majority of people more actively in preparations for military defence, and would tend to undermine the possibility of greater reliance on nonviolent methods.

What conclusions for Britain follow from this analysis? At a strategic level the case for territorial in-depth defence is less strong than for many European countries. We have no land frontier to hold, our terrain is not generally suitable, and most of England, South Wales and the lowlands of Scotland are too urban and densely populated to make in-depth defence attractive. The credibility of this approach might also be lower than in Yugoslavia and Switzerland where it is based on past experience and a clear political commitment. This caveat leads to the more explicitly political considerations. British historical experience has since the late nineteenth century not included emphasis on local defensive militias, and unlike many continental European countries there is not a strong radical commitment to the idea of a 'nation in arms'. There is one obvious exception to this generalisation — the response in Britain in 1940 to the threat of invasion, when there was a widespread popular willingness to mount determined armed resistance.[29] This precedent suggests that faced with a similar threat there might again be a strong popular response, but it is more doubtful whether it shows that the British people would be willing to commit themselves to universal military training in peacetime.

The arguments are less conclusive when we consider the possibility of territorial defence to *supplement* a frontier-based conventional defence, on the lines of Sweden, and so increasing deterrence by commitment to a more prolonged resistance. Lightly armed and not very highly trained territorial forces would also have more military credibility as an *additional* problem facing invading troops, who also had to contend with well armed and well trained regular soldiers. If we were part of a European association based on strong national defences and limited mutual assistance, the argument for a territorial defence element in our total strategy might be stronger. Apart from demonstrating resolve to both our allies and a potential opponent, the existence of territorial defence preparations could be important in hampering Soviet forces who landed in Britain in preparation for an attack on mainland Europe. The desirability of incorporating territorial defence into our defence would also depend on economic considerations and on domestic political attitudes. The idea of territorial defence is clearly attractive to some strands of opinion, and was urged in some submissions to the Commission; equally clearly it is viewed with grave doubts by others.

The balance of arguments for or against some kind of territorial defence depends a good deal on the scale envisaged. The Yugoslavs, for example, have a territorial force of a maximum of 3 million to cover a territory of 256,000 square kilometres; Sweden's land mass is 450,000 square kilometres, and its mobilised army, which would be partly engaged in territorial defence, is 700,000. If we were to emulate the seriousness of Yugoslav territorial defence, then since the UK is 244,000 square kilometres, we should need about 2.5 million territorials, 10 per square kilometre. But if territorial defence is seen as a back-up to a frontier defence, then it might be possible to go down to between 100,000 and 250,000. The numbers required would also depend on the strategy envisaged; if territorial forces are assigned to hold key points as long as possible, larger numbers will be needed than if the emphasis is on cutting communication lines, or harassing troops in the rear.

Partisan resistance and territorial defence

Territorial defence overlaps with partisan resistance. Both draw on the idea of a nation in arms, rely on the determination of the resistance to prevail against military superiority, and use the advantages of fighting on one's own ground to outwit the enemy, for example to organise ambushes. Nevertheless the underlying concepts differ. Territorial defence, as in the Swiss example, usually implies a willingness to stand and fight. Partisan or guerrilla resistance implies a strategy of hit and run, the partisans melting into the countryside (or in some cases the cities) and re-emerging to inflict further damage. Guerrillas normally avoid set-piece confrontations in which they will be at a military disadvantage. Although in some guerrilla campaigns the guerrillas may effectively control parts of the country, the main focus is not defence of territory.

Partisan warfare takes various forms. One type of partisan activity is to harry an enemy force in the rear, sabotage military targets, cut supply lines, ambush stragglers, and perhaps divert some of the enemy forces from their major front. This was the kind of role played by most partisans in World War II, for example in German-occupied areas of the USSR, and later by partisans in Western Europe.

This type of partisan warfare is a logical part of a commitment to defend a country in depth. An invading force could be harried by partisans in areas it has managed to occupy, while still confronting regular troops or militias in unoccupied territory.

If Soviet troops landed in Britain before attacking mainland Europe, there would clearly be a case for continuing partisan tactics even after Britain itself had been overrun, so long as fighting continued in Europe. If we were part of a loose European defence association we might be under an obligation to offer this type of assistance to our allies. Even if we had been strictly neutral, it might be judged to our advantage during the course of a war to undermine Soviet chances of final victory. These considerations would have to be weighed against the danger of severe reprisals if partisan tactics were used over a prolonged period.

Training for territorial defence and partisan warfare might well overlap. Both imply learning how to handle a rifle and a machine gun, knowing how to use simple anti-tank missiles, being able to lay mines and blow up bridges or railway lines.

There would, however, be some potential conflict between a policy of holding key points against the enemy, and the highly mobile warfare implied by partisan tactics — organising for swift strikes, tactical withdrawal and regrouping. The former suggests reliance on slightly more destructive firepower, the need for air defence (anti-aircraft guns or missiles), and a strategy of 'digging in' round built-up areas, power stations, civilian airfields or bridges. This strategy need not be wholly static, and may involve a series of pre-planned withdrawals — from one point along a road to another, or from the edge towards the centre of a town — but it does imply a 'last stand' commitment, ending in final surrender when the ammunition runs out. It also implies willingness to risk a high level of casualties.

A comprehensive territorial defence strategy might wish to set limits to this type of static defence, and give emphasis to destroying communications to slow down the advancing forces, staging ambushes, and avoiding direct confrontation. Territorial units trained to carry out these partisan-type tasks in a designated area could quite naturally transform themselves into partisan units continuing to operate behind the enemy lines.

Whatever the balance decided between static defence and hit-and-run tactics in territorial defence, it seems reasonable to envisage two branches of a territorial defence organisation, who would receive somewhat different training and be equipped with slightly different weapons.

Both branches would be uniformed soldiers, and the branch carrying out partisan tactics in an occupied zone would continue to wear their uniforms; this would be preferable to civilians engaging in sabotage. The case for reserving armed resistance to soldiers in uniform is that, if caught, they would in principle be covered by regulations governing prisoners of war, and that if a clear distinction between soldiers and civilians was maintained, there would be less likelihood of the occupation authorities undertaking reprisals against civilians.

If there was agreement to move into a further phase of guerrilla resistance, as a long-term strategy *after* the war was over, then remaining territorial units might discard their uniforms and go wholly underground, perhaps where possible returning to their civilian occupations in the locality. This long-term strategy of guerrilla warfare is discussed in detail in Chapter 6. While long-term guerrilla resistance may be a logical extension of a policy of total resistance embodied in territorial defence, as in Yugoslav defence planning, it is certainly not a *necessary* part of territorial defence, which ends when the enemy forces have been repelled, or have established some type of military control over the territory as a whole.

VII. Conscription

One question which must be faced in discussing a non-nuclear defence strategy is whether conscription is either necessary or desirable. As argued earlier, a purely conventional defence of Britain alone almost certainly does not require conscription, although selective conscription could ensure a much larger pool of trained reserves — especially if the quality of the Territorial Army is in doubt — if a convincing back-up in the event of an invasion is seen to be desirable. But one of the politically controversial aspects of territorial defence is that a strong commitment to it may require conscription.

The main purpose of territorial defence is to deter a possible attacker by demonstrating the universal will to resist to the last, so it is necessary to signal this convincingly by advance preparations. A system of conscription, which provided all men with a military training, and which might also provide training for women either in basic military skills or in the skills needed to supply the range of support required for combat units, would be a convincing demonstration of such will. A purely voluntary system, which involved only a minority of the population, would be less so. Conscription into the armed forces would be relevant to an in-depth defence conducted by regular troops drawing on a reservoir of trained conscripts. Training in the forces, or in some separate military organisation, would be required also if territorial defence were organised locally but drew on trained people.

It is arguable that the public here should be willing to take a more positive responsibility for defence, and that, since conscription was abolished after the Conservative government decided in 1957 to rely heavily on nuclear weapons, mass support for a non-nuclear policy should be translatable into willingness to shoulder the burdens of an alternative defence. Conscription is a way of ensuring that large numbers of trained people are available; it is also argued that conscription is more cost effective because it permits one to scale down the permanent armed forces and at the same time may be a means of recruiting permanent soldiers who would not come in through the normal route.

Political objections to army service may be less acute than in the early post-war period when conscripts were often engaged in holding down parts of the empire. The personal objections to military service might be reduced if military training were limited to eight months' basic training on the Swedish model, eliminating needless drill and concentrating on handling weapons and on military exercises and developing physical skills. It would be possible to consider using some conscripts for various forms of social service in lieu of military training. Although in present circumstances this is a highly controversial proposal which is liable to be interpreted as a coercive measure to deal with the unemployed young, it might be received more sympathetically if it was part of a general policy which could claim popular support.

It is sometimes argued that in principle a conscript army drawing on all citizens is politically preferable to having an elite professional force. But there are also strong arguments against conscription. In contrast to the concept of military service as a citizen's duty is the libertarian view that a decision to undergo training to kill other people should be a voluntary one — a choice to be made positively. Conscription which enforces military training, even if it allows for some form of conscientious objection, is in this perspective a violation of personal freedom. Conscription would be bitterly opposed in Britain by libertarian and pacifist groups, and probably others, as a retrograde step, and a proposal to introduce it would divide the peace movement whose continued development is likely to be crucial for the achievement of nuclear disarmament; this is an important consideration, though obviously it could not be an overriding one if conscription was seen as necessary for the security of the country.

But in fact at the military level too there are some reasons to doubt the efficiency of conscription. The professional army has to divert personnel and resources, including a large amount of quite expensive equipment, to training people, some of whom will have little aptitude or enthusiasm for military life. Moreover, a few years after training, conscripts will have only a limited value as soldiers, as equipment will have changed and they will have forgotten much of their training. These objections are particularly cogent for the British armed services which, since the ending of national service in 1963, have concentrated on becoming a highly professional force, proud of their skills. For these reasons any proposal to re-introduce conscription in Britain as part of a conventional defence policy is not on balance a persuasive military option.

If the purpose of conscription is to create the basis for a territorial defence policy, the military case for it may be stronger. It would be necessary to train most people only in relatively simple skills and with fairly cheap equipment, and this kind of training probably could be updated in civilian life by brief refresher courses as in some other countries. However, this might be better organised outside the regular army.

VIII. *Organisational implications of British-based defence*

If a non-nuclear Britain adopted a conventional, frontier-based strategy, the kind of restructuring of the armed forces needed would not require any radical changes in the organisation of the forces.

A strong commitment to a Yugoslav-style territorial defence would mean the creation of a new body to mobilise, train and deploy several million people, whether selectively conscripted or volunteers. The attraction of territorial defence for those who distrust the political composition and internal hierarchy of the armed forces and Territorial Army is that a new territorial defence could be brought under democratic and decentralised control, though this is not the only possible choice. It is hard to envisage Britain following the Yugoslav pattern of basing territorial defence units partly on the work place, but a territorial defence organisation could be devised which would be under the general direction of a central headquarters, but partly responsible to local government or to specially elected local committees.

A limited territorial defence provision of between 100,000 and 250,000 volunteers might not need a new organisation. It would be possible to convert the present local units of the TA to this role. Although this would require changes in present training and strategy, in principle the TA might be better able to plan for a purely local defence with light weapons than to prepare itself to fight with the regular army in unfamiliar terrain, as many units would at present. One possible disadvantage is that some people likely to be willing in principle to take part in territorial defence of a non-nuclear Britain probably would not join the TA, but there are obvious advantages in using an existing organisation with local facilities. In order to secure enough volunteers it might, however, be necessary to increase the meagre financial inducements to take part in regular training.

If the TA were given the task of local defence, a separate body might be set up to guard important civilian installations and military facilities, which would be likely targets of early attack by Soviet airborne troops, if the armed forces themselves lacked the personnel for this function. This task implies a rather high level of military training.

Diversion of the TA to local defence would of course mean a drop in the reinforcements available to the army. It would also be necessary to make alternative provision for logistic back-up for the armed forces, probably as a body directly under army control, and drawing on the existing specialist units of the TA as a starting point.

An extension of the present reserve system to encourage older ex-servicemen to serve a further period with local TA units, guard units, or specialist logistic units, would help provide a core of well trained men.

IX. *Summary of the argument*

This chapter has examined the policies for national defence pursued by the European neutral states of Sweden, Switzerland and Yugoslavia. All three aim to impose a 'high entry price' on an aggressor, but lay different emphases on the role of a high technology conventional defence, in-depth territorial defence, and commitment to long-term resistance after military defeat. Britain differs from all three countries in terms of geography, strategic position, population density, and social and political traditions, but is in most ways closest to Sweden, which combines a high technology frontier defence with an in-depth strategy. Because Britain has a much larger population than Sweden, it might not need to impose conscription to find the personnel for an effective conventional defence.

In order to assess what kind of defence policy would suit Britain best, it is necessary to decide on its basic purpose and rationale. A non-aligned Britain — or a Britain which was a member of a loose European defence association — should adopt a stance of 'defensive deterrence' conveyed by a mix of weapons, strategy and military deployment. We would have a choice between designing a policy primarily to fulfil a policing role for protection of our resources and territory from minor incursions, a slightly more elaborate role of symbolic military assertion of sovereignty, and a 'high entry price' stance. A merely symbolic military defence is hard to argue for, unless the aim is to put up token military resistance and fall back on alternative, nonviolent or guerrilla methods of resistance. Whether a policing role or high entry price policy is most appropriate depends on the likelihood of disarmament and on how we perceive possible threats. The more extreme threats of limited or total invasion (most probably in the context of a wider war) seem remote, but they have enough reality to make the high entry price stance worth serious consideration. It is also necessary to recognise that there are some threats — conventional, chemical or nuclear attack by missiles — which we cannot prevent directly by any military means, and that in some extreme scenarios (for example a Europe occupied by the Soviet Union as far as the Channel), our options would be extremely limited.

A high entry price strategy can be pursued either through frontier-based conventional defence, or territorial defence, or by some combination of the two. A frontier-based defence would of course have to make some provision for landings by air, and territorial defence for coastal defences, so the alternatives are not to be understood too literally.

Frontier-based defence would have solid advantages. It capitalises on our being an island, fits in with our historical experience, builds on existing military capabilities, and so would be fairly easy to adopt, and involves least disruption of the existing armed forces and reserve arrangements. In the short run — say, until the mid-1990s — it should be possible to adopt a conventional strategy with quite high force levels and actually reduce real costs in comparison with the present defence budget. In the longer term, the burden of a high technology defence may be unacceptably high.

An attractive case can be made for territorial defence in the abstract on political and economic grounds, and it can provide a convincing deterrent by demonstrating firmness of will to resist. It is, however, a policy which would be very destructive in time of war, and it requires a certain militarisation of society. For Britain it is not a convincing option, as it does not meet strategic needs, and neither our terrain nor our society is well suited to this approach, unlike those of Switzerland or Yugoslavia.

There is a stronger argument for adopting a territorial defence strategy *in addition* to a frontier-based conventional defence, if the possibility of an invasion is judged real enough to warrant this additional element of deterrence.

If territorial defence is an element in a total defence strategy, limited use of partisan tactics to harry invasion forces as they advance, and in the rear of enemy forces, is a logical component of an in-depth territorial defence while the war is still in progress. This role for partisan tactics does not imply any *necessary* connection between an in-depth defence and a long-term commitment to guerrilla resistance after a military occupation.

A switch to a non-nuclear military defence requires consideration of the case for and against conscription. It is unlikely that frontier-based high-technology conventional strategy would require conscription, but compulsory military service could be the basis for a territorial defence. Positive reasons can be cited for conscription, especially in the context of abandoning nuclear weapons for an alternative defence policy, but there are strong objections on libertarian grounds, and it is doubtful if the British armed services, proud of their professionalism, would be at all enthusiastic to have now the responsibility for training large numbers of conscripts.

A conventionally based defence would not necessitate any major reorganisation of the armed services. Adopting territorial defence on the Yugoslav scale would suggest the need for a new territorial defence force and create opportunities for some local democratic control. But a more restricted territorial defence commitment could probably be best organised by the local units of the TA if they were reoriented to this role. This would mean some reduction in reinforcements for the army. Logistic support for the armed forces could be met by an organisation directly under military control, drawing on existing specialist units of the TA. A separate well trained unit guarding special facilities against possible early attack might also be necessary if the TA were locally based.

X. Conclusions

The Commission takes the view that, unless substantial arms reductions can be achieved in Europe, the most appropriate basis for a military defence of an independent Britain would be a high entry price strategy. This would also be the most realistic strategy if we were a member of a loose European military alliance.

The Commission also believes that in view of the most probable threats, our geography and our social and political circumstances, Britain should concentrate on a conventional frontier-based military strategy involving investment in air and naval defences and a small professional, highly mobile, army. Britain should in general emulate Sweden's emphasis on a defensive strategy, though it might not choose to go as far as Sweden in forgoing an offensive capability. The aim, however, would be to adopt a posture which could not be interpreted as posing a serious threat to other countries.

No member of the Commission thinks Britain should be heavily committed to defence in depth on the Yugoslav model, but some members do favour a limited provision for territorial defence to supplement conventional forces, to be based on local volunteers.

Not all Commission members favour a heavy investment in military forms of defence; some would prefer a minimal military defence — primarily fulfilling a policing role — while switching the main emphasis towards non-military forms of resistance.

It was, however, generally agreed that a defensive conventional stance, possibly strengthened by some territorial defence preparations to enhance deterrence, was a reasonable option for a non-nuclear Britain to consider for the near future.

Notes on Chapter 4

1. A Report from the Swedish Parliamentary Committee on Defence took the view that: "military operations designed to secure control of areas of considerable importance to the great power blocs around the Northern Calotte and the Baltic Straits could be a reality in the early stages of a war in Europe".
   Summary in English of 1978 Parliamentary Committee on Defence Report, under the title 'Security Policy and Total Defence', Stockholm, February 1981, Ds Fö 1981: 1. (Mimeo)
2. These figures are taken from International Institute for Strategic Studies, *The Military Balance, 1982–83* (London, I.I.S.S. 1982),Table 5 — Comparisons of Defence Expenditure and Military Manpower 1975–81, pp. 124–5.
3. J. M. Luck, 'Modern Switzerland' (Swiss Embassy Pamphlet), 1978.
4. General Frank Seethaler, 'The Tactics of Dissuasion', *New Statesman*, 7 November 1980.
5. Report of the Study Commission for Strategic Questions, led by Professor Karl Schmid, rendered 4 November 1961, published in Zurich, 1971, pp. 56–7. (Cited in H. Mendershausen, 'Territorial Defense in NATO and Non-NATO Europe', *Rand Report*, R–1184–ISA, February 1973, pp. 79–80.)
6. Luck, 'Modern Switzerland'.[3]
7. A. Roberts, *Nations in Arms*, (London: Chatto & Windus, 1976), pp. 59–60.
8. Seethaler, 'The Tactics of Dissuasion'.[4]
9. The organisational relationship between the Yugoslav People's Army (YPA) and the Territorial Defence Forces is complicated. Under the 1969 Defence Law the Territorial Forces have considerable autonomy; the 1974 revised Law gave the YPA greater control, following the political trend to greater centralisation.

10. Bulgaria, which has a continuing quarrel with Yugoslavia over Macedonia and is the most faithful of Moscow's East European allies, is the most likely attacker.

11. Sources on Yugoslav defence are Roberts, *Nations in Arms*[7] and Mendershausen, 'Territorial Defense in NATO and Non-NATO Europe'.[5]

12. This commitment is underlined by a clause in the 1974 Yugoslav Constitution which forbids agreement to capitulate. See D. S. Gedza, *Borba*, December 7, 1975. Reprinted in *Survival*, XXVIII, 3 (May/June 1976) 116–17.

13. See P. Lyon, *Neutralism* (Leicester: Leicester University Press, 1963), p. 151, citing Arnold Toynbee.

14. A House of Commons Inquiry into policy on reserves and reinforcements under the Labour Government of 1974–79 found that only 75% of the Territorial Army would be available for mobilisation at any one time, and that the army only planned to use half its regular reserves. (Reserves and Reinforcements, HC 393, 1977: Evidence, pp. 107–08 and 111). The IISS figure of 609,300 for all services after mobilisation includes 7,400 in the Ulster Defence Regiment under Army Reserves.

15. In Table 5 of *The Military Balance 1982–83*, pp. 124–5 (referred to in Note 2 above), British defence expenditure in 1981 is shown as $24,223 million compared with Sweden's $3,431 million. (The table uses NATO definitions of defence expenditure and expresses all figures in terms of US$ for the sake of comparison.) The table shows that in 1981 Britain spent $433 per head of its population of 56 million, compared with Sweden's expenditure of $412 per head of its population of 8.3 million; Britain is shown to have spent 5.4% of GNP on defence, compared with Sweden's 3.1% of GNP. British defence figures reflect the inflation of recent years. Ruth Leger Sivard's figures, based on 1979, estimate British defence spending at that time as $19,156 million or $342 per capita, compared with Sweden's $3,383 million or $408 per capita. The proportion of GNP devoted to defence is shown as 4.8% for Britain, and 3.4% for Sweden. (Ruth Leger Sivard, *World Military and Social Expenditures 1982*, Leesburg, Virginia: World Priorities 1982).

16. This discussion excludes minor threats or incidents, e.g. illegal fishing in our waters, which would be covered by a purely policing role.

17. See P. Vigor, 'The Forward Reach of the Soviet Armed Forces: Seaborne and Airborne Landings', in J. Erickson and E. J. Feuchtwanger, eds., *Soviet Military Power and Performance* (London: Macmillan, 1979).

18. Norway could be attacked across the frontier in the Kirkenes area and by seaborne forces across the Kola Peninsula, and Denmark is in principle vulnerable to Warsaw Pact divisions in the north of Poland and East Germany. See A. L. King-Harman, 'Military Balance in the North', *NATO Review*, 24, 4 (August 1976), 10.

19. This is the lesson Soviet theorists have drawn from the failure of Arnhem, and it still seems to influence their strategy. (Vigor[17])

20. An example of simpler technology is a close support aircraft which is designed for that role only (e.g. USA's A-10). A classic example of 'gold-plating' is the Abrams XM-1 tank, with a jet engine which does not work with dust around, an inadequate gun-stabiliser and a fuel consumption of 3 gallons per mile. John Nott had started moving away from 'gold-plated' technology, and had suggested less elaborate equipment as one remedy for excessive costs. (*The Guardian*, 17 November 1981).

21. Statement of the Defence Estimates 1981, Cmnd.8212–1, pp. 27–28. The figure of 100,000 is a deduction from the available information, allowing for unavailability of reserves and TA cited in footnote 14.

22. John Nott's Statement to the House of Commons on his Defence Review. (*The Financial Times*, 26 June 1981).

23. See for example Philip Geddes, 'Messing About in Boats', *New Statesman*, 29 May 1981.

24. There is also a need for an effective means of detecting the movement of submarines in our waters, as the recent Swedish concern about Soviet submarines round their coasts illustrates. Britain does at present have a range of methods for submarine detection. Within limited areas detection can be undertaken by suitably equipped aircraft, but Britain relies primarily on cooperation with the USA in this field, in particular on the sonar listening devices on the ocean bed of the Atlantic, about 300 miles south-west of Ireland, which are linked to Brawdy in South Wales, and the chain of such listening devices which monitor submarine movements in the Scotland–Iceland–Greenland gap.

25. International Institute for Strategic Studies, *The Military Balance, 1982–83* (London I.I.S.S., 1982).

26. The TA was reorganised in 1967, and is made up of (1) local units which are locally recruited and have their own drill halls, and (2) units of specialists recruited nationally and run from a central headquarters, who receive less military training than the local independent units. About half the local units are intended for logistic support, and the rest are armoured gunners, or infantry units. Many TA units are now scheduled to reinforce BAOR, but others (including some more lightly armed home guard units) are assigned to British defence.

Recruitment has not been easy for the TA, and its real strength has been below the establishment figures. After an increase in TA bonuses and in pay for periods of training, which led to a net gain of 2,500, the TA's strength in February 1980 was 60,178 against an establishment figure of 73,666. Moreover, turnover of membership has been high, with many volunteers leaving after one or two years, although the increase in bonuses and pay, recommended by the Shapland Report, seems to have improved the retention rate. The training available to the TA has been criticised too, in particular the lack of training with regular forces. The number of days of training a year was raised in 1981 from 38 to 42, but in practice family and work commitments prevent many volunteers from attending weekend courses or the theoretically compulsory fortnight training camp. The specialist units can be criticised even more severely, because of inadequate military training, because of the difficulties of central call-up, and because in some cases they are not genuinely specialist. Finally, there is doubt about the quality of TA equipment or the appropriateness of the present arrangements for their deployment and control. It should, however, be possible to improve the quality of the TA, if enough importance is attached to it.

(Sources on TA: Debate in the House of Lords on the Reserve Forces, Hansard, 12 December 1979; Debate in the House of Commons, Hansard, 27 March 1980; *The Times*, 4 February 1980 and 18 April 1981; Debate on Reserve Forces in the Commons, reported in *The Times*, 4 March 1982.)

27. *The Daily Telegraph*, 14 February 1980.

28. This point was made forcefully by John Biggins in a helpful submission to the Commission on territorial defence in the UK.

29. David Fernbach, 'A New Look at Dad's Army', *New Statesman*, 24 October 1980, discusses the training school at Osterley Park run by Tom Wintringham, a veteran of the Spanish civil war. Charles Cruikshank, 'So Dad's Army Had Teeth After All', *The Times*, 2 January 1981, reports on special guerrilla units in the Home Guard organised on a cell basis in coastal villages to engage the initial wave of German assault forces until the British regular forces arrived.

Chapter 5
West European defence: the military options

I. Introduction

This chapter explores what kinds of non-nuclear military strategy could be pursued for a common defence of Western Europe, focusing particularly on strategies in a NATO context, and looking very briefly at what a purely West European defence association could do. The discussion does not cover defence arrangements which might be linked to a political settlement in Central Europe, for example the neutralisation of both halves of Germany. The Commission sees the dissolution of NATO and the Warsaw Pact as an important goal, but is concentrating here on measures which could be taken unilaterally by NATO or Western Europe, and on relatively short-term proposals to reduce the risk of nuclear war in Europe.

It is assumed, as set out in Chapter 3, that NATO forces would not possess battlefield nuclear weapons and that there are no inter-mediate-range nuclear weapons based in Europe or targeted for use in the European theatre, under NATO control. (What policies would be pursued by France is one of the major problems associated with a policy of de-nuclearising Europe in the NATO framework). It is also assumed that for the foreseeable future the United States would retain some kind of strategic deterrent force, but that the European countries should *not* seek to couple the American nuclear force to the defence of Europe, but rather the reverse.

The military case for NATO switching to a purely conventional war-fighting strategy is that, while there may be some loss of deter-rence without nuclear weapons, it is possible to fight a conventional war without totally destroying European society. Even if the worst happened and the Soviet Union was tempted to use its own nuclear weapons, it would have every reason to use them discriminately.

If a joint conventional defence of Europe is compared with other possible non-nuclear defence options it can claim some definite advantages. A collective system enhances the deterrent and defensive capacity of each individual country and many strategists see it as a much more realistic way of defending Britain than a purely British strategy.

The greatest disadvantage of this approach is that even a purely conventional war could be appallingly destructive and result in a great loss of civilian life. There are also obvious difficulties if NATO removed all its own battlefield and theatre nuclear weapons and the Soviet Union would not reciprocate. The Soviet Union would then retain the capability to use nuclear weapons in the event of war if it were to their overall advantage to do so. Nevertheless there is a strong military and political case for de-nuclearising Western forces, and the constraints on Soviet first use of nuclear weapons should not be underestimated (see Chapter 1). But the ultimate possibility of nuclear escalation or nuclear blackmail means that the anti-occupation strategies of guerrilla warfare or nonviolent resistance have to be taken seriously; these are examined in the following two chapters.

The discussion in this chapter is inevitably fairly technical, but there are a number of important political and human issues central to the debate, which should be understood clearly at the outset.

II. *Non-military issues*

The first central fact is that the main battleground for NATO would be West Germany, which is a highly industrialised and urban country, with its major cities in the North growing rapidly, and which has traumatic memories of the devastation of the Second World War. So the West German government is naturally sensitive about military strategies which are likely to increase the risks to the civilian population in the event of war. Official NATO pronounce-ments tend to dodge the question of what will happen to German cities, but the West German government seems committed to avoiding fighting in urban areas, even though it is unlikely that fighting in built-up areas could be avoided. Although Soviet forces might often try to bypass towns in the interests of a speedy advance, they might also at times find it convenient or necessary to drive straight through them or to try to take control of them. West German concern to limit a war being waged over its territory also influences NATO strategy, which is based on the concept of 'forward defence', which in this context means attempting to hold the line near the East German frontier.[1] NATO strategy at a conventional level is therefore primarily defensive (although it certainly includes some provision for counter-offensive attacks on East European and Soviet territory), but has so far excluded serious preparation for a defence in depth.

The vulnerability of West Germany in the event of a conventional war limits the choice of defence policies by its European allies. The existence of a multi-national force on West German territory is a visible commitment by other West European countries that they will defend German territory. As a result it is politically difficult to reallocate NATO resources in a way which might point to withdrawal of non-German troops. A number of strategic commentators have over the years suggested that Britain could contribute most cost-effectively to NATO by removing the British Army of the Rhine and investing more in the British naval contribution to NATO, but this option has not been seriously pressed.

Germany's European allies are not only constrained to join in a defence at the East German frontier; they are inhibited in advocating alternative strategies. If a country like Britain, which is less vulnerable to conventional attack, argues strongly for policies of in-depth defence in Germany, this may look like a willingness to fight to the last German. Despite these problems, it is important to look at alternatives if NATO's reliance on nuclear weapons is to be replaced by conventional military deterrence. The movement within West Germany against cruise and Pershing II missiles makes such a discussion timely.

Another political factor which has military implications is the peculiar position of the East European countries inside the Warsaw Pact. At a political level the West expresses solidarity with the peoples of Eastern Europe and supports popular movements which have tried to reform or challenge the Soviet-style communist regimes in Hungary, Czechoslovakia and Poland. But if war breaks out, Eastern Europe will be enemy territory. So while the West expresses support for the Polish people, present nuclear strategy means it may be making Poland a primary target in a war with battlefield nuclear weapons. A really radical shift in defence policy would make peace-time political perceptions of the differences in aims and interests between Eastern Europe and the Soviet Union, and between peoples and governments not only in Eastern Europe but the USSR itself, intrinsic to a defensive campaign. This would involve abandoning the orthodox commitment to defend frontiers and territory in favour of a more specifically political and ideological form of 'defence' through guerrilla or nonviolent resistance, designed to encourage resistance inside the Soviet bloc (see the next two chapters). Conventional military methods fall in between the indiscriminate destructiveness of any major use of nuclear weapons, and the discriminative nature of a political struggle. Conventional strategy can also be planned to reduce the degree of destruction caused, or to limit the military threat posed to East European countries by NATO forces.

Not only is it morally and politically important to try to limit the damage to Eastern Europe if there should be a war, but it may also affect the course of the actual war. The East European members of the Warsaw Pact may not prove wholly reliable allies of the Soviet Union, and the potential unreliability of East European forces and the possibility of popular resistance in the rear of Warsaw Pact armies are clearly significant factors which could influence the outcome of a conventional war in Central Europe. Popular attitudes in various countries to the Soviet Union vary; some East European forces are regarded by Western observers as more professionally competent and more likely to be reliable than others; and distinctions have to be made between the probable attitudes of the officer corps and those of conscripts, and between the response of communist parties and governments and of the majority of the people.

The attitudes of East European troops and civilians may depend on the specific circumstances of the war. For example if the Soviet Union could present the war as a defensive response, pre-empting a Western threat, then given the historic fear of Germany in much of Eastern Europe there might be real support for the Soviet Union. Secondly, East European armies are more likely to put up a vigorous defence of their own territory against NATO counter-attacks than to participate enthusiastically in an offensive. The East European troops thought most likely to be included in an attack are the East Germans and the Poles, but the former would be engaged in fighting against fellow Germans, and the latter are at the time of writing deployed in enforcing martial law on their own people. The third and possibly most crucial factor is the speed and success of a Soviet attack. If Warsaw Pact forces were mobilised for an attack with little advance warning, the pressures of military discipline would probably ensure initial obedience; and if the Soviet forces achieved rapid military success, both the East European troops and people would probably accept a *fait accompli*. As a recent Rand study of the East European military concludes: "The strategy of 'lightning war' may even constitute a primary Soviet lever for ensuring substantial Northern Tier military participation in a Warsaw Pact offensive."[2] If on the other hand NATO forces blunted an initial Soviet drive into West Germany, and demonstrated the possibility of winning the war, the chances of East European disaffection would increase considerably. Demonstrable Western ability to defeat a Soviet offensive would therefore constitute a significant deterrent at the conventional level.

Creating a credible conventional military deterrent to possible Soviet attack cannot, however, be pursued in isolation from other goals. One important goal is to reduce tension between NATO and the Warsaw Pact and to avoid the danger of war through miscalculation. This includes avoiding strategies which in the event of a crisis would put pressure on either side to take pre-emptive action through fear that the other side will act first. It is even more important in the longer term to bring about substantial reductions in arms on both sides and to promote forms of political and military disengagement which will remove the danger of a major war in Central Europe. If tension reduction and arms limitation are seen as essential to European security, then the defence policy adopted should be compatible with the disarmament proposals being tabled, and the requirements of seeking disarmament should shape defence policy. It is for these reasons the Commission prefers a military posture which can be seen as clearly defensive.

By a defensive strategy we mean renunciation of the intention and the capability to carry out a major offensive against Eastern Europe and the Soviet Union, even in response to an invasion. Such a strategy need not mean giving up the means to counter-attack enemy forces *within* NATO territory, a capability which many strategists would regard as essential.

The problem with renouncing counter-attacks against Soviet targets is that it ties the hands of military commanders in a way they may find unacceptable and unrealistic. Whilst it is possible to construct persuasive strategies based on a defensive stance, and many experts would accept that on balance present technological developments in conventional weaponry tend to favour the defence, to forgo all opportunities of taking the offensive must mean abandoning some military advantage. This problem is more acute in the context of trying to modify NATO strategy than it would be if Britain withdrew from NATO and pursued an independent policy, because a restructuring of NATO strategy implies a greater emphasis on orthodox military concern to create a satisfactory conventional defence against the Soviet Union. The second reason why it is especially difficult to impose this kind of restriction on NATO commanders and soldiers is that if NATO unilaterally abandons battlefield nuclear weapons, its forces will face Warsaw

Pact troops who not only have access to such weapons, but also at present appear to envisage using them. A purely military case can be made out against deploying battlefield nuclear weapons, especially on one's own territory; nevertheless it is a fact that if this policy were agreed, NATO troops would have to accept limitations which would restrict their freedom of manoeuvre on the battlefield.[3]

Despite the military objections which can be raised against proposals for a defensively oriented strategy, variations on defensive deterrence should be weighed carefully, not only because of the political and disarmament advantages of this approach, but also because it would be less threatening to Eastern European countries and might be more likely to elicit resistance within these countries to a Soviet attack on Western Europe. This chapter does however include consideration of the possible case for a greater counter-attacking capability to take the war into Eastern Europe.

The status of West Berlin is a special problem. It is the result of the post-war division of Europe, and a permanent solution must be part of a wider political settlement. The presence of US, British and French garrisons is as much a symbol of political as of military commitment, but the element of uncertainty as to whether the US would risk a nuclear war over Berlin may now discourage any Soviet thought of trying to take over West Berlin. If NATO switched to a non-nuclear strategy in Europe it is hard to see how it could credibly threaten to start a major European war to recover West Berlin — even if it possessed the necessary level of offensive capability, which itself would be undesirable. But provision could be made to exact a military and political cost for an attempt to take over Berlin, either by strengthening existing garrisons and preparing to airlift further troops and supplies into Berlin in an emergency, or by preparing for a street by street defence of the city and for long-term guerrilla resistance by Berliners. Either option would result, if it came to a conflict, in appalling destruction, but would mean the USSR could not expect an almost bloodless *fait accompli*. The alternative would be to look for stronger political deterrents, for example to consider locating an international organisation in West Berlin, or to plan seriously for nonviolent resistance in Berlin to an occupation regime, in the hope of promoting popular unrest inside East Germany as a whole.

There is no ideal method of defending a city divided in half and surrounded by hostile troops: limited conventional preparations, territorial and guerrilla resistance, or nonviolent resistance, are appropriate to the specific and limited threat of a Soviet take-over of the city, and could make that threat more remote. Whatever decision is taken about the best means of defence, there is a political case for maintaining the existing garrisons so as not to downgrade Western commitment to Berlin.

III. Military options for a non-nuclear Europe in NATO

Bearing in mind the general considerations which have just been outlined, this chapter looks briefly at seven broad military options within the framework of NATO. (1) The simplest course would be to remove battlefield nuclear weapons and replace nuclear warheads and shells by conventional explosives, while keeping forces at approximately their present level, and retaining the present emphasis on a forward defence. It would be possible within this brief to consider measures to increase the efficiency and fighting capability of existing forces. (2) The second possibility is to switch the emphasis of the strategy from 'forward defence' to one of preparing to mount counter-attacks into Warsaw Pact territory. This need not necessarily imply higher force levels but probably would. (3) The most obvious choice would be to increase the size of the conventional military forces stationed in West Germany and the numbers of the available military reserves; there would be scope for debate about the kinds of weapon to be made available to the additional troops. An increase in manpower would make it possible to deploy larger numbers of simpler tanks, missiles and aircraft in preference to investing exclusively in the most elaborate technology. (4) A compromise possibility would be to keep roughly the present level of conventional forces, but to reinforce them with lightly armed territorial defence units who could operate in specific zones or provide an in-depth territorial defence, thus emphasising the defensive element in NATO strategy. (5) A more radical approach to be considered is restructuring NATO's conventional strategy to present a purely defensive stance, emphasising the role of precision guided munitions. (6) Taking the logic of a purely defensive strategy further would involve abandoning a front-line defence altogether in favour of a more radical in-depth deployment. (7) Finally, NATO could abandon its present integrated command and multi-national force structure, and become a more loosely linked defence association of the type suggested by the actual terms of the NATO Treaty.

While the main emphasis of this chapter is on the range of military options available in Europe, it is important to note that some strategies are consistent with, and might be strengthened by, supplementary preparations for guerrilla or nonviolent civil resistance, either to be used as a means of harassment and sabotage in the rear of the Soviet armies while they are still engaged in fighting, or as a fall-back strategy to be adopted after an occupation.

Proposals for a purely conventional defence of Western Europe require an assessment of the balance of conventional forces in Central Europe. This is a highly controversial issue, since some political sources (including some NATO generals) greatly exaggerate Soviet conventional superiority, and underplay political and military factors which should favour the West. Questions to be resolved include the quality of Soviet forces and weapons, the numbers of men and weapons the Soviet Union could put into the European theatre, and how East European forces would be used. On the Western side the balance of forces depends considerably on getting reinforcements into place in time, so it is necessary to look at speed of reinforcement and at the possibility of a Soviet surprise attack. The detailed technical issues are set out in Appendix 3. Here is it only necessary to note, firstly, that the conventional military balance at present does not greatly favour the USSR, especially when one takes into account the advantages always accruing to the defence; secondly, that NATO does, however, rely heavily on the USA for reinforcements to counteract Soviet troops and aircraft; and thirdly, that NATO's current concern to provide for rapid reinforcement in time of war is relevant to a convincing defence.

Whether there is a case for increasing the number of NATO troops in Germany, or for any major reorientation of strategy, depends primarily on broader political and military calculations.

One question which has to be considered is what rationale should underlie NATO strategy in Europe. We discussed in the previous chapter how an independent British defence might be based on a minimal, symbolic military capability, or might aim to exact a high entry price from an aggressor (on the Swiss or Swedish model) or aim at a winning capacity, and suggested the middle road as most realistic. In a European, as in a non-aligned, context, a symbolic military stance would make sense only if the main emphasis was on non-military, or para-military, methods — nonviolent resistance or guerrilla warfare. A high entry price policy has some logic in a European context, but a strategy which is not expected to avert defeat but simply to make a victory very costly for the opponent is more appropriate to neutral countries — which are more likely to be threatened in the context of a wider war, and which cannot in any case acquire the means to defeat alone a major power — than to NATO. In principle NATO could muster the military capability to make winning a conventional theatre war against Soviet forces a credible goal. But in practice it implies an unrealistically high investment of resources in defence, and is also unnecessary as a lower level of conventional forces is likely to be a quite adequate deterrent. In addition a war-winning strategy implies planning to wage a prolonged conventional war, which is the strategy most likely to prompt eventual escalation to the nuclear level. The most satisfactory policy in Europe is probably therefore to aim at something more than a high entry price policy but less than the total defeat of opposing forces: that is to ensure that Soviet forces could be denied victory unless the Soviet government undertook massive mobilisation or nuclear escalation. Such a policy of 'defensive balance' is to some extent already inherent in NATO strategy but needs to be translated into a purely conventional defence.

We next examine the military options listed at the beginning of this section.

(1) Keep present levels of conventional forces

This approach would imply that NATO should take steps to match Soviet moves towards greater technological or numerical superiority, but that switching NATO strategy towards a purely conventional defence of Europe would not in itself require a major build-up of conventional forces.

Staying within present force levels also implies continuous measures to increase the efficiency of the existing forces. Since the Mutual and Balanced Force Reduction Talks began in Vienna in 1973, NATO strategists have had political as well as military incentives to turn their minds to this question. There are many ways to improve the efficiency of existing manpower which have been raised in debates about NATO forces. Possible changes include increasing the proportion of combat troops, adding to their equipment (for example more anti-tank and anti-personnel mines), stationing forces in Germany closer to their front-line positions, better training of reserves, improving transport facilities and call-up methods for reserves to be transferred to Germany, and better co-ordination and rationalisation of communications and weapons systems so that NATO operates more like a collective unit than loosely linked national forces. Robert Komer, who advocated most of these measures in 1977, commented: ''Militarily, NATO's crying need is not so much for 'more' as for 'better' ".[4] There are difficulties in implementing such proposals, which may increase costs in some areas, or run into political or industrial opposition, or (as in the case of moving barracks in West Germany) raise considerable practical problems. But it is worth noting that NATO could improve its capability without actually increasing its forces and some expert commentators believe there is ample scope for it to do so.

The option of working with the existing troop numbers and force structure implies also keeping to the present NATO strategy of forward defence, since any radical shift in strategy would require changes in deployment, weaponry and force levels.

The strategic case for maintaining approximately present levels of conventional arms in Europe is that present conventional defences are strong enough to prevent an easy Soviet victory, and are therefore an adequate deterrent to Soviet attack. It is also likely to be politically and economically more acceptable to West European governments to maintain present conventional defence commitments than to increase them, or to contemplate a more radical restructuring of defence policy.

There are, however, strong arguments against simply removing battlefield nuclear weapons from the NATO arsenal but otherwise continuing as before, even if the actual efficiency of existing forces is improved. The present strategy rests on the possibility of fairly rapid escalation to the nuclear level by NATO forces, which is one of the main grounds for objecting to it. It is arguable that to maximise military deterrence to a Soviet attack the West needs greater conventional ability to ensure it could defeat a purely conventional offensive.

This approach is unlikely to reassure sectors of military and political opinion who fear a Soviet attack and worry about Western weakness. Neither on the other hand is it likely to appeal to those who have pressed for nuclear disarmament and look for further arms reduction. Keeping present conventional force levels could be justified as a temporary measure by governments seeking negotiated arms reductions, but cannot be seen as a strategy positively promoting prospects for disarmament or disengagement in Europe.

An additional objection to relying on present force levels is that the onus for matching Soviet numbers rests heavily on the United States, and its willingness to rush in reinforcements. This is not satisfactory for West European countries which seek greater military and political independence, nor is it by any means certain that future US Administrations will wish to commit themselves to fighting a major conventional war in Europe. Therefore, even assuming that over 200,000 American ground troops will still be committed to the defence of West Germany, there are good reasons why European countries should play a larger part in reinforcing NATO defences.

Two other considerations weigh against merely accepting present NATO force levels and strategy without the nuclear element. The first is that NATO, like its members, has become caught in the trap of 'gold-plated technology' (see Chapter 4, section V).[5] One possible solution to this problem is consciously to reverse the trend, and for the armed forces to order and deploy larger numbers of simpler types of weapon system. If NATO adopted this policy it could boost the number of its weapons *vis-à-vis* the Soviet Union and presumably its combat effectiveness. It would, however, need to increase the number of its military personnel to make use of additional tanks or aircraft.

The second reason for not simply retaining the present conventional status quo is the desirability of using the opportunity which would be presented by a decision to de-nuclearise NATO European forces to rethink NATO's overall military strategy and its political implications.

(2) Changing NATO strategy

NATO's present strategy is based on a commitment to try to hold the front line by massing forces as far forward as possible. There is strong political pressure from Germany for retaining this emphasis on 'forward defence'.

The main alternative which has been canvassed in various debates about NATO strategy is to plan for a war of manoeuvre.[6] This may mean greater willingness to allow opposing forces to enter Western territory before launching counter-attacks. It also implies a much greater willingness than now to launch counter-attacks deep into Warsaw Pact territory and to give priority to disrupting communications and reinforcements in the rear. This strategy requires reliance on tanks for counter-attacks on the ground and giving a central role to combat aircraft. It may also imply heavy investment in the most recent precision guided weapons to attack Soviet reinforcements. The US has been developing a system able to destroy tank formations deep inside enemy territory.[7] All these elements are involved in the 'air–land battle' strategy being debated in NATO circles in the autumn of 1982.

If considered in a narrow military framework, taking the war into the enemy rear, rather than concentrating on holding the line inside one's own territory at great cost, is clearly attractive. But in a broader political–military perspective there are major drawbacks. One central fact which is simultaneously a potential asset and a problem for NATO is (as noted on page 149) that despite the incorporation of East European forces in the Warsaw Pact under Soviet command, the majority of East European peoples are hostile to the USSR.

Whether this means the East European armed forces are likely to rebel or to drag their feet is much more debatable, but the Eastern European forces will be unenthusiastic and perhaps only partially co-operative allies in the event of war, especially if the Soviet forces suffer setbacks.

But if NATO appeared to be launching a counter-attack against Eastern Europe, these forces might fight seriously in self-defence. If war had been started by miscalculation or as a result of a border incident, there might even be East European suspicion that the West had manufactured an excuse to launch an attack eastward; while this might be seen as a chance for liberation from the Soviet Union, it might equally be viewed with serious alarm. Moreover if Eastern Europe is a potential friend rather than an enemy, it is politically undesirable to wreak destruction in East European territory, quite the reverse.

So NATO attempts to disrupt Soviet supplies and reinforcements should concentrate not only on strictly military targets, but as far as possible on *Soviet* military targets or military lines of commun-ication, and should be sufficiently limited in scale to signal their purely defensive intent. In practice this would probably mean eschewing ground offensives and either attacking from the air or infiltrating specialised sabotage teams into Eastern Europe and the USSR. Long-range conventionally armed missiles could also be used to disrupt communications or reinforcements; there is, however, a danger that the use of certain types of missile such as cruise, which can be fitted with a conventional warhead, would be misinterpreted by the Soviet Union as the start of a nuclear attack.

Apart from the political and military dangers of emphasising a strategy of counter-attacks into Warsaw Pact territory, there is the additional problem that highly complex technology systems are liable to go wrong. The use of high technology does not always bring greater efficiency.

A strategy which would give greater priority to taking the war into Eastern Europe need not be linked to an increase in NATO's conventional forces; it could instead mean a re-deployment of forces and a change in their composition. However, it probably would mean a significant increase in some types of military equipment and might well result also in higher force levels.

(3) Reinforcing the NATO front line

The most obvious option for a non-nuclear Europe in NATO is to strengthen its front-line conventional defences by increasing the number of troops and weapons available in West Germany, or for immediate reinforcement. The size of the increase and the form it took, for example what types of weapon were given priority, would affect the military, political and economic implications of this approach.

A policy of reinforcing the front line would not necessarily imply any change in present research, development and procurement of NATO weapons, but it could be compatible with switching to a simpler technology, thus having more troops armed with more but cheaper models; or some mix of modern technology supplemented by older models which would also be possible with greater numbers of troops. This policy would also be compatible with either the present strategy of holding a Soviet attack at the border, or with a strategy of much more actively disrupting the Soviet rear; a significant increase in the number of forces would presumably make it easier to do both.[8]

Several proposals have recently been made for strengthening NATO's conventional forces. For example, the Supreme Allied Commander of NATO, General Rogers, suggested in September 1982 that if all NATO members achieved an annual 4 per cent increase in defence spending in real terms (i.e. 1 per cent more than the 3 per cent annual increase to which they have already in principle committed themselves until 1986), then NATO could strengthen its forces to the point of being able to absorb a conventional attack by the Soviet Union without resorting to battlefield or other nuclear weapons. General Rogers wants to invest mainly in better reconnaissance and in new precision guided weapons able to strike second-echelon reinforcements well behind the Soviet front line.[9]

In July 1982, *The Economist* made a number of more specific proposals for increases in NATO conventional forces in an interesting article on the possibility of a non-nuclear defence of Europe which was based on advice from strategic experts.[10] According to *The Economist*, the increases needed to ensure that NATO could hold an attack for 30 days include: 30 more combat battalions (about 30,000 men) to stiffen defences in the North German plain, plus 200 more support battalions; 800 more tanks (over and above those assigned to the extra combat battalions); 300 more combat aircraft, 600 more anti-aircraft missile launchers and a large increase in anti-tank missiles and artillery ammunition. The estimated requirements for more aircraft and ammunition are in part to counteract combat losses. The proposed figures take account of increases already planned by NATO, and augment them.

The Economist's proposals imply a 5 per cent increase in troops in fighting units on the Central Front, a minimum 12 per cent increase in the number of tanks in West Germany, and roughly a 14 per cent increase in the total of combat aircraft available to NATO throughout Northern Europe. Since the main emphasis of the proposal is on weapons regarded as primarily defensive, and since the Soviet Union already has a clear superiority in numbers of tanks and aircraft, increases of this nature could not be regarded as provocative and would not suggest any change in NATO strategy, though it is questionable in political terms whether this is the best way to increase NATO equipment. *The Economist* suggests that a 4½ per cent increase in real defence spending could purchase these additional troops and weapons, but this seems optimistic. Field Marshall Lord Carver takes the view that keeping NATO forces up to date with equipment "absorbs more than the 3 per cent increase in real terms which NATO countries have agreed to find".[11] Moreover, *The Economist* article points out that NATO is already short of storage space and would have to provide more barracks and stores for the extra troops and equipment, at a possible cost of $2–3 billion.

The increases proposed by *The Economist* are based on two assumptions which they spell out. The first is that NATO will not have to meet a surprise attack, but that troops will be moved into position and reinforcements brought over to Germany before fighting starts. Belief that NATO might be taken by surprise, or that NATO governments would not be willing to move troops and reinforcements in a crisis, would suggest the need for larger forces in place in West Germany. Secondly, the estimates are based on a 30-day war. If the aim is not simply to be able to hold a Soviet attack for a month, but to have the forces and equipment to fight a much longer conventional war in Europe with the expectation of victory, then an increase in conventional force levels of a much greater magnitude is implied: perhaps a 30 per cent increase in NATO forces in Europe, and in reinforcements available.

The advantage of demonstrably strengthening NATO's conventional forces would be that it could provide a greater margin of military security than at present, and an increase in numbers could provide political reassurance to those nervous of Soviet intentions. There are, however, very substantial disadvantages. Firstly, there are clearly political and economic problems in envisaging any major increase in ground forces available to fight in West Germany. While the economic burden could be lessened by equipping some forces with cheaper weapons, the considerable difficulty of finding the troops to deploy them would remain. A 30 per cent increase would imply another 200,000 men stationed in Germany and perhaps an additional 500,000 reserves committed to the Central European front.

Now Spain has joined NATO a portion of its fairly substantial armed forces might conceivably be stationed in West Germany. However, in view of the French refusal to participate in NATO's integrated military command structure, and assuming Italy is committed to defence of NATO's 'southern flank', a major increase in European NATO forces in Germany would have to mean a much larger UK contribution — probably at least 100,000 *additional* men, which is about twice the present size of BAOR. Even a 10 per cent increase, which is a more realistic target, would imply our finding another 35,000 for BAOR and perhaps 50,000 more reserves.

Secondly there are political objections to actually building up conventional forces at this stage. As a means of meeting the fears of the more vocal groups convinced of a Soviet desire to conquer Western Europe, it may well be counter-productive, by conceding too much to those fears. Multiplying military defences often heightens fear, partly for psychological reasons, and partly for political reasons, since requiring social and economic sacrifice for defence means politicians have to stress the need for it.

Most important of all is the effect a significant conventional arms build-up would have on the prospects for disarmament, detente or disengagement in Europe. It would mean abandoning altogether any attempt at agreed force reductions. To combine withdrawal of battle-field nuclear weapons with a build-up of NATO conventional forces might create suspicion about Western intentions in the Soviet Union, and Soviet military interests are very likely to insist on an increase in their own conventional forces, especially in the light of their general stance of pre-emptive deterrence. This could maintain political tension, and create a context in which there would be political and military pressure to reintroduce nuclear weapons and so negate one of the purposes of removing battlefield nuclear weapons. These results would not be inevitable, since NATO willingness to denuclearise its European forces unconditionally should signal a desire to avoid war, and might be accompanied by diplomatic moves stressing a desire for further disarmament. The impact of a conventional build-up would also be influenced by the strategy associated with the new force levels. However, if the Soviet Union gained the impression that NATO was more willing to risk war than it had been in the past, the likelihood of the Soviet Union either increasing its own conventional arsenal, or refusing to renounce its own battlefield nuclear weapons, would be increased.

To sum up the argument in this section, an attempt to achieve a substantial increase (of say up to 30 per cent) in numbers of troops, tanks, artillery and combat aircraft available for a war in Central Europe is probably not practicable in terms of West European willingness to make available the required resources, and is almost certainly not desirable in terms of its likely impact on the Soviet Union and the danger of a mutual conventional build-up in Europe. A change in NATO strategy towards disruption of the enemy rear, which is open to interpretation as a guise for aggressive designs on Eastern Europe, would exacerbate the negative repercussions of a conventional arms increase, and is inherently a mistaken strategy if it results in treating Eastern Europe as an enemy.

A more modest increase in NATO's conventional forces, based on a more limited strategy of being able to hold a Soviet attack for 30 days, and so being able to exact a heavy penalty for aggression, would not raise the same kind of problems in relation to the Soviet Union. If increases were concentrated in anti-tank and anti-aircraft weapons, the possibility of some limitation on 'offensive' weapons would be kept open. Relatively modest increases in force levels also seem more likely to be politically and economically acceptable to West European countries. But increasing force levels by even 5–10 per cent still promises to be economically costly, especially if the emphasis is on the most recent technology. Acceptance of the more limited case for a conventional build-up may also pave the way for pressure from some political and military groups on both sides to engage in a further conventional build-up.

It is therefore important to look at methods of reinforcing NATO's conventional forces which would be construed as more clearly defensive, and would demand fewer resources than multiplying regular forces.

(4) Territorial reinforcement

The two goals of emphasising the defensive element in any methods used to reinforce NATO's regular forces and of minimising the cost and personnel requirements of such reinforcements merge if it is proposed to use territorial forces to back up the NATO divisions. Territorial forces can be equipped with simpler and cheaper types of defensive weapon — hand-held anti-tank and anti-aircraft missiles — and can be used to man anti-aircraft batteries, lay mines, guard installations and communications, and in general play a defensive and supplementary role in the rear. They need not necessarily be used for static duties; territorial forces lightly equipped can also be very mobile, and may be deployed to lay ambushes and harass the enemy, using their local knowledge of the terrain to give them an advantage. In either case the equipment and strategy usually assigned to territorial forces, plus their inherent nature as a citizen militia, normally designate them as a primarily defensive body (though it is of course possible to arm and train them to form part of regular forces). The relative simplicity of their weapons and the fact that they are composed primarily of part-time volunteers or reserves, reduces the difficulties involved in maintaining large professional military forces.[12]

Not all territorial forces are made up of citizen volunteers, and it is possible for regular troops to be deployed like territorials. Both these caveats apply in the case of West Germany, whose Territorial Army is of particular relevance to this discussion. After an initial and unsuccessful attempt to raise a purely volunteer force, it was based on conscription in 1965, and in 1969 made a component of the Army; and like the rest of the Army it is a mix of conscripts, volunteers and full-time professionals.[13]

There are two ways in which the German TA, or an additional German force drawing on further manpower, could be used to strengthen NATO defences: first by organising, training and deploying it more effectively to support NATO front-line forces; or second by deploying territorial units in suitable front-line zones such as forests and built-up areas, which would leave NATO armoured and mechanised divisions free to concentrate on the corridors of open land. The first option is implied in a critical analysis of the role of the German Territorial Army by Horst Mendershausen, and the second is advocated by Steven Canby in an article in *Armed Forces and Society*.[14]

The first strategy might mean that in addition to its scheduled tasks of providing transport, communications and medical support for

NATO forces, of defending specific facilities against sabotage or attack, and defending rear areas against enemy breakthroughs, the TA could undertake a more extensive defence role. The gaps in its strategy identified by Mendershausen were: lack of prepared static defence positions or plans to lay minefields or tank traps, and inadequate facilities for destroying bridges or roads; absence of plans for the territorial forces to move forward to fill the gap should NATO forces advance into Eastern Europe; and more crucially an assumption that if NATO forces retreated the TA would retreat with them and remain in the NATO rear, rather than remaining in place and creating pockets of armed resistance, harrying the Soviet forces in the rear and providing intelligence for the NATO forces.[15] This unwillingness to plan for armed resistance in enemy-occupied territory (which appears to be logically linked to unwillingness to plan for last-ditch defensive and delaying tactics against an advancing Soviet army) stems from the refusal of the Federal Republic to consider the possibility of partisan warfare.

The German authorities' total opposition to partisan warfare seems to be based upon reasonable doubts about its usefulness in German conditions, and acute awareness of the likely costs of last-ditch and partisan resistance to soldiers and civilians. There are certainly good grounds for any government to hesitate before requiring from its people the sacrifice which could be involved in a determined territorial defence and partisan tactics — the previous chapter pointed to its major disadvantages. But there are counter-vailing arguments: that an effectively prepared territorial and partisan resistance can be a significant deterrent to occupation; that there is a distinction between uniformed troops engaged in action in the enemy rear during a war and an indefinite campaign of guerrilla resistance by unidentifiable guerrillas, the latter being more likely to result in deliberate reprisals against civilians; and given that a conventional war would be very destructive, the deterrent value of territorial defence preparations on an extensive scale may, for a country vulnerable to land attack, outweigh the danger of additional suffering involved.

The extent of extra destruction incurred by territorial forces maintaining armed resistance in the enemy rear may depend partly on whether or not they operate in towns and cities. German policy is to protect urban areas only from the surrounding countryside, and to attempt to prevent massive destruction of buildings and industry by declaring cities 'open' and by making no military use of them. Mendershausen stresses the military advantage which can accrue from fortifying and holding cities against an enemy, the possibility of using the city as a base to harass an enemy force seeking to bypass it, and the danger that if cities are undefended an advancing force may seize them and use them to its own advantage. Canby also advocates perimeter defence of cities, on the grounds that the advancing troops will probably lack the time and fire-power to try to seize or destroy defended built-up areas, that being forced to avoid urban areas will channel the attacking forces and may lead to congestion on the remaining roads, and that cities can be used to shelter defending troops.

The case for a perimeter defence of towns and cities and using them as military bases is questionable on moral and political grounds, and the military case does not seem foolproof. It is impossible and probably counter-productive to try to evacuate large towns and cities, so if the attacking forces did fight for the cities very many civilians would be killed. Both Mendershausen and Canby refer to the effective defence of Russian cities in World War II, but do not seem to allow for the potential scale of air or missile bombardment which could supplement a ground attack. Even if the military case for defending cities and using them as a base for military harassment were strong, it would be politically very difficult for other countries to ask West Germany to sacrifice its cities.

Canby makes a more persuasive case for defence of villages along the frontier and in the open corridors likely to be used for enemy advance. He envisages that territorial units would hold the villages, but be supplemented by mobile regular forces which would create networks of villages by blocking enemy attempts to move between villages. The political objections here are less strong, since it might in favourable circumstances be possible to evacuate civilians from villages most at risk, and it seems inevitable that frontier villages would become involved in fighting.[16] Whether it is wise to rely on local village militias to defend frontier villages seems dubious. Canby himself concedes the advantage of using professional troops to stiffen the resolve of village militia "understandably nervous and prone to flight", and to expect them to hold their villages against the advance guard of an invading army is unrealistic.

Although schemes for maximising the potential for territorial defence in the Federal Republic of Germany are unlikely to be politically acceptable, a more limited case for using flexible forces, taking advantage of the terrain and supplementing regular NATO divisions with more lightly armed territorial units with different objectives, is persuasive. While such forces alone cannot halt an armoured attack, they can harass infantry and support units, lay ambushes, plant mines, and may damage some tanks. The existence of such a defensive network would greatly increase the difficulty of Soviet forces who could no longer concentrate solely on defeating NATO regular troops, and therefore would add significantly to conventional deterrence. Canby's suggestion that light infantry should be deployed in Germany's considerable areas of forest for example is certainly worth further examination, as are possibilities of using territorial forces to delay and harass an advancing enemy. Field Marshal Lord Carver suggested in 1976 that the ideal pattern would be to use mobile armoured forces to concentrate against an enemy attack, "while reserves for strengthening up and thickening those areas in which penetrations have not taken place come principally from reserve indigenous territorial organisations, plentifully supplied with easily transportable anti-armour weapons and mines".[17]

Should a strategy of using territorial reinforcements for regular NATO forces rely on German territorial reserves? Commanders of the present German TA might reasonably object that their forces are already fully stretched by their existing duties. There are also political objections to laying the onus on the Federal Republic, which already supplies considerable manpower to NATO forces. In principle it would be possible to build up multi-national reserves specifically trained and earmarked for providing a supplementary defence. One way of extending the available reserves and including territorial defence tactics in NATO preparations would be to draw on older age groups of men with military experience, but no longer sufficiently familiar with modern weapons to be part of the reserves who reinforce the regular troops.

There would, however, be considerable problems in deploying an international territorial force effectively. It could be difficult to call them up and get them into place in time (it is hard enough with existing reserves), it would be necessary to train them in Germany, which might cause social and practical difficulties, and an international force would lack many of the advantages of a home-based militia such as familiarity with the local terrain and commitment to fight for one's own home. Therefore the most practicable solution on military grounds would probably be to organise and train a German 'Home Guard' in addition to the existing TA with the specific task of harassing Warsaw Pact forces. In order to make this politically more acceptable, those NATO countries who do not already have such in-depth territorial defence arrangements might have to undertake them. An additional possibility would be for Britain and other countries to release some Germans from the Regular Army by increasing the size of their own forces stationed in Germany, thus compensating for the additional burden undertaken by the Germans.

In principle it is quite possible to increase the number of reserves by adopting the policy of European neutrals like Austria and Switzerland of periodic training for reservists.[18] Austria can mobilise 12.8% of its population and Switzerland 10.2%. At present West Germany mobilises only 2% of its population (1,245,000 out of 61,665,000), Belgium 2.5%, and the Netherlands 1.9%. Whether more frequent training and a longer period in the reserves would be politically acceptable is another question. The desirability of such a policy may also be queried. The main objection to it, considered in the previous chapter, is that an emphasis on territorial defence may involve a further militarisation of society. It tends to conflict with the goal of mobilising people to achieve disarmament, and it also runs counter to any attempt at encouraging people to develop their capacity for unarmed political defence to military threats.

(5) A defensive deterrence strategy

If a primary purpose of restructuring NATO forces and strategy is to promote prospects for disengagement, disarmament and the eventual dismantling of the military blocs in Europe, then there is a strong political case for adopting weapons and deployment which denote more clearly a purely defensive stance. This strategy can overcome some of the difficulties of finding a 'balance' in multilateral disarmament, because the goal is not to offset the offensive forces on the other side, but to have an adequate defence against them.[19]

Signalling purely defensive intent ideally requires a combination of weapons, deployment and strategy which indicate that no offensive action is intended or possible. Taken individually no weapon is purely defensive; even anti-tank missiles or anti-aircraft missiles can be deployed to screen and assist an attack — indeed this is how Western commentators tend to interpret Soviet military preparations. But if a defence posture depended on this type of weapon, played down or abandoned tanks or ground-attack aircraft, and deployed dispersed forces committed to fight only in their own territory, then it is not likely to be misconstrued. If one considers how much Western fears of Soviet attack relate to numbers of tanks, and to the conversion from fighter aircraft to fighter–ground-attack aircraft in Europe during the 1970s, the psychological impact of weapons which *look* offensive is clear. Therefore a defence posture which looks solely defensive should decrease tension.

Since the political advantages of this approach are indisputable, the argument hinges on whether or not the military advantages are equally clear. Technological developments in weaponry, involving production of increasingly accurate missiles designed to destroy tanks, aircraft and ships, have given substance to this concept of defensive deterrence, by reinforcing the traditional advantage accruing to the defence with the latest techniques for precision guidance, and by offering in addition at least a partial answer to the modern problem of air attack. As a result a number of commentators have argued that NATO should seek to counter Warsaw Pact armoured divisions and air power by investing heavily in precision-guided munitions (PGMs) and at the same time adopting a purely defensive posture.[20]

Developments in PGMs are undoubtedly promising for advocates of defensive deterrence; the problem is to decide how decisively and how permanently the evolution of PGMs (or 'smart' weapons) has given a further advantage to the defence, and secondly how relevant this new generation of defensive weapons is to the problem of NATO defences. Unfortunately the scientific and strategic experts disagree.

The nature of the debate may be divided into technical, geographical and strategic considerations.[21] The primary debate is about anti-tank weapons. Technical factors involved are that anti-tank missiles can hit and knock out tanks with a high degree of accuracy (though the simpler wire-guided types of missile must be properly aimed by a soldier who keeps his eye on the target for at least ten seconds), but that many missiles have limitations such as a relatively slow firing rate or being useless in darkness or fog, and that a whole range of counter-measures have been devised, such as smoke screens, electronic counter-measures, and tougher tank armour. Whether anti-tank missiles can keep one technological step ahead of counter-measures, or whether some measures, like Chobham armour for tanks (which is more impenetrable without adding weight to the tank), are too expensive to be practicable on a large scale, are both unresolved questions.

The geographical issue is whether the terrain in Central Europe favours or impedes use of anti-tank missiles in comparison with the Sinai desert or Golan heights (the examples of their successful use in the 1973 Arab–Israeli war). Forests, hills and urban areas make it easier for anti-tank units to hide, and tend to channel the attacking forces who thereby become more vulnerable, but the same terrain tends to hinder anti-tank units by blocking their line of fire.

Possible military measures to counteract anti-tank missiles are: to overcome anti-tank units with intensive artillery fire (a tactic used successfully by the Israelis in 1973 on the Egyptian front once they realised the threat posed by the Egyptian anti-tank missiles);[22] to increase the number of tanks (possibly opting for simpler and cheaper models); to ensure a surprise attack so that anti-tank weapons will not be deployed in time; or to overwhelm defences by air attack. These possible measures in turn raise further questions: if tanks can advance only after massive artillery fire, does this make impossible rapid advance by armoured divisions in a blitzkrieg attack,[23] can use of remote-controlled anti-tank missiles foil attempts to destroy the crews operating them, and can air attacks in turn be met by surface-to-air missiles? They do, however, indicate the degree of uncertainty surrounding a defensive strategy based on anti-tank missiles. They also suggest that a defensive posture relying heavily on precision guided munitions could possibly encourage an offensive build-up on the other side, or put a premium on surprise attack, so that such a strategy is not absolutely guaranteed to reduce tension.

One of the important issues in this debate is that of costs. Advocates of reliance on PGMs suggest that not only are they an effective and non-provocative form of defence, but that they are cheaper than aeroplanes or tanks. For example a missile costing $50,000 may bring down a plane costing $10 million, or a missile costing $4,000 could destroy a tank worth $1 million. However, to transpose high rates of accuracy for missiles in test conditions to the battlefield may be misleading, as in practice precision-guided munitions might not achieve this degree of accuracy.[24] Accounts which rely heavily on such accuracy and the corresponding cheapness of PGMs may be over-optimistic.

The other issue which bears on how far a switch towards defensive missiles would be cheaper than reliance on armoured divisions and combat aircraft, is how NATO forces should best be organised to deploy them. It is possible to imagine a strategy incorporating different types of PGM and different kinds of unit operating them. Forward-based units, committed to hold a given position, could have fairly sophisticated missiles and means of target acquisition, and perhaps have protective armour for missile launchers. Highly mobile units to be rushed to major areas of fighting might include anti-tank missiles on helicopters which proved effective in the Vietnam war, and were appraised optimistically in 1972 NATO war games in

Germany, although in some circumstances they would be fairly vulnerable to being shot down.[25] Territorial forces in the rear could be equipped with simple anti-tank and anti-aircraft missiles, and simpler line-of-sight anti-tank missiles to be used in conjunction with artillery. Professional soldiers would need to be highly trained to operate the more sophisticated technology, whereas conscripts or part-time volunteers could be trained in handling the simpler weapons. A strategy based on PGMs implies decentralisation of responsibility and initiative to a large number of dispersed units, which has implications for organisation and training of the armed forces. Whether such a strategy would require more men than the present disposition of NATO forces would depend on the numbers of weapons to be deployed.

There are important strategic objections to be raised against relying exclusively on defensive weaponry and tactics, but before discussing them it is worth examining briefly an even more radical version of a defensive deterrent strategy in Central Europe, that of a purely in-depth defence designed to ensure attrition of enemy forces and to obviate unacceptable destruction of life and property in the area.

(6) In-depth dispersed defence

Horst Afheldt has argued that a credible and effective defence could be organised by dispensing altogether with frontier defence, which he thinks creates too many targets and a possible incentive to the other side to use tactical nuclear weapons. We should note that in Afheldt's own writing this strategy, while designed to eliminate battlefield nuclear weapons from NATO's armoury, does rely heavily on the use of sea-based US nuclear weapons. In a modified form, however, it can still serve as a useful model for a purely conventional defence of Western Europe.

The strategy envisages a network of defensive commando units thoughout West Germany equipped with short- and long-range anti-tank weapons, mines and light infantry weapons. There might in addition be surface-to-air missiles for air cover. Afheldt estimates that a commando unit of 20 men covering an area of 20 square kilometres, which they would know inside out, would be able even with present technology to destroy on average three tanks using short-range anti-tank missiles, and if in addition each commando unit had six soldiers with long-range missiles they would be able to destroy advancing tank columns. To cover West Germany 10,000 commando units would be needed, a total of 200,000 men. Each unit should in addition have five men per commando unit for air defence. Afheldt assumes reserves would be mobilised to supplement forces combatting landings, and that reserves might also be used for liaison between techno-commandos and the central command.

Total numbers required in peacetime for this network of commandos would be 310,000 regular soldiers, plus reserves of 30,000 for liaison and a minimum of 50,000 to meet air landings. The regular soldiers need not all be German, since troops from other NATO countries could be deployed as techno-commandos and familiarise themselves with their local terrain. The numbers required should pose no problem at all for a multinational NATO force, and the existing German Field Force and TA could provide over 300,000 men and all the required reserves. It should be stressed that Afheldt's concept differs from the usual concept of territorial defence because it envisages the use of sophisticated weapons and highly trained professional forces, rather than a less well trained and more simply armed citizens' militia. It is seen as an alternative to the present deployment of regular troops.[26]

Afheldt raises the possibility of air cover by an air force but does not go into detail. The rationale for this strategy is to provide a credible form of defence which would be an effective deterrent, and which could be put into practice if war broke out without resulting in appalling damage to Germany. Afheldt also stresses that such a defensive posture would promote arms control and make possible one-sided reductions in weapons without offering the other side a military advantage.

There are a range of possible objections to Afheldt's specific proposals, plus some more general drawbacks to any purely defensive stance. Some of the objections can be convincingly met by Afheldt, others clearly challenge his approach.

Afheldt's strategy seems able to deal with the central difficulty of safe-guarding cities from destruction at least as well as, if not better than, present NATO thinking about conventional defence. He proposes that, as at present, cities should be declared open and that NATO should make no attempt to defend them militarily. But in order to hamper occupying forces trying to establish a military or political base in the cities, the citizens should be organised in advance to offer nonviolent resistance and non-co-operation to any attempt to establish an occupation regime. Military defence in the countryside would therefore be complemented by a political form of defence in urban areas. As there would be no set-piece battles in Afheldt's scenario, the danger of towns being caught up in fierce fighting would not be inherent in the strategy, and there would be no military rationale for the attacking forces to try to destroy built-up areas, except as a terror weapon.

Three possible objections that he can meet convincingly concern problems of central control and communication, the dangers of extreme decentralisation of responsibility and the degree of dependence on PGMs. Whilst a central command centre would be vulnerable to destruction, Afheldt can argue that it matters much less in his strategy, where techno-commandos have clearly defined tasks, than it does in a strategy much more dependent on efficient communications between forces and on grouping and regrouping them. Thus decentralisation can be seen as a considerable strength, and though it is open to the objection that too much initiative is placed in the hands of small groups of men not subject to higher discipline, who may panic in the event of an attack, it can be argued that the defection of a small number of commandos would not be disastrous to the defensive strategy. As regards the reliance on PGMs, it is easier to justify an estimate that each commando unit could knock out three tanks than to postulate that anti-tank weapons could automatically hold a major tank attack; the advantage of Afheldt's proposal is the emphasis on general attrition.

But a strategy of pure attrition is open to forceful criticism in terms of its practicality. It may have some deterrent value, but in the event of an attack it is not possible to halt an advance early without some form of frontier defence, and counter-attacks to regain territory require the ability to concentrate one's own troops. It is also arguable that a strategy of allowing enemy forces to advance deep into one's own territory would be extremely demoralising, and undermine resistance. Perhaps an even more important objection is that a pure dispersion strategy makes it impossible to contain minor incursions or border incidents by military means. The absence of any specific front-line defence is likely to be unacceptable on political grounds, since there is a psychological significance in defending frontiers. It also creates considerable practical problems if there is no possibility of delaying an attacking force long enough at the border to mobilise reserves, bring civil defence measures into operation and make the necessary political preparations to conduct a war. Ability to hold an attack also creates a brief opportunity to try to mobilise international diplomatic channels before being committed to a major war.

Therefore it is worth seriously considering modifying this type of strategy by making provision for a visible frontier defence, reinforced by a highly mobile armoured force, which could be used to try to hold an attack initially and to block an offensive thrust. These provisions would contravene Afheldt's intention of avoiding any concentration of troops which might provide a military rationale for use of tactical battlefield nuclear weapons, but would not seriously undermine the defensive emphasis of the whole strategy, since a limited mobile force could not be construed as offensive.

Since increasing thought is being given by both military strategists and peace researchers in Europe, and especially in Germany itself to alternative defence strategies, Horst Afheldt's proposals are not the only ones available. The emphasis of a number of these alternative defence plans is on the need to substitute an in-depth purely defensive strategy for NATO's present dispositions. One proposal being considered sympathetically by the authors of a study of an alternative defence policy for Holland is that made by Hans Joachim Löser for the division of the Federal Republic into three defence zones: an Eastern zone of 50 to 100 kilometres in which there should be a frontier defence emphasising sophisticated anti-tank and anti-aircraft missiles; a central zone of 200 kilometres for a defence in depth by reorganised forces to use territorial defence tactics; and a western zone to be defended by a territorial force.[27] These proposals give priority to simplifying logistic support and increasing the numbers of combat troops.

(7) Abandoning NATO's integrated command structure

The last option to be glanced at here is reorienting NATO strategy from a multinational force towards a loosely linked system of national defence. This step would clearly be consistent with primarily relying on in-depth defence, replacing the goal of holding a Soviet attack at or near the West German frontier with the concept of cumulative attrition and harassment of Soviet forces, each country providing a kind of 'hedgehog' defence. It is certainly not an impossible scenario, relying on the willingness of national forces to defend their own countries tenaciously, and following the kind of strategy already adopted by a number of European countries not directly dependent on military alliances, such as Yugoslavia and Switzerland (discussed in the previous chapter).

There would be obvious political advantages in this sort of development, which is quite consistent with the actual terms of the NATO Treaty, and which would allow for the withdrawal of most US troops, if the central aim is to move towards withdrawal of the great powers from Europe and to break down the division of Europe into opposed military and political blocs. A loose defensive arrangement would allow for some symbolic multinational commitment, for example contingents in a frontier force along the West German border, and for agreed co-operation in early warning and monitoring systems, and possibly in air defence. It would also be possible to write in guarantees of specific types of aid to individual countries attacked, which could include not only arms supplies or limited forms of military aid, but also medical, financial, and diplomatic assistance, aid for refugees and an emigré government if necessary, and help in maintaining communication with an occupied country.

This type of defensive arrangement could not rely on defeating a really major Soviet attack. The logic of this approach suggests the need to maximise deterrence in each country by providing for determined resistance even after military defeat, either by partisan methods, as the Yugoslavs intend, or by nonviolent civil resistance. Hence mutual defence commitments should extend to the types of limited but potentially vital aid which could be given to such internal resistance movements.

Apart from the deterrent possibilities of a commitment to continued resistance after military defeat, there is also a case to be made for some provision for partisan and guerrilla tactics to be used during the period fighting continues in Europe. Just as at a national level partisan harassment of the enemy in the rear and disruption of supply lines is a natural extension of an in-depth defensive campaign within an individual country for the duration of formal hostilities, so at a European level it would make sense for partisan activity to be undertaken in an occupied country while Soviet forces were still operating in other parts of Europe. That is, a strategy of in-depth territorial defence can, even whilst organisationally the emphasis is on national defence, be envisaged at a West European level. This would tend to mean that West German units should be committed to partisan tactics after Soviet forces had entered France and Belgium, but also that Norwegian and Danish units should be prepared to harry the Soviet rear if an initial strike were made in Northern Europe. By the same logic Britain should be prepared to undertake partisan warfare in the event that Soviet forces seized the UK as a strategic base before concentrating an attack on Central Europe. Partisan tactics can be undertaken by either soldiers (the SAS has this kind of 'stay behind' role now), or separate units, or *ad hoc* by civilians. In terms of credible advance planning, and effective and disciplined use of partisan tactics, there is a case for allocating partisan duties to special units of the armed forces.

A 'hedgehog' approach to European defence would be rejected by those who see the main value of NATO in attaching the USA as strongly as possible to the defence of Europe, and by those most fearful of Soviet attack. But it is likely to be attractive to those in nuclear disarmament movements who do not favour a total disbanding of NATO, but wish to move decisively towards a form of defence compatible with nuclear disarmament and other measures of arms limitation and disengagement in Europe.

Apart from broad political and strategic judgements, however, the value of this option, and other options discussed which rely on adopting a purely defensive stance, depends on a practical judgement on how well this approach would work in the field.

IV. The problems of a purely defensive strategy

The idea of a purely defensive strategy can be interpreted partly in terms of weapons, since even if no absolute distinction can be drawn between offensive and defensive weapons, some types of weapon have much clearer offensive uses and connotations than others. But weapons cannot be judged in isolation from their deployment and the total strategy. So the political rationale for a strategy, and the public indications of strategic planning, must point clearly in the direction of a commitment to defence and a renunciation of aggressive aims.

If a defensive stance means forswearing use of certain types of weapon, the first question to ask is whether it is possible to dispense with tanks, which are popularly seen as offensive weapons, perhaps because of their central role in a blitzkrieg strategy. A tank can play various military roles. One is in knocking out opposing tanks with its anti-tank guns. Whether or not a tank is a better anti-tank weapon than the new PGMs is, as indicated earlier, a complicated issue, but technological and military evidence suggests that it could be tactically effective and cheaper to replace tanks by anti-tank missiles for this purpose. The second role for tanks is to provide both mobility and fire power, and most military commanders would probably be reluctant to dispense with tanks altogether as an element in a mobile force. The case for keeping tanks for this second role is at the heart of the tactical objection to a purely defensive strategy: that at least a limited counter-attacking capability, which may be designed to regain one's own territory and need not mean crossing frontiers, is an essential part of defence.

The argument for abandoning bombers seems more clear cut, since these will normally be used inside enemy territory, though whether they are used against military or civilian targets is a matter of choice. But a crucial part of a successful defence may be to destroy enemy aircraft on the ground, for which ground-attack aircraft may be less provocative than missiles. Since it is harder to defend oneself against a missile attack, possession of long-range missiles may well look more menacing to the other side than bombers.

The central issue, therefore, is not whether to keep particular types of weapon but the nature of the strategy and the overall shape of the forces adopted. There is clearly a strong military case for reserving some capacity for disrupting enemy communications, or destroying enemy planes before they reach our own airspace. The possible danger of this approach is that an effective capacity may create the impression of willingness to strike first, and in a situation of crisis and mutual mobilisation create a strong temptation to launch a pre-emptive strike. In addition, if NATO possesses large numbers of aircraft capable of attacking targets in Eastern Europe or the Soviet Union, there will be a Soviet incentive to strike first. If therefore priority is given to reducing tension and the possibility of war by miscalculation, it may make most sense to concentrate on purely defensive capability against air attack. A combination of surface-to-air missiles, anti-aircraft guns (found to be very effective against US planes in the Vietnam war) and fighter cover at higher altitudes should be capable of providing a fairly efficient screen.[28]

If the general political and arms control case for a defensively oriented strategy is accepted, but the military case for some offensive capability is also conceded, the possibility of a compromise in which NATO's potentially offensive weapons would be so limited as to pose no serious threat to the Warsaw Pact is worth considering. It is arguable that NATO has already moved in that direction by emphasising anti-tank weapons and maintaining a limited conventional bomber force, so the issue would be how much further NATO strategy should be tilted towards a demonstrably defensive stance. Similar considerations would apply to a West European defence association should NATO be disbanded.

V. *Strategies for a European Defence Association*

There is no need to elaborate on the range of possibilities here, since the seven strategies outlined for NATO could all in principle be adopted by a European defence organisation without the USA. In practice it would be politically and economically unrealistic to attempt to increase the level of conventional forces and armour in West Germany at the same time as replacing US troops and weapons withdrawn. Maintaining NATO conventional forces at their existing level would not be impossible, but a great deal would depend on the attitude of the French both in terms of their willingness to adopt a non-nuclear strategy and to commit more troops to West Germany. Without French co-operation, an integrated multinational European conventional force in Germany, and an orthodox conventional defence strategy, would be very difficult to sustain. It would however be possible without French involvement to mount some form of in-depth defence of West Germany, drawing on British, Belgian and Dutch contingents but relying heavily on the existing German forces. This approach could allow for British support for air defence and a naval role in a European defence body.

It is perhaps more likely that a purely European defence association would move towards the option of a much looser defensive alliance (hypothetically possible for NATO but less probable). The advantages of this approach in terms of contributing to a breakdown of military blocs dividing West and East Europe have already been summarised. The most obvious disadvantages would probably be fears of a repetition of the disastrous failure to co-ordinate defence against German attack in 1940, and a sense of greater vulnerability to Soviet pressure. Public awareness of the need to move away from reliance on nuclear weapons, and serious efforts by individual countries to complement orthodox conventional defence by territorial in-depth resistance or preparation for more prolonged guerrilla or civil resistance (measures adopted *ad hoc* in World War II but not seriously envisaged in advance), might however enhance the deterrent value of decentralised national defence preparations and conduce to greater public confidence in such an alternative defence strategy.

VI. *Summary of the argument*

This chapter has suggested seven possible strategies which could be adopted by NATO if its European members abandoned all reliance on nuclear weapons. Before assessing them a number of central political factors must be taken into account. These are: the West German concern to protect its cities and to avoid ceding territory to the Soviet forces, which favours a defence along the East German frontier; the pressure on Germany's allies not to place excessive responsibility on German forces and people for resisting a Soviet advance; the desirability of restricting damage in Eastern Europe and encouraging disaffection there in the event of Soviet military action against the West; the need to reduce tension between NATO and the Warsaw Pact and to devise a defence strategy which is compatible with measures of disarmament; and finally the importance of devising a strategy which could be accepted by the military, who would be expected to fight a war in Europe. These considerations do not always lead to the same conclusions.

A conventional defence must be credible in relation to the opposing conventional forces. There is dispute about the relative strength of Warsaw Pact forces, but whilst there is some numerical superiority this does not on reasonable assessment add up to the kind of real military superiority required for an attack on Western Europe. NATO is at present, however, dependent on rapid reinforcement, especially from the USA.

The following options have been briefly examined: (1) retaining present conventional forces and the forward-based NATO strategy, possibly with some reforms to increase combat efficiency within the existing force levels; (2) a strategy of taking the war more actively into Warsaw Pact territory; (3) a significant increase in conventional force levels; (4) maintaining existing conventional forces but reinforcing them by substantial provision for defensive territorial-type units, equipped with light weapons; (5) switching to a purely defensive strategy using anti-tank and anti-aircraft missiles; (6) abandoning front-line defence altogether in favour of an in-depth defensive posture; (7) moving away from NATO's present integrated command structure and multinational forces deployed in Germany in favour of a much looser coalition of national forces stressing in-depth defence.

The viability of purely defensive strategies depends to a considerable extent on assessment of how far the new precision guided anti-tank and anti-aircraft missiles have tipped the conventional military balance in favour of the defence. While it would be unwise to see these weapons as a miraculous solution to military problems, there are good grounds for thinking that they do enhance the effectiveness of a defensive strategy.

Measures to discourage the use of battlefield nuclear weapons and to provide as few tempting targets as possible also suggest the desirability of troop dispersal and a defensively oriented strategy.

VII. Conclusions

The Commission takes the view that the rational basis for a European defence policy is to provide a credible deterrent to conventional attack, by preparations for military resistance which would deny easy victory to an invading force. This aim might be met either by having the ability to hold an attacking force for several weeks or by an in-depth deployment which would ensure serious attrition of advancing forces. It means eschewing an attempt to build up Western forces to the point where they could expect to win a prolonged conventional war. Such an attempt would promote an arms build-up in Central Europe and impose substantial and probably unrealistic demands on European members of NATO. It is also ultimately an untenable strategy, because of the appalling devastation which would result from even a purely conventional war, and because of the increasing danger in a war prolonged over several months that one or both sides would resort to nuclear weapons, whatever their initial non-nuclear commitments.

The Commission's general position is that ultimately our security depends on achieving substantial disarmament, and on reducing the political tension and distrust which promotes arms proliferation and the risk of war by miscalculation. Part of the intention in rejecting a nuclear strategy is to improve the prospects for reductions in conventional forces. The Commission would therefore prefer that priority should be given to alternative strategies most likely to promote arms limitations and detente, especially as the military–technological case for relying on a purely defensive stance is itself reasonably strong, though controversial. Whether this means eschewing altogether military action against the home base of the attacking forces once hostilities have broken out is by no means certain; it does imply forgoing a preventive strike against Soviet aircraft on the ground or of armoured excursions deep into East European territory, and therefore means possessing few, if any, offensive missiles or long-range ground-attack aircraft, and limiting the number of tanks to those required for a mobile defence.

The Commission is also impressed by the arguments in favour of a dispersed defensive system, which would reduce the likelihood of Soviet forces using nuclear weapons on the battlefield and could ensure a high attrition rate for advancing Soviet forces. This kind of in-depth defensive strategy, relying heavily on PGMs, and possibly reinforced by lightly armed territorial units and by a strategy of partisan tactics in the rear of an enemy force, meets the political requirements of posing a minimal threat to Eastern Europe, of tension reduction, and of being compatible with agreed measures to limit forces with a primarily offensive capability; it is therefore conducive to future possibilities of disarmament and disengagement.

A pure in-depth defence would, however, contravene two relevant criteria. First, it would not be likely to find favour with a West German government, since it requires immediate cession of territory to the opposing forces in the event of conflict. Whilst a future German defence policy might accept that the deterrent advantages of an in-depth strategy, in conjunction with the political advantages of an unequivocally defensive stance, outweighed the disadvantages of preparing to fight throughout German territory, any government is likely to insist on some form of frontier defence to deal with limited incursions and hold the line initially. There are also political arguments for creating a multinational frontier force to demonstrate European commitment to come to the defence of West Germany, as long as NATO is committed to an integrated command structure and a multinational force. Secondly, there are strong military arguments for a frontier force, and for a highly professional mobile armoured force able to strengthen resistance at key points. With these modifications, an in-depth defensive posture involving defensive deployment of some regular forces is an attractive proposition.

There is a compromise position worth serious consideration, that is to maintain approximately the existing levels of the regular forces minus the nuclear element, while considering various forms of re-organisation of the existing forces to improve military capacity. This does not pose major problems for a West German government, involves least disruption of present military planning, and at least as an interim measure is compatible with goals for force reduction and other disarmament measures, which NATO might seek to negotiate more seriously than in the past. Since NATO conventional strategy and force structure is, once the nuclear element has been removed, primarily geared to a defensive war in West German territory, this option should not be alarming to the Soviet Union.

If there were, as is quite likely, pressure to enhance NATO's defensive capability, the most satisfactory way to achieve this would be to reinforce present forces and the German TA by some kind of additional territorial units. This approach would increase military security, but by concentrating on clearly defensive measures would not jeopardise prospects for various forms of arms limitation. Indeed it would create a defensive framework which does not at present exist in NATO deployment, and so create a possible basis for a later shift towards a more clearly defensive stance if political conditions were favourable. It is an approach already being advocated by some strategic theorists in Britain and the United States (although they would disagree with the Commission's totally non-nuclear approach), and it chimes with the thinking of some commentators and political movements in Germany and other European countries. Moreover this approach, although it would mean additional costs and more reserve manpower, would not pose the prohibitive demands implied by a major increase in professional conventional forces with high-technology weapons.

There is scope for considerable debate about the precise nature and deployment of such additional territorial forces, how far the burden should fall entirely on the West German government, and what compensatory contribution could be made by other NATO countries. If the British government did press for this kind of solution it would have to be prepared to make some additional military contribution to NATO, perhaps in the form of making available some additional troops to replace West German regular army contingents or by demonstrating its own willingness to make similar territorial defence preparations. This solution would therefore involve real costs for Britain.

The other approach to strengthening NATO is of course to raise present force levels in Central Europe. The Commission accepts that an argument can be made out for a *limited* increase, especially if the main emphasis is on primarily defensive weapons, and provided there is no attempt to link such an increase to a change in NATO strategy towards a greater counter-attacking capability. It is, however, concerned that acceptance of this approach could lead to further pressure for a conventional build-up on both sides, and is sceptical whether even a fairly limited increase could be achieved without costing much more than the 3 per cent annual increase in defence spending in real terms to which NATO countries have in principle committed themselves until 1986. But a non-nuclear Britain could not reasonably refuse to make some increase in its own conventional contribution to the defence of Europe if other members of NATO opted for a limited rise in force levels.

Notes to Chapter 5

1. Forward defence is also sometimes used to mean defending Britain on the Rhine rather than nearer home, or simply defence of frontiers. In this chapter it is used in its technical sense. For a statement of the German position, see: G. Leber, 'Principles Underlying German Defence Policy', *NATO Review*, 24,2 (April 1976), 9: "It cannot be our wish that, in the event of attack, our land would first have to be retrieved; rather, defence of the Federal Republic of Germany must be conducted as far forward as possible."

2. A. R. Johnson, R. W. Dean and A. Alexiev, 'East European Military Establishments: The Warsaw Pact Northern Frontier', *Rand Report*, R-2417/1-AF/FF (December 1980), vi. See also D. R. Herspring and I. Volgyes, 'Political Reliability in the Eastern European Warsaw Pact Armies', *Armed Forces and Society*, 6,2 (Winter 1980), 270–96.

3. If NATO has forsworn use of battlefield nuclear weapons in advance and the Warsaw Pact has not, one consequence is that Pact forces could concentrate their forces, whereas NATO would be inhibited from doing so.

4. R. W. Komer, 'Ten Suggestions for Rationalising NATO', *Survival*, XIX,2 (March/April 1977) 68. See also S. L. Canby, 'European mobilization: US and NATO reserves'. *Armed Forces and Society*, 4 (2) (February 1978), 227–244.

5. In relation to PGMs, there is clearly a case for having more but simpler weapon-systems, see for example Walther Stützle, 'The Impact of New Conventional Weapons Technology on NATO Military Doctrine and Organisation', in C. Bertram, ed., *New Conventional Weapons and East–West Security* (London: Macmillan for I.I.S.S., 1978), p. 24; "five relatively simple tanks, each with only a fifth of the firepower of a highly sophisticated tank and costing only a fifth as much, have higher survivability against PGMs than one complex with the firepower of five."

6. C. Gray, 'NATO Strategy and the Neutron Bomb', *Policy Review*, 7 (Winter 1979), 13–14, distinguishes forward defence in the literal sense, which means massing firepower on the edge of the battle area, from a war of armoured manoeuvre. See also D. Gouré and G. McCormick, 'Debate on Precision-guided Munitions; PGM: No Panacea', *Survival*, XXII,1 (January 1980), 18: "NATO planners can either continue to implement a 'strategy' of forward defence based on halting a Soviet–Warsaw Pact armoured offensive at or near the point of attack or they can abandon current practice and prepare for a counter-offensive war of manoeuvre." The authors refer to an article on the need for a manoeuvre strategy for NATO by D. K. Anderson, 'The Counter-Mobility Potential in the NATO Context', *Strategic Review*, 7,1 (Winter 1979), 67–75.

7. See P. F. Walker, 'Precision-guided Weapons', *Scientific American*, August 1981, p. 27: "The most ambitious US Army smart-weapons program, designated Assault Breaker, is an effort to create a long-range battlefield missile system to strike the support areas of an enemy army. New side-looking and forward-

looking radar in airplanes, helicopters or remotely piloted vehicles would locate tank columns deep in the territory of the enemy; the radars would supply the position coordinates to a tactical missile battery, which would launch a warhead filled with homing submunitions.''

8. See for example R. Kennedy, 'Precision ATGMs and NATO Defense', *Orbis*, 22,4 (Winter 1979), 925: "NATO is likely to wage a 'dynamic defense'. Such a defense would include a variety of 'tactically offensive' operations such as amphibious assaults, armored probes and armored counter-attacks." See also Statement on the Defence Estimates 1981, Cmnd. 8212–1, p. 23, para 326 on 'interdiction': "This would fall to the Buccaneers and Jaguars and would involve attacks against units behind the line of battle, and the disruption of second-echelon formations, road and rail communications and the movement of enemy reserve forces." The Statement also refers to the effectiveness of counter-air operations against airfields and command centres.

9. *The Guardian* (29 September 1982), 1.

10. *The Economist*, 284, 7248 (31 July 1982), 30–32.

11. Field Marshal Lord Carver, *A Policy for Peace* (London: Faber & Faber, 1982), p. 108.

12. For a general survey of territorial defence, see A. Roberts, *Nations in Arms: The Theory and Practice of Territorial Defence* (London: Chatto & Windus, 1976).

13. H. Mendershausen, 'Territorial Defense in NATO and Non-NATO Europe', *Rand Report*, R-1184-ISA (February 1973), pp. 79–80. The West German TA now comprises 38,000 men, but after call up of reserves would number about 480,000. Unlike the West German Field Army it is not directly under NATO Command, but has a role in assisting NATO forces, and Mendershausen found that in the Schleswig-Holstein area the TA was integrated into the NATO Command and that the Area TA Commander was also a NATO commander. Some motorised infantry brigades of the Field Army were deployed to act like territorial forces in hill country though officially assigned to NATO.

14. Mendershausen, 'Territorial Defense in NATO and Non-NATO Europe',[13] and S. L. Canby, 'Territorial Defence in Central Europe', *Armed Forces and Society*, 7,1 (Fall 1980), 51–67.

15. Although the West German Army has undertaken reorganisation of its reserve structure in recent years, the role of the Territorial Army does not appear to have changed. A more recent paper by H. Mendershausen, 'Reflections on Territorial Defense', *Rand Report*, N-1265-AF (January 1980), stresses that the West German territorial forces "are always supposed to stay behind the NATO-assigned regular forces; they have no mission in enemy-occupied territory . . . The West German territorial army does not appear to have a city defense mission." p.6. An article by Lieutenant General E. Burandt, Territorial Commander of the Bundeswehr, in *NATO's Fifteen Nations*, Special, 2 (1981), stresses the supporting role of the Territorial Army, its role in the Rear Combat Zone and liaison with civilian authorities.

16. See P. Bracken, 'Urban Sprawl and NATO Defence', *Survival*, XVIII, 6 (November/December 1976), 255: "A typical defensive position for a NATO armoured brigade on the East German border contains about eighty-five villages . . . Warsaw Pact forces attacking tanks would be unable to bypass one village without almost immediately running into another."

17. *Survival*, XIX, 1 (January/February 1977), 37 (Address delivered by Field Marshal Lord Carver on 15 November 1976).

18. See J. L. Clarke, 'NATO, Neutrals and National Defence', *Survival* XXIV 6, November/December 1982, 260–265.

19. A point strongly made by A. Boserup in 'What Can be Done?', a paper given at the Conference on Nuclear War in Europe, Groningen, 22–24 April 1981 and sent by the author to the Commission. Published as 'Nuclear disarmament: Non-nuclear defence' in M. Kaldor and D. Smith (eds.), *Disarming Europe* (London: Merlin Press, 1982), pp. 185–192.

20. Two of the most important articles advocating a new form of NATO defence based on the defensive potential of PGMs are G. H. Quester, 'Can Europe Really be Defended?' *Encounter*, LI, 3 (September 1978), 6–19, and P. Morrison and P. F. Walker, 'A New Strategy for Military Spending', *Scientific American*, October 1978, 36–49.

21. A good summary of the pros and cons of PGMs in relation to NATO is the article by Kennedy, 'Precision ATGMs',[8] which is fairly sceptical about PGMs. An excellent analysis of the impact of PGMs on strategy, which suggests that defensive missiles will tend to maintain a technological edge over any countermeasures devised is provided by the article by Walker, 'Precision-guided Weapons'.[7] See also J. K. Miettinen, 'Can Conventional New Technologies and New Tactics Replace Tactical Nuclear Weapons in Europe?' in *Arms Control and Technological Innovation*, D. Carlton and C. Schaerf, eds. (London: Croom Helm, 1977). See also F. Barnaby and E. Boeker, 'Defence Without Offence', *Peace Studies Paper No. 8* (Bradford: Bradford University School of Peace Studies, and London: Housmans, 1982).

22. J. A. C. Weller, 'Middle East Tank Killers', *Royal United Services Institute Journal*, 119 (1974), 28–35.

23. The arguments in support of the thesis that PGMs make it much easier for the defence to thwart a blitzkrieg attack are set out by J. J Mearsheimer, 'Precision-guided Munitions and Conventional Deterrence', *Survival*, XXI, 2 (March/April 1979), 68–76; the arguments against by Gouré and McCormick, 'Debate on Precision-guided Munitions; PGM: No Panacea'.[6]

24. The point is made, as part of a forceful argument against a defensive strategy relying on PGMs, by O. Even-Tov, 'The NATO Conventional Defense: Back to Reality', *Orbis*, 23, 1 (Spring 1979), 35–49, who quotes the cost estimates cited here from Quester, 'Can Europe really be defended?'[20] and Morrison and Walker, 'A New Strategy for Military Spending'.[20]

25. See Walker, 'Precision-guided Weapons'[7] on a 1972 NATO exercise in which helicopters with TOW missiles 'killed' on average 18 tanks for one helicopter 'lost'. But see L. Whetten and M. Johnson, 'Military Lessons of the Yom Kippur War', *The World Today*, March 1974, p. 109: "In the Middle East both sides used helicopter-borne commandos and almost 50% of the helicopters were reported to have been destroyed in the air."

26. Dr Afheldt has elaborated his ideas over a number of years. The version of his proposals cited here is based on: H. Afheldt, 'Tactical Nuclear Weapons and European Security', in SIPRI, *Tactical Nuclear Weapons: European Perspectives* (London: Taylor & Francis, 1978) pp. 262–95, and on Dr Afheldt's remarks at a seminar in Oxford on 6 November 1981.

27. H. J. Löser, 'Vorneverteidigung der Bundesrepublik Deutschland? Ein Beitrag zur Strategiediskussion im NATO-Bundnis', *Oesterreichische Militärische Zeitschrift*, 2 (1980). Cited in F. Barnaby and E. Boeker, 'The Case for a Non-Nuclear Defence', 10 August 1981 (First Draft).

28. See Walker, 'Precision-guided Weapons',[7] who also argues that in the Iran–Iraq War fighter aircraft were effectively countered by "older radar direct anti-aircraft guns" as they were in the Middle East in 1973. Mearsheimer, 'Precision-guided Munitions and Conventional Deterrence',[23] also claims: "The 1973 Middle East War demonstrated that a sophisticated air defence belt can exact a heavy price from attacking aircraft."

Chapter 6
Strategies against occupation
I. Protracted guerrilla warfare

I. Introduction

In Chapter 4 we considered briefly and in a purely British context the use of guerrilla tactics in the course of an in-depth resistance to invasion. The territorial forces, it was noted, would normally operate in conjunction with conventional forces and this phase of resistance would continue as long as the latter were still in the field and the government to which they gave their allegiance still existed and could reasonably claim to control at least part of the territory. In this chapter we consider protracted guerrilla resistance to an occupation or client regime once it has been established — that is to say guerrilla warfare mainly as a strategy against occupation rather than against invasion as such.

Protracted guerrilla warfare relies on a process of attrition to wear down the enemy forces, on progressive demoralisation to reduce their effectiveness and on a variety of political and economic pressures. In favourable circumstances it can permit small countries to overcome, if not to slay, the nuclear-armed Goliaths seeking to impose their political will. By making certain kinds of warfare inoperable, or at least much less effective, it partially disarms the opponent. The American defeat in Vietnam provides the classic example of what can be achieved given the right circumstances and the political will to resist; Vietnam and Afghanistan illustrate the problems guerrilla resistance can create for an occupying power.

Guerrilla resistance has found advocates who see it as either a means of complementing conventional defence or, more radically, providing an alternative to it. Guerrilla warfare is also seen by some as a complementary strategy to civil resistance — strikes, boycotts and other forms of non-co-operation and obstruction — as a means of making a society virtually ungovernable and bringing an administration and an economy to a standstill.[1] Such a 'mixed strategy' might be particularly appropriate in highly industrialised and urbanised societies where the military possibilities of guerrilla warfare are restricted but where social and economic conditions tend to favour mass civil resistance.

A pure form of protracted guerrilla warfare would be one where no frontal defence at all was put up, and the guerrilla resistance began only after the occupation had occurred. It is more likely, however, that there would be, at the very least, harassment of advancing enemy forces by territorial or militia units who might at times be concerned to hold areas of strategic or tactical importance, even if they mainly employed the hit and-run tactics of guerrilla warfare.

If we grant this, two principal models for defence by protracted guerrilla warfare emerge. In the first, more radical, version, there is little or no emphasis on frontal defence: territorial and militia forces alone are assigned the task of harassing invading forces, with the main burden of deterrence and defence falling on the preparations for resistance to occupation. In the second model, protracted guerrilla warfare would be a fall-back option to be employed when resistance by a combination of regular and territorial forces had failed to halt the invasion. This second approach is broadly speaking the one adopted by countries such as Yugoslavia, China and Vietnam where guerrilla warfare has played an important part in recent history.

Putting up no frontal defence grants an opponent a freedom of manoeuvre and control that one would normally seek to prevent. It could, however, make sense in a small country facing an over-whelmingly superior military opponent, such as Denmark facing German invasion in 1940; more generally it would be a reasonable course of action in situations where engaging in conventional warfare was judged to carry a high risk of leading to nuclear war — a case which could apply to a major European war involving one or both of the superpowers. Defence by guerrilla warfare would greatly reduce the likelihood of nuclear weapons being used by an opponent, since their own forces and officials would be in the country and there would be no obvious military targets for such an attack. America's nuclear weapons were of little avail in Vietnam, and it is not likely that the Soviet Union would contemplate using them in Afghanistan.

Deterrence is one of the functions of defence by guerrilla warfare, as with any defence strategy. If an opponent knows that an occupation is going to be followed by years of debilitating struggle which may cost them dearly in political, economic and moral terms as well as putting a strain on their military capabilities, they may think twice before embarking on an attack. We suggest later that there are limitations to the deterrent aspect of guerrilla war as a defence strategy on its own while acknowledging that in combination with other strategies it can enhance deterrence. But its effectiveness as a deterrent depends, as with all deterrents, on its credibility. To be convincing there must be evidence that preparations for guerrilla warfare are solidly based and could in fact be conducted and sustained in the event of the deterrent failing. What forms could guerrilla resistance take in the setting of Western industrial societies like Britain, and how realistic are the prospects of its being able to achieve eventual success?

II. The main forms of guerrilla warfare

The following categories are not hard and fast, and there is often considerable overlap between them, but it seems useful to distinguish three main types: *partisan warfare, urban guerrilla warfare,* and *political terrorism.*

By *partisan warfare* we mean professional or semi-professional forces operating from rural strongholds in a military campaign which is normally aimed at inflicting eventual defeat on the enemy in conventional warfare. The partisan forces may operate in conjunction with regular forces, as in China in the war against Japanese occupation and in the revolutionary war, or on their own as in Cuba and in other instances of internal struggle where a revolutionary army had to be built from scratch from below; in either case the aim is to transform the level of warfare from the guerrilla to the regular form. The main theorists and practitioners of this kind of guerrilla warfare – Mao in China, Giap in Vietnam, Guevara in Cuba — agreed that only through regular warfare could the opponent be finally defeated and the revolution established.[2] This accords with the post-revolutionary practice of relying on a combination of regular and guerrilla warfare for national defence. In all versions of revolutionary guerrilla warfare, the political element is assigned an important place, especially the task of political mobilisation against the opponent; nevertheless what Mao and the others are describing is still essentially a *military strategy,* designed to inflict defeat on the opponent's forces.[3]

The two other forms fall, broadly speaking, into the category of *para-military strategies* in so far as their aim is not so much to destroy the military forces of the opponent as to erode the political, economic and psychological basis of domination and thus bring about either the collapse of internal regimes or a political decision by an outside occupier to withdraw.

Urban guerrilla warfare employs sabotage of military and economic targets and attacks on military personnel to sap the morale of the opponent and to make the task of running the country and economy increasingly difficult. It may often be linked to types of political resistance or non-co-operation, and, as we have suggested, normally constitutes a para-military strategy. In two situations, however, the goal may have a specifically military character. One is where a disciplined underground army keeps the embers of rebellion glowing but holds back from a major strike until it can co-ordinate its efforts with those of regular forces; the underground resistance to German occupation in Northern Europe in World War II was mainly of this character.[4] The other is where the aim is to overthrow a weakened and overstretched army of occupation by a general uprising of the population. The obstacles to success in such a strategy are, however, formidable and the cost of misjudgement extremely high.

Political terrorism may accompany partisan or urban guerrilla warfare, though it is most closely associated with the latter. It is a form of political pressure to which the Commission is strongly opposed. By political terrorism we mean the indiscriminate use of violence for political ends, aimed for instance at civilians of the same nationality as the occupying power, or at civilians of one's own side where there has been a reluctance to support the resistance, or to support it wholeheartedly. It includes, for instance, placing bombs in pubs, taking random hostages of people who simply happen to be passengers on a particular plane, and so on. Most political assassinations also come into this category, especially where the victims could not be regarded as combatants in any normal definition of the term; thus during an occupation members of the indigenous population whose work necessarily involves a certain degree of co-operation with the occupying regime, such as minor officials, may be selected for attack. There are borderline cases here, and room for argument as to when and under what circumstances attacks on individual members of the opponent's armed forces, or on those directing a campaign of repression, could be considered legitimate acts of guerrilla warfare, but the distinction itself is a crucial one. It is an application in a particular setting of the notion of discrimination in the conduct of war.[5]

III. Guerrilla warfare and West European defence

In Britain, and probably in most of industrialised Western Europe, partisan warfare over a protracted period is not a serious possibility.

It is a form of warfare particularly suited to, and perhaps only possible in, a society with a strong rural-peasant economy. The pattern of British commercial agriculture, the concentration of the population in the major cities and towns, the centrality of industry in the economy, the relative sparsity of terrain suitable for establishing guerrilla strongholds, and the remoteness of such terrain from most of the large cities, means that partisan warfare on a strategically significant scale cannot be expected. Thus if we rule out terrorism on moral and political grounds, urban guerrilla warfare remains as the one realistic guerrilla option for Britain and many other industrialised societies. In these settings mass non-co-operation is central to effective resistance, especially where liberation from outside is not in prospect, and the significance of urban guerrilla warfare may depend largely on its capacity to spark off, sustain and complement campaigns of non-co-operation and political resistance. An example of such a dynamic relationship between para-military resistance and political struggle is provided by the independence struggle in Ireland during the 1919–21 period.[6]

In *The War of the Flea*, Robert Taber draws attention to increased leverage populations have gained as a result of the interlocking and interdependent structure of industrial societies.[7]. He concentrates on people's economic power, as producers, distributors and consumers. Modern communications and the need for higher educational standards in technically advanced societies greatly facilitate the spread of ideas touching upon wider issues throughout society. These factors and the increased opportunities under industrialisation for organising corporate action have led to an important shift in the centre of gravity of power within industrial and semi-industrial societies. Greater attention has to be given to securing the acquiescence and co-operation of the population. This is one reason why radio and TV stations are key strategic points in any attempt to wrest control from an existing regime.

In wartime the mobilisation of the population and the economy has become crucial and this partly explains the totality of war between modern industrial states in which the aim is to cripple the enemy's economic production and demoralise the population by massive bombing and shelling. It also accounts for the increasing importance of propaganda as a specialised arm of warfare. These points are worth stressing since they show that guerrilla warfare and civil resistance are not some esoteric deviation but are rooted in political and economic developments which have profoundly affected the conduct of warfare even in its orthodox forms.

IV. The resistance in occupied Europe in World War II

The resistance movements in occupied Europe provide useful examples when considering the possibilities of guerrilla warfare in Britain, especially since Britain played a key role in stimulating and supporting that resistance. The experience of France and countries to the north of it — Belgium, Holland, Denmark and Norway — is particularly relevant since the resistance was aimed against established occupation regimes, whereas in Yugoslavia, for instance, there were areas where the Axis powers never achieved effective control, and in the Soviet Union the large-scale guerrilla resistance took place in the context of a continuing struggle for the control of the country. Even in Northern Europe, however, the World War, and the prospect of eventual liberation from outside, were of critical importance and this has always to be borne in mind.

British support was organised through the Special Operations Executive (SOE) set up in July 1940 under the auspices of the recently formed Ministry of Economic Warfare headed by Hugh Dalton. Dalton's writing at the time shows a keen appreciation of the dynamics and the potential significance of a para-military and civil resistance campaign. He identified the task of the organisation as that of creating "movements in the enemy occupied territory comparable to the Sinn Fein . . . or — one may as well admit it — to the organisations which the Nazis themselves have developed" who would engage in "industrial and military sabotage, labour agitation and strikes, continuous propaganda, terrorist acts against traitors and German leaders, boycotts and riots".[8] This shows an awareness that in an industrial society guerrilla warfare needs to be accompanied by civil resistance. It also suggests the fine line that divides urban guerrilla warfare from campaigns of political terror.

The pattern of resistance in occupied Europe supports the argument that only in societies with a strong rural-peasant base is partisan warfare likely to develop on a scale where it can pose a serious military threat to an enemy and escalate from guerrilla to regular warfare. In Southern and Eastern Europe — Yugoslavia especially, but also Albania, Greece, Italy after 1943, and in Poland and the occupied parts of the Soviet Union — partisan warfare became a significant and in some instances a major force.[9] In parts of France, too, where the terrain was favourable, the Maquis reached sizeable proportions and achieved notable successes in the latter part of the war, especially in conjunction with Allied offensives.[10] In Northern Europe the military resistance mainly took the form of sabotage, especially blowing up railway tracks, attacks on military personnel and ambushes and skirmishes on a relatively small scale. Serious attempts to engage the enemy militarily were generally held back until they could be co-ordinated with Allied offensives and then they were frequently combined with industrial strikes and sabotage to create the maximum disruption.

Overall, the most important achievement of the resistance movements was at the political level. In Northern Europe especially, the Germans had expected their New Order to be largely welcomed by those whom they regarded as fellow Aryans and they were clearly taken aback by the extent of the political opposition they encountered. There is, for instance, a note of genuine dismay as well as resentment in the official response of the German authorities' broadcast on Berlin radio to the wave of strikes that paralysed Amsterdam, Hilversum and other Dutch towns in February 1942, following attacks by the Dutch Nazi Party on the Jewish quarter of Amsterdam.[11] Denmark, which was officially occupied for its own protection, was permitted to hold parliamentary elections in March 1943; there was the highest turn-out in Danish history, and 97% of the votes cast were for non-Nazi candidates.[12] In August 1943 Copenhagen was paralysed by a 'people's strike' supported by all sections of society, and the Germans took over direct control of the country. In France the settlement establishing the Vichy government was at first widely accepted and resistance was limited; but as the war progressed, and particularly after the introduction of labour conscription in February 1943, drafting French workers to German factories, opinion turned against the Vichy regime and the German occupiers. By the latter part of the war the Nazis were detested in every country they had occupied and whatever limited support there had been for the New Order in Europe crumbled. German military defeats partly account for this, as well as the brutality of Nazi policies in occupied countries, but credit is also due to the resistance activities, both military and civilian.

The global war was the crucial backdrop to the resistance in occupied Europe. Firstly, the prospect of eventual liberation played an important part in sustaining morale. Secondly, the resistance movements depended on Britain and other Allies for the supply of arms and equipment, and benefitted also from the trained personnel who were parachuted or smuggled into occupied Europe, in many cases nationals of the country concerned. Thirdly, the resistance movements were often most effective militarily when their attacks were co-ordinated with Allied strategy. Where uprisings took place prematurely, as in Naples in September 1943, or help from the regular forces failed to arrive, as in the Warsaw uprising in August 1944, the result was a massacre because the undertrained and ill-equipped insurgents were no match for the professional German forces. This is not to underestimate the achievements of the resistance movements or to suggest that no resistance at all would have occurred had the context been different; it is simply to note the importance of that context and to recognise how different the situation would be if Britain and Western Europe were to experience Soviet occupation with no serious prospect of liberation from outside. If US forces were still in the field and committed to the liberation of Europe, the parallel with World War II might hold, but this raises the question as to whether it is at all realistic to imagine a prolonged war between the superpowers that did not become nuclear or at least did not bring utter devastation to the countries of Europe.

V. Costs of guerrilla warfare

The human and social costs of guerrilla warfare can be severe. First, it has a tendency to create and exploit an ambiguity between combatants and non-combatants, thus blurring the distinction that is essential if limits and constraints are to be observed. Second, it tends, especially in the urban variety, to degenerate into terrorism and criminal violence. Third, it can intensify divisions within society and heighten the danger of internal feuding or civil war.

Combatants and non-combatants

The blurring of the distinction between combatant and civilian is likely to be most acute in the case of urban guerrilla warfare. Partisan units sometimes wear a distinctive dress or uniform, but even if they do not the battle lines tend to be more clearly drawn. For the urban guerrilla, civilian dress is in effect a disguise which facilitates sabotage operations, surprise attacks, and the ability to melt back into the general population after an attack. But this almost invites reprisals against the population and general repression, and certainly weakens the constraints on attacking civilians. Even with partisan war, the close dependence of the guerrillas on the local community tempts anti-guerrilla forces to resort to collective punishments such as taking hostages, destroying villages thought to be helping guerrillas, and herding populations into guarded 'strategic hamlets' — in fact the familiar horrifying pattern of counter-guerrilla strategy from the Peninsular War to the US war in Vietnam.

Terrorism

Terror may also be employed by the guerrillas. First, innocent people may be killed or taken hostage as a way of putting pressure on the opponent to grant political concessions, release prisoners, etc. Second, in colonial situations where there is a settler population, or where a civilian comunity has become established in conjunction with occupying forces, officials and advisers, indiscriminate violence may be part of a general psychological campaign to destroy morale. Third, terror and intimidation may be used as a means of securing the compliance of the population.

It is sometimes argued that terror cannot be the main basis for guerrilla support among the population since beyond a certain point terror becomes counter-productive as people's anger and resentment get the better of their fear, leading in this case to their supporting the forces of the status quo; thus it is argued that the very success of a guerrilla movement is a measure of the popular support it commands. The equation is not so neat, especially where the guerrilla forces are receiving considerable support from outside, and populations can find themselves caught in a vice of terror and counter-terror. Thus while both the communist guerrillas in China during the war against the Japanese and subsequently against the Kuomintang forces, and the Vietminh and NLF guerrillas in Vietnam, observed a strict code of conduct in their dealings with the peasantry on whom they depended for support, the same was not true — and is not true today — of the Khmer Rouge guerrillas in Kampuchea.[13]

We have argued that there is an objective distinction between guerrilla warfare and terrorism — it is not simply a matter of the viewpoint from which events are judged. Guerrilla warfare is, or should be, discriminate and narrowly aimed at the armed forces, or — more controversially — at aspects of the system of military/political control of the opponent; terrorism is indiscriminate, drawing no distinction between combatants and non-combatants, between legitimate and non-legitimate targets. In practice, however, the divide is often a fine one and urban guerrilla warfare especially, where there is likely to be a stronger emphasis on assassination and seizing hostages, is liable to degenerate into terrorism.

Guerrilla strategy may sometimes include the calculation that the repression set in motion by guerrilla action will show the regime in its true colours. Crushing a particular rebellion often proves to be less than a total victory for an occupying power or repressive regime, since the rebellion may inspire later struggles and create a climate and tradition of resistance which may prove invincible in the long run. To calculate on provoking repression, however, implies a willingness to use people as pawns, to contemplate the loss of civilian life in the hope of political dividends. It is, moreover, a calculation that is liable to go badly awry. In several countries in Latin America over the last two decades, guerrilla warfare and political terrorism have frequently led to a consolidation of the repressive machinery of the state and the increasing use of state terror by death squads.[14]

Social divisiveness

Guerrilla warfare heightens social divisions. Rival guerrilla groups, each enjoying a measure of popular support, may engage in murderous feuds with each other. The availability of weapons, and the generalised climate of violence means that political differences are more likely to be settled violently — a tendency that can be observed in the bitter divisions and feuds within the Republican movement in Northern Ireland. Similarly, long-standing divisions within society as a whole, of a political, religious or ethnic character, are more likely to be given violent expression, sometimes leading to full scale civil war. Sometimes it can be difficult to define who constitutes the enemy. During World War II some of the governments in exile and responsible Resistance leaders attempted to curtail political assassinations and attacks on individual members of the occupying forces;[15] collaborators and traitors on the other hand were considered fair targets and most of the resistance movements had special squads to carry out this work.[16] Where, however, does unavoidable co-operation end and culpable collaboration begin? The tendency is for the battle lines to be drawn deep inside one's own community. For all these reasons, where regular warfare against an outside enemy generally has the effect of reinforcing social cohesion, guerrilla warfare tends to destroy it.

The Resistance in Europe during World War II did not escape these negative repercussions. German reprisals themselves were savage, and, at the end of the war, especially in France and Italy, the spate of revenge killings of 'collaborators' reflected in part the intense bitterness and social division caused by guerrilla war. In France some 40,000 people are estimated to have lost their lives in the wave of killings that followed the liberation, approximately one per thousand of the population.[17]

The indiscriminate violence that might occur during a guerrilla war has to be compared with the alternatives. Terrible though it would be, a protracted guerrilla war would not have the destructive finality of a nuclear war, and even a major conventional war would be immensely destructive. Perhaps the concept of the just war, with its criteria of discrimination and proportionality, must now in practice increasingly disqualify major wars, though it might be more realisable in limited military engagements. This is not an argument for abandoning the notion of the just war, but rather one for intensifying the search for military and non-military methods of pursuing a struggle that would be consonant with the concept of justice, and of due restraint in the use of violence. The examples of underground resistance in Northern Europe during the occupation, which was disciplined and restrained and confined mainly to acts of sabotage, show that at least in certain contexts, and within particular organisational frameworks, guerrilla resistance can be controlled and used with discrimination. The term *guerrilla sabotage* could be used to identify guerrilla warfare confined largely if not entirely to acts of destruction against property rather than people.

Finally it has to be borne in mind that whatever the official policy, some guerrilla activity would be almost certain to occur in the event of an occupation. If — though only if — guerrilla warfare of some kind is considered to be a legitimate and worthwhile activity, there is a case for attempting to control it and channel it in a creative way by making advance plans and preparations for it.

VI. *The limitations of guerrilla warfare*

In face of repressive dictatorships, guerrilla warfare may sometimes be the only form of military struggle that is possible. However, there is an enormous difference between deciding to launch guerrilla warfare in circumstances where no other form of military struggle is available, especially if it is judged that civil resistance on its own is unlikely to succeed, and deciding in advance of an occupation to rely on it as the main component of a defence policy. Even those countries that have had most experience of using guerrilla warfare in recent history have not thought it advisable to take such a step, though plans for guerrilla warfare are an important part of their overall defence policy.

The limitations of guerrilla warfare stem in part from the fact that it is a strategy of protracted struggle. First, if it was the sole defence strategy it would not be able to provide a concentration of force to meet an attack aimed at seizing specific strategic objectives, such as ports, airfields, power plants and so on. If the principal reason for an invasion of Britain were to seize certain strategic points, this would be rather a serious drawback; regular forces could, however, act as a first stop against this type of attack, leaving guerrilla warfare as a fall-back possibility.

Second, there are limitations to the deterrent aspect of guerrilla warfare as a strategy on its own, though in combination with other strategies it can enhance deterrence. The prospects of having to deal with a stubborn guerrilla resistance would certainly not be welcome but, if this was to be the only military resistance, a potential aggressor might well be prepared to risk this in some situations for the sake of a short-term gain such as the seizure of strategically important areas. Where benefits are immediate and costs and penalties mainly a future possibility, nations — like individuals — may be tempted to take a risk. Moreover, the success of a protracted guerrilla struggle is far from being assured and an aggressor might calculate, sometimes correctly, on being able to break the resistance in the long run.

Third, guerrilla resistance against a major power, or the client regime of a major power, is likely to need outside assistance if it is to have a significant military impact or achieve military victory. This need not compromise the independence of the resistance movement or the post-war government — as Tito for instance demonstrated — but it creates pressures which can be difficult to resist. Despite the notion that guerrilla resistance is a self-sufficient form of defence or of revolutionary agitation, this frequently turns out not to be the case.

VII. Guerrilla warfare in British defence

One difficulty in discussing protracted guerrilla warfare as a strategy against occupation is to imagine the circumstances in which it might have to be put into operation. As things stand at the moment, Britain would not be occupied in the event of war — it would in all probability be destroyed. A Soviet occupation would become likely only in the course of a European war or following Soviet occupation of mainland Europe, and — short of very radical changes in the defence arrangements throughout Western Europe and a very different approach by the USA — it is hard to imagine how in these circumstances of superpower confrontation a nuclear war could be avoided.

However, some of the policies we have put forward for consideration in this Report would involve just such radical changes, so the exercise is worth undertaking. One possibility, some time in the future, is that following the removal of battlefield and theatre nuclear weapons from Europe, a war involving the superpowers might be kept to the conventional level because neither side would want to risk unleashing the holocaust. Another is that if NATO were to break up and the USA to withdraw from Europe, it might become militarily possible for the Soviet Union to occupy Western Europe, even if one thinks that for political and other reasons it would be unlikely to do so.

In this discussion we consider chiefly the scenario in which Britain has been occupied by the Soviet Union and where guerrilla forces are seeking to restore constitutional government and British independence. There could, however, be more ambiguous situations – for instance if the Soviet Union had established control over Western Europe and under threat of invasion, or as a result of a blockade, a pro-Soviet Quisling government was established here — perhaps even with some semblance of constitutional propriety; similarly US economic sanctions and political pressure in response to a request for them to close their bases in Britain could result in the democratic process being thwarted, or, in the extreme instance, in an unconstitutional take-over of power by right-wing forces.

Aside from the use of guerrilla tactics by territorial forces resisting invasion which we considered in Chapter 4, guerrilla warfare could have a role in British defence in three main contexts:

(1) an underground military organisation could operate along the lines of the 'secret armies' of Northern Europe during World War II, co-ordinating its strategy with that of an outside power — effectively the USA — still engaged in a military, non-nuclear struggle to liberate Europe.

(2) guerrilla warfare might be conducted on a European-wide scale, in conjunction with other forms of disruption, to put military, political and economic pressure on the Soviet Union to withdraw;

(3) civil resistance, again preferably at a European level, might be in the forefront with guerrilla actions having a supportive role. The distinction between the second and third options here is one of emphasis, but the shift is sufficiently important for this to be regarded as effectively another option.

We explained earlier why we think that partisan forces operating from strongholds in the British countryside could hardly build up to the point of being able to challenge and defeat the occupying power in regular warfare; this is likely to be true also for other countries in Western Europe. Here, however, we are talking mainly about urban guerrilla warfare with possibly some supportive military action in the countryside.

The first context mentioned above may be considered improbable, but could arise, for instance, if both superpowers refrained from using nuclear weapons and from wholesale destruction. In that event, a secret army poised to act in support of US forces could perform a useful military function. In order to retain its credibility and momentum, it would need to carry out sabotage and perhaps other para-military operations, despite the risk of reprisals. If this underground resistance were to operate with the kind of restraint and discipline shown by the secret armies of Northern Europe — for instance, confining their activities to acts of sabotage and avoiding assassinations and activities bordering on terrorism — the repression might well be more limited and the crucial distinction between combatants and non-combatants largely retained.

If one accepts that there won't be any US cavalry to come to the rescue, we are left with the second and third possibilities listed above. Considering Britain on its own, the prospect of a straightforward *military* victory developing out of urban guerrilla warfare is virtually negligible. The observations of Mao, Giap, Guevara and others on the need for guerrilla warfare to support, or develop into, regular warfare, the tragic experience of premature urban uprisings against the German occupation in parts of Europe, and the many failures of urban guerrilla warfare on its own to achieve even political success, underline the difficulties and the risk of provoking repression.

However, if one imagines a situation in which Soviet and Warsaw Pact forces are greatly overstretched and face urban and other guerrilla warfare activities across Western Europe, and possibly in parts of Eastern Europe too, in combination with other forms of civil unrest, then it is possible to see how this could force a Soviet withdrawal, or some compromise arrangement, and how the prospect of having to face such a resistance could enhance deterrence. The period in which successful resistance of this kind would be most likely to occur would be in the first few years following an occupation before client regimes had had time to consolidate their position.

There remains the third possibility listed above, namely that in which civil resistance would be central, with limited guerrilla activity occurring in conjunction with it. Non-co-operation is likely to be of critical importance in any protracted struggle, and it is the method by which the majority of people can participate in the resistance, especially where the possibilities of guerrilla warfare are limited. The problems associated with this kind of combination are considered in the following chapter.

Organisation of guerrilla resistance

The organisational base for such protracted resistance could be units of the regular army plus territorial or local defence forces, both specially trained in advance in the techniques of sabotage and possibly other guerrilla warfare activities. Upon the defeat or dispersal of the regular forces, these groups would merge into the population and provide a trained corps for continued resistance. It might be worth setting up separate, locally based forces, distinct from the present Territorial Army, who would be assigned to the defence of their areas during an invasion, and to resistance activities if the occupation were established. The intimate knowledge of the locality which such forces would have could be especially valuable during the phase of protracted resistance. Such preparations would, however, involve a considerable militarisation of society, in the sense of involving a large sector of the civilian population in military organisation and training, and perhaps even to the re-introduction of conscription, and this has to be taken into account when the notions of territorial defence and guerrilla warfare are being considered.

A structure of alternative political authority, as well as a specifically military chain of command, would have to be established to co-ordinate, and provide a focus for, the underground resistance, and plans for this would need to be made well in advance. Here again the experience of Europe under German occupation in World War II is instructive; thus a government in exile might be established in, say, Canada or the United States, while the resistance movements within the country were represented in a Provisional Government or Freedom Council, similar for instance to the Milorg organisation in Norway during the German occupation.

One populist version of the notion of defence by guerrilla warfare favours the arming of the total population and the disbanding of all regular forces, and in some cases of the structure of state authority altogether. The vestiges of such a notion are to be found in the constitutional right of US citizens to possess firearms which relates to the hostility in the early days of the founding of the American republic to having a standing army and to the popularity of the notion of the citizen-soldier. But arming the population makes military sense only if there is organisation and training as well as the distribution of arms. In so far as the proposal to arm the population takes account of this it may be simply another way of expressing the notion of a citizens' militia and universal military training to replace conventional defence. If it is taken literally to mean that arms would be distributed at random without any formal control, organisation or training, it does not make sense. It looks like a radical solution but is in fact a technical fix since it assumes that simply giving someone a weapon turns him or her into a soldier capable of taking on organised military units. The proposal in this form ignores the central importance of the human factor in warfare — the need for organisation, the importance of acquiring confidence and specialised skills through training, the importance of group morale in the face of appalling dangers, and the role of military tactics and strategy. Without such training and direction most people would not fight except in the most desperate circumstances, and those who did would not be likely to hold out for long. The proposal also raises the spectre of rival para-military organisations with a ready access to arms making war upon each other and competing for the control of the state.

Finally, guerrilla warfare does not necessarily, as is sometimes claimed, create momentum towards a decentralised and libertarian form of social organisation. Individual guerrilla units have to have a certain kind of freedom of manoeuvre and decision-making, as Mao for instance acknowledges. But Mao was no less insistent that the units must operate within the framework of a strategy and discipline if they were to be effective and this of course can be laid down centrally and rigorously imposed. Nothing in the way guerrilla movements have to be organised and to conduct operations of itself prevents the establishment of authoritarian modes of ideology and control either during the struggle itself or in the post-war period. China, Cuba, Vietnam, Kampuchea — however one might want to evaluate the regimes that followed the successful guerrilla resistance in these countries — bear out this point.

Guerrilla warfare as a total or partial strategy

Where do plans for guerrilla resistance (in some conjunction with civil resistance) fit into the overall defence policy of the country? The most radical proposition would be to dispense altogether with preparations for a serious conventional defence on the grounds that if one renounces nuclear weapons one effectively gives up the possibility of fighting a major war against a nuclear-armed opponent. Variants of this argument are that even a conventional war in Europe would be prohibitively destructive, and that the risk of a conventional war becoming nuclear in the European context would be too high to be worth taking. These are serious arguments, but tell us nothing about how likely guerrilla warfare would be to succeed. If an invasion occurred, guerrilla warfare on its own could not be expected to halt it and there is no assurance that it could dislodge an occupation, even in conjunction with civil resistance.

If one takes a long-term view (decades rather than years), the indirect strategies of guerrilla warfare and civil resistance hold out hope for maintaining essential human values and for eventual liberation. It is therefore possible to hold the view that it would be morally preferable, and make better sense in terms of ensuring human survival, to be willing if necessary to accept occupation and look to guerrilla warfare (or nonviolent resistance) as a means of continuing the struggle, rather than engage in warfare which might lead to nuclear destruction.

Normally, however, protracted guerrilla warfare is a fall-back option, linked to plans for in-depth defence by regular and territorial forces, as in Yugoslavia. It is perfectly compatible with orthodox defence plans even in principle with a defence policy involving some reliance on nuclear weapons. On the other hand by extending the options available it can permit a re-casting of the entire defence policy. There is a case for instance for a defence package that could be adopted throughout Western Europe in which there would be very mobile regular forces, sufficiently dispersed to avoid presenting an obvious target for nuclear attack, territorial and militia forces to operate in conjunction with the regular forces in resisting an attack, and back-up plans for what can be regarded as in-depth resistance over time in the form of guerrilla and civil resistance.

It seems to us that there is a strong case for planning some kind of anti-occupation strategy to back up whatever more orthodox defence plans are adopted. Even if one maintains strong conventional forces, there could be circumstances in which the only rational course of action would be to decide not to use them against an attacker, and it would be especially important to have such an anti-occupation strategy if one renounced the capacity to threaten nuclear retaliation in response to nuclear blackmail or attack.

VIII. Summary of the argument

Guerrilla warfare may be chiefly a *military* or a *para-military* strategy. As a military strategy it aims at gradually building up the guerrilla forces until they are in a position to engage and defeat the enemy in regular warfare. As a para-military strategy it aims not at the physical destruction of enemy forces but at exerting political, economic and a certain degree of military pressure for their withdrawal or to bring about the collapse of an internal regime. The difference, however, is one of degree and all guerrilla warfare tends to put a considerable emphasis on the political and economic aspects of armed conflict.

Three principal forms of guerrilla warfare have been identified: *partisan warfare, urban guerrilla warfare* and *political terrorism*. Partisan warfare can sometimes aim realistically at achieving a military victory; the other two fall into the category of para-military strategies and are often associated with forms of political resistance. In Britain, protracted guerrilla warfare would be predominantly of the urban variety, with or without a campaign of political assassination and terrorism.

The chief attraction of guerrilla warfare is that it is a military strategy which makes it possible for a militarily weak country to resist domination by a major power, even a major power possessing nuclear weapons. Its drawbacks are that it tends to erode the distinction between combatants and non-combatants and so easily degenerates into political terrorism and criminal violence, especially in an urban context. For these reasons it weakens the constraints on the use of violence against civilians and often leads to intensified repression; it tends also to be destructive of social cohesion.

Military limitations of guerrilla warfare are that it is not well equipped to deal swiftly with an attack, or to defend islands or outlying areas, and this could be a particular disadvantage where an attack was aimed at seizing specific strategic assets. By itself its deterrent value is limited because the military response it threatens is delayed and cumulative, and therefore might be seen by an opponent as a risk worth taking in order to gain some immediate advantage. However, in conjunction with other strategies it can enhance deterrence.

Some of the problems raised by guerrilla warfare in international conflicts are reflected in the state of international law on the subject which is reviewed in Appendix 4. However, changes in the law embodied in the 1949 Geneva Conventions and the 1977 Geneva

Protocol I have had the effect of recognising its legal existence as a method of struggle, as well as proposing norms for the way it should be conducted and opposed.

In the British context, the scope for guerrilla warfare is limited. Guerrilla *tactics* could be used to some extent by territorial units acting in support of the regular army, but this is different from the notion of a protracted guerrilla struggle against an established occupation or client regime. But a prolonged guerrilla struggle could have a role in Britain in three possible circumstances. Firstly, a 'secret army' might operate in co-ordination with outside regular forces, as occurred in occupied Europe in World War II, though these conditions seem less likely to recur in a future war. Secondly, urban guerrilla warfare, coupled with general agitation and unrest, could exert significant military and political pressure on an occupying power, especially if it occurred in a number of European countries. Thirdly, guerrilla warfare in a restrained form, for instance confined largely to acts of sabotage, could support a campaign based on civil resistance.

The organisational base for guerrilla warfare could be units of the regular forces plus territorial or militia forces. An alternative structure of authority would also have to be established to operate during an occupation, probably involving a government in exile and a Provisional Government or Freedom Council within the country on which the resistance bodies would be represented.

IX. Conclusions

The Commission rejected the notion of making guerrilla warfare the central element in a defence policy for Britain. In view of Britain's conventional military resources and of the kind of threats it is most likely to face, it does not seem desirable to substitute reliance on guerrilla warfare for a conventional frontier military defence. Nor did the Commission think that guerrilla methods should be central to a fall-back strategy of resistance to an occupying regime, since non-violent forms of political non-co-operation are better suited to British conditions than protracted guerrilla resistance.

In general the Commission members were acutely aware that guerrilla tactics were likely to result in severe repression and quite possibly in indiscriminate retaliation by opposing forces, and that guerrilla fighters are themselves tempted to use ruthless and indiscriminate methods. The Commission was also strongly opposed to any reliance on a campaign of political assassination or terrorism. It recommends that nonviolent resistance should be the central element in a fall-back strategy.

Some members of the Commission did see a strictly limited role for guerrilla tactics as parts of a broader strategy of prolonged resistance, but others were sceptical about guerrilla warfare even at this level and thought that combining nonviolent and guerrilla methods would be unsound.

Notes to Chapter 6

1. On the notion of a 'mixed strategy' see for example J. Galtung, 'What Kind of Defence Should We Have?' in *The Dynamics of European Nuclear Disarmament* (Nottingham: Spokesman Books, 1981), pp. 157–168

2. See for instance Mao Tse-Tung, 'On Protracted War', *Selected Works of Mao Tse-Tung,* 5 vols. (Peking: Foreign Language Press, 1975), Vol. II, p. 172: "When we say that in the entire war mobile warfare is primary and guerrilla warfare supplementary, we mean that the outcome of the war depends mainly on regular warfare, especially in its mobile form, and that guerrilla warfare cannot shoulder the main responsibility in deciding the outcome . . . guerrilla warfare will not remain the same throughout this long and cruel war, but will rise to a higher level and develop into mobile warfare. Thus the strategic role of guerrilla warfare is twofold, to support regular warfare and to transform itself into regular warfare."

   Similarly Che Guevara in *Guerrilla Warfare* (Harmondsworth: Penguin, 1975), p. 19: "Thus it is clear that guerrilla warfare is a phase that does not afford in itself opportunities to arrive at complete victory . . . Triumph will always be the product of a regular army, even though its origins are in a guerrilla army."

   Vo Nguyen Giap in 'The Political and Military Line of our Party', reprinted in *The Military Art of People's War: Selected Writings of General Vo Nguyen Giap,* R. Stetler, ed. (London: Monthly Review Press, 1970), pp. 163–84, also speaks of the need in the situation then existing in Vietnam "to promote an extensive guerrilla war which will develop gradually into regular war combined with guerrilla war" (p. 177)

3. Mao, and Giap follows Mao, identifies three aspects of warfare: *mobile* and *positional warfare,* both of which involve the use of regular forces, and *guerrilla warfare.* It is regular warfare in its mobile form that is at the heart of Mao's military strategy rather than guerrilla warfare as such. Mobile war emphasises the inflicting of heavy casualties on the enemy and ultimately destroying the fighting capacity of their forces, rather than on retaining or re-capturing territory (positional warfare), though this does have a role, especially in the final phase of the struggle when the enemy is being forced out of the country. Mobile warfare permits greater flexibility and freedom of manoeuvre than positional warfare and therefore, Mao argues, the establishment of the proper balance between the human and technological factor in warfare; positional warfare, epitomised by the trench warfare of World War I, allows too little scope to the human factor.

   Mao's concept of the relation between these forms in the context of a protracted war are summed up in 'On Protracted War' p. 173: "In the first stage mobile warfare is primary, while guerrilla and positional warfare are supplementary. In the second stage guerrilla warfare will advance to the first place and will be supplemented by mobile and positional warfare. In the third stage mobile warfare will again become the primary form and will be supplemented by positional and guerrilla warfare. But the mobile warfare of the third stage will no longer be undertaken solely by the original regular forces; part, possibly quite an important part, will be undertaken by forces which were originally guerrillas but which will have progressed from guerrilla to mobile warfare.''

4. See for instance J. Haestrup, *Europe Ablaze* (Odense: Odense University Press, 1978) p. 476: ''the Norwegian underground army, or 'Home forces', was an organised force in waiting position, and here as in Denmark, the forces only went into action in connection with the German capitulation, after which these Resistance forces took over a number of guard duties. Although some of these Western and Northern European forces were engaged in reception of weapons and sabotage operations etc. before the capitulation, this makes little difference to the fundamental fact.''

5. For a discussion of this distinction, see the chapters on Guerrilla Warfare and Terrorism in M. Walzer, *Just and Unjust Wars: A Moral Argument with Historical Illustrations* (Harmondsworth: Penguin, 1980).

6. See R. Kee, *The Green Flag: A History of Irish Nationalism* (London: Weidenfeld & Nicolson, 1972), especially pp. 630–31 and 678–81.

7. R. Taber, *The War of the Flea: A Study of Guerrilla Warfare Theory and Practice* (London: Paladin, 1970), p. 25.

8. Cited by K. Macksey, *The Partisans of Europe in World War II* (London: Hart-Davis, MacGibbon, 1975), p. 47.

9. Tito is estimated to have had about a quarter of a million available armed soldiers by November 1943, including, in the words of M. R. D. Foot, ''a decent proportion of artillery units''. See M. R. D. Foot, *Resistance: An Analysis of European Resistance to Nazism, 1940–45* (London: Methuen, 1976), p. 196. In Italy the figure for partisans by late 1944 is put at about 300,000, of whom 45,000 were killed in action; some 3,000 tons of supplies were parachuted to them, two-thirds by British and the rest by American aircraft (p. 227). Accurate figures for the partisan war in the Soviet Union are difficult to obtain. The East German historian, Heinz Kuehnrich, in *Der Partisanenkrieg in Europa 1939–45* (Berlin: Dietz Verlag, 1968) puts the number of Soviet partisan forces at 1,993,000 — a figure that includes both partisan and resistance members. His estimate of German and Axis casualties at the hands of partisans is around half a million for the Soviet Union, and approximately the same for the Balkans. (Cited by Haestrup, *Europe Ablaze*,[4] p. 471).

10. For an account of the Resistance in France see Foot, *Resistance: An Analysis of European Resistance to Nazism, 1940–45*,[4] pp. 234–54.

11. ''The fact that the strike made an impression in Berlin became apparent when an appeal was broadcast over the Berlin radio to the Dutch people. The appeal was not without concessions. It declared that Germany was 'deeply shocked' and complained at 'the provocative attitude and increasing resistance'. The tone of the appeal was defensive, offended and apologetic, and revealed deep uncertainty at the first serious outbreak of an occupied people's unforeseen reactions.'' Haestrup, *Europe Ablaze*,[4] p. 103.

12. Foot, *Resistance*,[9] p. 275.

13. See for instance *The Guardian*, 16 February, 1982, report from P. Quinn-Judge: ''In contrast to the generally impeccable behaviour of National Liberation Front

and North Vietnamese troops towards peasants during their war with America, the Pol Pot forces seem to have lost none of their brutality . . . one hamlet was attacked the night before my visit to Prey Chruk, and inhabitants report that Khmer Rouge troops stripped them of their year's supply of rice and took away as many pigs, chickens and cattle as they could find. Then, before they left, a villager claimed, they burned several houses 'for no reason at all'."

14. J. W. Sloan, 'Political Terrorism in Latin America: A Critical Analysis', in M. Stohl, ed., *The Politics of Terrorism* (New York and Basel: Marcel Dekker, 1979), p. 306.

15. De Gaulle, broadcasting on the BBC on 23 October 1941, discouraged this kind of random killing on the practical grounds that the population was in the power of the enemy, and the Dutch government in exile addressed a similar appeal to the Dutch Resistance in February 1943 — see Haestrup, *Europe Ablaze,*[4] p. 446, who also cites other examples.

16. Haestrup, *Europe Ablaze,*[4] pp. 453–54.

17. See Macksey, *The Partisans of Europe in World War II,*[8] p. 205, and Foot, *Resistance: An Analysis of European Resistance to Nazism, 1940–45,*[9] p. 253.

Chapter 7
Strategies against occupation
II. Defence by civil resistance

I. Introduction

We argued in Chapter 1 that a system of conventional military defence in the nuclear age would require a fall-back strategy to deal with the possibility of nuclear escalation or blackmail. If protracted guerrilla war could not be expected to play a major role in the British context, as we concluded in chapter 6, the alternative — or additional — fall-back option is defence by civil, nonviolent, resistance.

There are, however, many other types of situation that might be best dealt with by a combination of political pressure and nonviolent resistance. A small country, for instance, threatened by an overwhelmingly stronger opponent — such as Czechoslovakia when it faced the Soviet and Warsaw Pact forces in 1968 — might decide not to use the military forces at its disposal but to concentrate on nonviolent forms of resistance. Similarly a country might decide to respond with nonviolent resistance to relatively marginal infringements of its territorial integrity rather than resorting to war. The notion of nonviolent defence in fact pre-dates the nuclear age and has long been advocated by many of those who reject war as a matter of principle.

There are arguments in favour of shifting the emphasis of defence still further towards nonviolent methods. The ultimate vulnerability of conventional defence in face of a sufficiently ruthless nuclear opponent is seen by some as pointing in this direction, at least in the long term. There is also the consideration that a major war between modern industrial states would in any case be immensely destructive, and unlikely to be conducted with the discrimination enjoined by the concept of the just war. And if one side alone pursued a consistent policy of limiting itself to discriminate forms of warfare during a conflict it could put itself at a major disadvantage against a less scrupulous opponent, even if the latter did not use nuclear or chemical weapons. Finally, there is the urgent need to check the prodigious level of global military expenditure which is indirectly costing millions of lives because of the diversion of resources from economic and social development.

Britain and Western Europe do of course face a potential nuclear adversary, so the argument for preparing for nonviolent resistance, at least as a fall-back strategy, is a strong one. How central its place in an overall strategy should be depends in part on how likely one thinks it is that the Soviet Union would resort to the use of nuclear weapons, or would deliver a nuclear ultimatum in a war or major crisis, and the importance one attributes to the role of conventional defense in deterring a Soviet attack. Some of the advocates of defence by civil resistance argue that if one is going to place a considerable reliance on moral and political disincentives, these are more likely to prevent the Soviet Union from attacking a substantially disarmed Britain or Western Europe in the first place than to prevent the use of nuclear weapons (much less the indiscriminate use of conventional weapons) once war has started. They also argue that a country that has chosen to rely centrally on civil resistance has a better chance of being able to control the circumstances under which this resistance is conducted than one which has adopted it as a fall-back strategy; in the aftermath of a particularly destructive war, for instance, it might take some time before mass civil resistance could be initiated. There is also the risk of a conventional war escalating to the nuclear level before a fall-back strategy could be put into operation, since one has to allow for the irrational dynamic that can take control once war has started and thousands of people are being killed.

There are then four main ways in which civil resistance could contribute to defence. Firstly it could replace military preparations altogether, as many pacifists advocate. Secondly it could become the central element in a defence strategy, but with some military forces being retained for basically 'policing' functions, to deal with limited threats, etc. Thirdly civil resistance, as we suggested above, could be seen as an option to be used in particular circumstances, or against particular types of threat. Finally it could be regarded solely as a fall-back option to be employed if one's armed forces met with defeat, or if the country had to capitulate in face of a nuclear ultimatum; in this case it might be accorded a rather marginal significance, or it could be given greater importance if the risk of occupation was thought to be substantial.

Examining the concept

Civil resistance is resistance by the civilian population in the form of strikes, boycotts, civil disobedience, mass non-co-operation — the methods that have played a central role in economic and social struggles, particularly since the 19th century and have become increasingly important in political and liberation struggles in the present century. Examples of its role in the latter context are the Indian independence struggle, the resistance to the Kapp putsch in Germany in 1920 and to the Franco–Belgian occupation of the Ruhr in 1923–25, much of the resistance in occupied Norway, Denmark, Holland and other countries during World War II, Czechoslovak resistance to the Soviet and Warsaw Pact invasion of 1968 and the Solidarity movement in Poland.[2] The proposition examined in this chapter is that this form of resistance could be incorporated into the national system of deterrence and defence.

Defence by civil resistance rests on the proposition, discussed earlier in relation to guerrilla warfare, that states and governments rely upon the co-operation, or at least the compliance, of the majority of the population. Its aim is to deprive any illicit or occupation regime of this basis of social power, to encourage international sanctions against an aggressor, and to seek support among the population, or within particular circles, in the aggressor state. Advance preparation is central to the notion and a period of transition is normally envisaged during which there would be a gradual shift from reliance on military defence to defence by civil resistance.

The notion of relying on forms of civil resistance as an alternative to military defence has been strongly associated with pacifism and philosophical nonviolence.[3] However, the achievements of civil resistance, together with concern about weapons of mass destruction, have led to an interest in the idea among a much wider circle. In Britain the military historian Basil Liddell Hart and Sir Stephen King-Hall were interested in the possibilities of civilian resistance in the 1930s, and King-Hall advocated it in 1938 as a suitable response by the Danish government and people in the event of a Nazi occupation.[4] King-Hall also played a key role in the post-war revival of interest in the notion. The coming together in Britain during the early 1960s of people from a pacifist and peace movement background with historians, strategists and political analysts can be said to have produced the first systematic studies.[5] During the 1960s and 1970s the notion has been further explored by analysts and research institutes in a number of countries. Several governments too have taken an interest in the notion and have commissioned studies and research projects into its possibilities.[6]

II. The political basis of civil resistance

Classic strategic theory maintains that the purpose of war is ultimately political — the 'continuation of policy by other means' to quote Von Clausewitz.[7] Frequently the political objective will be achieved without the total military defeat of the opponent, for instance when military setbacks or stalemate coincide with rising social, economic and political costs in continuing the war.

The political dimension of warfare has become increasingly important during the present century even in conventional war. It is particularly important in guerrilla warfare, but civil resistance shifts the struggle still more decisively to the political arena. It has been described as the political equivalent of war.[8] It cannot match conventional or guerrilla warfare with regard to certain tasks and objectives. Unlike conventional warfare, it cannot physically halt or destroy invading forces, and unlike guerrilla warfare, it cannot deplete them by the cumulative effect of many small engagements. It resembles guerrilla warfare, however, in that it is normally a form of protracted struggle, achieving its effects by gradually undermining the morale and confidence of the opponent, making their task increasingly difficult and costly.

Civil resistance can plausibly aim to:

(1) make governing a country difficult if not impossible. Sometimes it can thwart an attempted military takeover, as during the attempted Kapp putsch of 1920 in Berlin, and the Generals' Revolt in Algeria in 1961;

(2) maintain the values, institutions and general culture of an occupied country;

(3) deny to the opponent many of the political and economic benefits that it might seek to gain from an occupation.

These are essentially defensive tasks. But the resistance must also aim to take the struggle into the opponent's camp, and inflict costs in its turn. Thus it can aim to:

(4) sow dissent and disaffection among the armed forces and officials entering the country, or carrying out the occupation. In Czechoslovakia, for instance, there is evidence that some of the troops were nonplussed by demonstrations and passive resistance during the 1968 invasion;[9]

(5) disrupt economic and cultural exchanges that existed between the countries before an attack, so that the invasion not merely fails to

bring advantages to the aggressor but brings tangible disadvantages. The Swiss threat to blow up certain tunnels through the Alps during the last war in the event of a German invasion is one illustration of this kind of sanction. In the East/West context, the aim would be to signal to the opponent that there was more to be gained economically and in other respects from continuing normal, peaceful trading relations, than from any attempt to seize assets by force;

(6) mobilise international opinion against the attacker, for instance through the United Nations, and various governmental and non-governmental bodies in other countries;

(7) work to bring about divisions, or widen existing divisions, within the opponent's forces and officials, and leaders in the opponent's own country, culminating in the extreme case in a change of government, or revolutionary upheaval.

The extent to which these objectives can be carried out will vary according to the circumstances, including the soundness of the tactics and strategy. Some observations on these are made later.

The support of the international community can be an important source of pressure on the opponent, and a country adopting a policy of defence by civil resistance would probably want to strengthen its international links and seek the maximum support, short of military action, in the event of an attack. There might be an agreement for instance that a variety of economic and diplomatic sanctions would be applied if an attack occurred. The notion of a general strike against war, across national boundaries, collapsed with the onset of World War I. It, or a partial strike, could be applied, however, in response to aggression against a state offering no armed resistance. Now that Solidarity has been suppressed in Poland, independent unions do not exist in the Soviet bloc, so here we are looking mainly to future possibilities, as far as East/West conflicts are concerned. Later we discuss novel forms of international direct action and the possibility of having a specially trained nonviolent action corps or 'Peace Army' for such purposes.

If Vietnam provides the classic case of a successful guerrilla war in an anti-imperialist struggle, India provides the classic parallel for nonviolent struggle. The campaigns of civil disobedience, non-co-operation, boycotts of British goods and other measures made British rule increasingly untenable. Moral and psychological pressure was exerted by the nonviolent discipline of the resistance, and anti-colonialist sentiment mobilised within Britain (partly by Gandhi himself during his visit to Britain in 1931) and in other countries, notably the United States.

Gandhi was of course working under more favourable circumstances than countries under occupation from totalitarian regimes have experienced. Organising resistance of any kind in such circumstances is difficult and hazardous and the problem of making contact with, let alone influencing, the population of the aggressor state is particularly acute. Yet there was resistance, both guerrilla and nonviolent, under Nazi occupation in Europe and at certain levels at least the latter was effective. Severe repression has also failed in some cases to end civil resistance or to prevent it from achieving its objective, notably in the campaign in Iran in 1978–79 which brought down the Shah's regime. In Poland, the imposition of martial law in December 1981 has, for the time being at least, driven Solidarity underground. Nevertheless the methods of civil resistance, coupled in the early period particularly with a nonviolent discipline to prevent the authorities from having any reason or excuse for sending in the militia or armed forces, brought some of the most remarkable changes ever seen in a state within the Soviet bloc. We have not come to the end of the story and Poland is unlikely to go back to what it was before August 1980 when the movement was born.[10] These and other examples show that civil resistance is not some marginal phenomenon that can be effective only against relatively non-repressive regimes. Whether or not it is formally adopted by any country as part of its defence policy, the political importance of civil resistance is likely to grow and to play a role in the regulation of power within and between states.

However, when we come to consider its possible role in defence policy a number of questions arise:

(1) What types of action would be involved and what would be their function in the overall campaign?

(2) Can these actions be structured into a general strategy of civil resistance against occupation or other external and internal threats?

(3) Do plans for civil resistance have a credible deterrent value?

(4) Would civil resistance be effective against a dictatorial or repressive opponent?

(5) Could civil resistance constitute a defence strategy on its own?

(6) What are the possibilities of combining it with a military strategy?

(7) To what extent is it an option that would suit the strategic needs and social and political conditions of Britain?

(8) What measures of organisation, training and other prepar-

ations would be needed to facilitate effective resistance during an occupation?

(9) What international arrangements could be made to strengthen defence by civil resistance and provide an element of mutual security?

These questions are briefly surveyed in the rest of this chapter.

III. Types of action and their function

Nonviolent action can be categorised in various ways. Here we group activities in terms of their function in the overall resistance. We suggest three broad categories of action, while recognising that many actions perform several functions simultaneously.

Communication, persuasion and mobilisation

Actions in this category would include marches, vigils, leafletting, painting slogans and symbols — like the V for Victory sign which appeared everywhere across Europe under German occupation — displaying national flags or colours, singing patriotic or resistance songs, and holding public fasts, or even token strikes.

The communication is aimed at the opponent, though more at the troops and functionaries than at a leadership which would probably be impervious to such appeals, at third parties (other governments and populations) and most crucially in the early stages at one's own population, especially elements who may be tempted to collaborate. Mobilising the population and maintaining morale should be seen as the key defensive task, just as undermining the morale of the opponent is the key offensive task. So it is important to find the right words and actions that will strike a responsive chord among the population, appealing to shared experience, tradition and values.

Action may be still more eloquent, and this is the key to understanding the importance of 'symbolic' acts. Gandhi's Salt March in 1930 was in one sense no more than a defiant gesture. It was also an action that was understood right across the sub-continent, and a signal for tens of thousands to begin a campaign of defiance and non-co-operation.[11] In the context of a guerrilla war, Castro's attack on the Moncada barracks in 1953 had a similar symbolic yet mobilising function. Thus symbolic action is not to be understood as merely token. At its most effective it can rouse a population to action, and mobilise international opinion in favour of the resistance.

Denial actions

The objective here is to prevent the occupier or usurper from reaping the expected political, economic and other advantages of their action. Strikes, boycotts, go-slows may prevent the production or flow of goods upon which the occupier was counting. During the winter of 1941/2 the Belgian government in exile could report a drop in Belgian coal production under German occupation of 36% [12] Similar instances of strikes, go-slows and obstruction occurred throughout occupied Europe.

Obstruction and non-co-operation can also hamper or bring to a standstill the administration of an occupying or illicit regime. An occupying force might bring in its own administrators, but this is frequently not practicable. Historians of the German occupation of Europe have noted the German dependence on the national, regional and local administrations of the countries they occupied, and the opportunities this provided for hampering and obstructing German plans.[13]

Non-co-operation does not have to take the form of outright defiance; forms of semi-resistance, such as go-slows, or deliberately misunderstanding instructions may be the predominant mode, particularly if repression is severe.

The denial of legitimacy to an occupying regime is another important aspect of this form of struggle. Governments in exile, provisional governments, alternative elected assemblies and other bodies may claim the allegiance of the population and so deny it to the opponent. Setting up provisional revolutionary governments and assemblies and other institutions at every level of society has occurred in a number of anti-colonial struggles, though usually in the context of guerrilla war.

Interventions, such as the occupation of buildings and worksites, obstruction, such as forming human barricades in front of tanks as happened in cities in Czechoslovakia in 1968, the selective destruction of property, like removing street signs, and possibly limited forms of sabotage that did not involve risk to human life, such as cutting power and telephone lines — all deny access to goods, services and property as well as fulfilling in many cases important symbolic functions.

The denial of ideological objectives is a still more crucial objective. The refusal of churches, trade unions, teachers and other organisations to cooperate with the plans of the Quisling regime in Norway to construct a corporate state on National Socialist lines was one of the outstanding successes of the civil resistance to the German occupation of Europe. The resistance to, and obstruction of, Nazi persecutions of Jews and others in occupied Europe is another example of an effort to deny the occupier important ideological and policy goals; the most notable success here was in Denmark where 95% of the Jewish population were smuggled to Sweden in October 1943.[14]

Undermining the opponent

Undermining the opponent's sources of power and legitimacy represents the 'offensive' element of civil resistance. In the case of an invasion and occupation, it includes putting pressure on soldiers and officials on the spot to refuse certain orders such as firing on unarmed strikers and demonstrators, to use go slow or obstructive tactics, for instance turning a blind eye to resistance activities or collaborating with the resistance by giving it tip-offs when police or army raids are going to take place. This pressure would be exercised not only by written and broadcast appeals, but by actions designed to put the discipline of the opponent's forces to severe test, for instance disciplined symbolic protests where the clear rejection of the occupation is combined with the absence of any physical threat to the safety of soldiers or officials. Under-cover support and help for a resistance from occupation personnel is not uncommon,[15] and the dynamic of a nonviolent opposition would tend to make it more likely to occur than if the resistance is violent.

The second aspect of the attempt to undermine the opponents' sources of power would be to take the political struggle back to their homeland. We discuss in Section VI the difficulties of achieving this against an aggressor state that does not allow free political association and discussion among its citizens. Sometimes even in such circumstances there may be divisions within the army or ruling group that can be exposed or that develop as a result of the failure to establish a credible client regime in the occupied state and a loss of face internationally; sometimes the weak link in the opponent's armour may be in other allied or subjugated states — in the case of the Soviet Union some of the countries of Eastern Europe. International pressure could be important here, in particular countries which had strong ties with the aggressor state but which were nevertheless prepared to put pressure upon it to withdraw; movements and parties aligned ideologically to the aggressor state may also be willing and able to exert pressure. A number of Western communist parties protested to no avail against the Soviet and Warsaw Pact invasion of Czechoslovakia in 1968, but the disunity of the international communist movement as a result of Soviet actions in Hungary, Czechoslovakia and Afghanistan represents a net loss of Soviet power and influence. Possibly one of the factors inhibiting a direct Soviet intervention in Poland to crush the Solidarity movement is the likelihood that this would be the final blow to pro-Soviet sympathies among the majority of outside communist parties.

The morale and political will of the opponent is at the heart of their endeavour and is therefore the ultimate target of the offensive strategy of a resistance. Even where direct contact with the opponents' population or ruling elite is not possible, the goal of striking back at their base of power may still be achieved by thwarting political and economic goals in the occupied territory and by fomenting disaffection and a breakdown of discipline among the forces and officials who have been sent there. Such a failure is likely to have repercussions among the political and military leaders of the aggressor state and may even trigger off sweeping political changes.

IV. The strategy of civil resistance

A detailed strategy for defence by civil resistance would have to relate to particular situations; here we want only to make some general observations.[16]

The problem can be stated in this way: given that quick victories in civil resistance cannot normally be expected, especially where resistance to a foreign occupation is concerned, what pattern of activity or plan of campaign is best calculated to sustain the momentum of opposition and lead to eventual success? Are there discernable stages in a campaign of resistance with activities appropriate to them?

It can be argued that the notion of an indefinite general strike in response to invasion is not realistic. It could probably not be sustained and, unless there was a plan for continued resistance, its collapse could bring demoralisation and failure.

It seems too much to expect the majority of the population to be capable of a prolonged and heroic resistance. In the event of occupation, society is likely to divide into three groups; a small strong-willed and highly motivated minority would refuse allegiance to the conquerors; the majority would accommodate themselves to the situation, however unwillingly and resentfully; and another minority would actively and treasonably collaborate with the occupiers.[17] Can we devise a strategy that takes this likely pattern into account and still holds out the prospect of success?

There could be three principal stages in resistance to invasion or *coup d'état*: an initial phase of intensive resistance; a second phase of consolidation characterised mainly by selective, passive and 'semi' resistance; and a third stage of counter-offensive and renewed mass action aimed at achieving a final victory.

There is an approximate correspondence here to the phases of military resistance envisaged by Mao and other writers on guerrilla and revolutionary war.

In the initial phase two main responses are possible. The first is all-out defiance and non-co-operation — what Gene Sharp calls 'Nonviolent Blitzkrieg'.[18] All-out defiance is appropriate where there is some possibility of a rapid victory, for instance where the attacker is perceived to be acting out of weakness, the defending society is confident and well-prepared, and the line-up of international forces is such as to make a quick success possible. However even if a rapid victory is not possible, the all-out resistance policy can serve to mobilise the population for the longer-term resistance, and provide dramatic evidence to the outside world that aggression has taken place and that the population is determined to resist it.

The second possible immediate response of communication, mobilisation and warning differs from the first chiefly in that it does not attempt to force a quick decision. Underground propaganda and symbolic acts of resistance will play a larger part.

Where there is no quick resolution of the conflict, the initial phase will be followed by one of consolidation and of substantive but generally lower-key resistance. *Selective resistance* is likely to play an important role during this period, that is to say resistance focused on areas or objectives of critical importance in the struggle. It could be focused on preventing the attacker from obtaining major economic or political objectives, or defending institutions and freedoms which are regarded as central to the indigenous culture and to continuing resistance. In Norway the resistance of teachers to the introduction of a Nazi-style curriculum in the schools and to the establishment of a state-controlled union was one example of selective resistance in a critical area; there was also similar resistance by the churches, trade unions, sporting and cultural organisations.[19] One advantage of this selective resistance is that it tends to shift the burden of responsibility from one section of the community to another, rather than involving the whole society all at once in a defiance that would be difficult to sustain. Even in this phase, there will be occasions when all-out resistance by the community would be appropriate — for instance in response to severe brutalities or as a means of supporting particular groups under attack.

Passive and 'semi' resistance is also likely to be important during this phase. This can involve go-slows, economic and administrative obstruction, and the kind of general bloody-mindedness that characterised the popular response to occupation in Europe and for that matter is a common feature of trade union and working class resistance to demands which are seen as unreasonable or exploitative. The great advantage of this kind of resistance is that it is difficult to detect and may therefore be carried out with relative impunity even during periods of intense repression. Other forms of indirect resistance may accompany it such as wearing badges, singing resistance songs, observing days of national mourning or celebration and other collective actions which can sustain morale by an open and visible expression of resistance and yet are not so challenging as to bring down on the population the full repressive wrath of the regime.[20]

A campaign which combines this kind of passive and semi-resistance on the one hand, with periodic climaxes involving mass open defiance on the other, could probably be sustained over a long period. It corresponds for instance to the pattern of resistance in Denmark during the German occupation, where low-key resistance in the form of the 'civil consciousness' programmes led by Dansk Samling and the Union of Danish Youth, and the *alsangs* — the mass patriotic singsongs — was interspersed with two major 'battles' — the rescue of the majority of the Jewish population in October 1943, and the Copenhagen general strike of July 1944.

The last phase of the resistance aims, like Gandhi's Quit India campaign of 1942, to dislodge finally the occupation or client regime. In this phase, open and large-scale resistance will again predominate. It can occur when the balance of forces favours the resistance — when the opponent is weakened and the occupying forces are over-stretched, and when the population has built up the confidence and strength for an all-out effort to achieve liberation.

V. *Civil resistance as a deterrent*

The prospect of having to face determined political opposition and mass non-co-operation would not be welcome to any would-be occupier, and the forces that civil resistance bring into play are well understood by governments. Moreover there are instances where the threat of civil resistance has had a dissuasive effect on an opponent. Thus following the successful resistance of the teachers in Norway in 1942, the Quisling regime felt it prudent to drop plans to create a corporate labour system for the country rather than risk a similar confrontation with the unions.[21] And during the Revolt of the Generals in Algiers in 1961, the massive demonstrations against them throughout France, including a token general strike, was certainly a factor in the decision of the generals to abandon any attempt to mount an invasion from Algeria.[22]

But because civil resistance is, generally speaking, a strategy of protracted struggle, an opponent might be tempted in some circumstances to risk facing problems in the longer term for the sake of an immediate advantage. Even so, acts of aggression bring international opprobrium and sometimes immediate and damaging political consequences, and these costs could be much higher where the aggression was against a state resisting solely in a nonviolent way. The prospect of civil resistance by itself may not deter aggression in some situations, especially as no country has yet tried to rely on it as a defence strategy. If it is envisaged as a back-up to military defence, however, it could enhance deterrence by adding to the difficulties of maintaining control after an invasion.

One can distinguish between dissuasion in general and deterrence which is one type of it. Deterrence is generally considered to rely on the threat of destructive reprisals to prevent attack, but it is only one of a number of dissuasive factors. Moreover, 'offensive deterrence', epitomised by the nuclear threat to destroy the opponent's society, may actually precipitate pre-emptive war under some circumstances. Thus a policy which reduced the element of deterrence in a defence policy would not necessarily increase the overall likelihood of war.

There is also a temptation to oversimplify the social psychology of conflict, to reduce it to a matter of the credibility and effectiveness of the threats by one side or the other. However, in the emotional fervour that can accompany a military crisis, the armed forces of the other side may be seen less as a deterrent than as a challenge to be met and overcome, even as an opportunity to vindicate the military prowess of one's own side. A policy of defence by civil resistance might help to defuse this process of psychological escalation, and thus sometimes be more effective in preventing war than a policy of military deterrence. There is not much glory in occupying a country when the only engagements are between the invading forces and unarmed civilians.

The assessment of the risks that Britain or Western Europe would run in adopting a policy of defence by civil resistance depends partly on whether one thinks the Soviet Union is determined to establish control over Western Europe if ever this becomes militarily possible, or whether one expects the Soviet Union to see political and economic advantages overall in developing peaceful relations with Western Europe, and to be daunted by the enormous problems of trying to impose its will by force on complex industrial societies with long traditions of democratic organisation. It is certainly debatable whether the Soviet leaders would want to take on the problem of Poland several times over, especially if plans for civil resistance were well prepared and publicised in advance.

VI. Civil resistance against dictatorial or repressive regimes

Has civil resistance any reasonable prospect of succeeding against a dictatorial regime, or in any circumstances in which the opponent is prepared to resort to extreme repression? The difficulties involved in such circumstances ought not to be underestimated, and the defeat of any particular resistance movement is always possible. Nevertheless, civil resistance has achieved significant successes against dictatorial regimes, and has sometimes persisted in the face of repression.

Civil resistance contributed to the decisive political defeat of the Nazi plans to establish a New Order in Europe. The significance of that defeat can hardly be overstated. The Nazis had expected the New Order to be welcomed, especially in the 'Aryan' countries of Northern Europe, and to be able to mobilise people in the occupied countries in an anti-Bolshevik crusade. Instead they created a political fiasco by a crude reliance on violence, failing even to exploit the political opportunities that were open to them, for instance in the Ukraine where there was considerable anti-Bolshevik sentiment.

The Danish historian Joergen Haestrup notes that "the two dictatorship movements (Nazi and Fascist) showed a surprising ability to gather the great masses, not, as they had expected, under them, but unexpectedly, against them".[23] Some of the credit for this achievement must be attributed to the illegal press and other resistance activities.

The precise contribution of civil resistance to the political defeat of Nazi and Fascist ideologies is hard to assess. This resistance took place in the context of a world war, and alongside guerrilla resistance. The prospect of eventual liberation through the military defeat of the Axis powers contributed to the will to resist, and as the tide of war turned, political support for the occupiers or client regimes naturally ebbed still faster.[24] But courageous, principled civil resistance occurred, and to some effect, during the early period of the war when Hitler's armies seemed invincible, including the strike of Norwegian teachers, the student strikes in Leiden and Delft in Holland in the winter of 1940 in protest against the dismissal of Jewish lecturers, and the strikes in Amsterdam, Hilversum and other Dutch towns in February 1941, again in protest against anti-Jewish activities.[25]

Basil Liddell Hart has argued that the nonviolent resistance in occupied Europe was more troublesome to the Germans than the guerrilla war except in the Balkans and Russia, where the terrain favoured guerrilla action,[26] though this conclusion has been challenged by other historians of the resistance.[27] It is clear, however, that the totalitarian nature of the Nazi regimes did not make them invulnerable to the pressures which civil resistance could bring to bear. And if direct contact with the German population by resistance movements was not generally possible, the fiasco of the occupation policies did lead to sharp divisions within the ruling clique.[28]

Civil resistance can realistically hope to exploit divisions among the wielders of power, if not initially among the general population of the invading country, in the attempt to undermine the policy and morale of a dictatorial opponent. There is a rather close parallel here with the guerrilla war in Portugal's African colonies, which opened up divisions within Portugal's dictatorial regime and led to the coup that overthrew Caetano, so paving the way for wider reforms and for the rapid ending of colonial rule.

Of more immediate relevance to the East/West confrontation is the dramatic civil resistance to the Soviet and Warsaw Pact invasion of Czechoslovakia in August 1968. It failed either to halt the invasion or to prevent the eventual re-establishment of a hardline pro-Soviet regime which is now one of the most rigid in Eastern Europe (presumably because it enjoys so little public support). But the 1968 resistance did achieve important short-term results. During the ten days of street demonstrations and mass popular protest, the Soviet Union lost the political initiative and had to release the arrested Czechoslovak leaders and negotiate a settlement which kept Dubcek in office until April 1969. This was a remarkable climb-down and a decision that can only have been taken with extreme reluctance; it seems likely, moreover, that had it not been for the widespread resistance Dubcek and his colleagues would have been executed, as Imry Nagy had been 12 years previously after the Hungarian uprising.[29]

The terms of the Moscow Accords signed by Dubcek and Svoboda were clearly disadvantageous to the Czechoslovaks, enabling the Soviet Union to tighten its grip inexorably, and eventually remove Dubcek from office, carry out a massive purge and rescind the liberalising reforms of 1968. However, it was not the popular nonviolent resistance as such that failed, but the political leadership which did not appreciate its scope and potential, and therefore made a settlement that was much more disadvantageous to the Czechoslovak side than it need have been.[30] Once the Moscow Accords had been signed, the resistance could only have been continued at the price of a rift in the unity of the campaign, something which the Czechoslovaks were understandably anxious to avoid.

It is a matter of judgement whether and under what circumstances civil resistance could defeat the attempts of a dictatorial opponent to impose its will on a people through an occupation or the establishment of a client regime. But it is clear that authoritarian regimes are not impervious to the pressures of civil resistance, that significant successes have been achieved in the past, and that divisions can open up within states, however apparently monolithic. Further study is needed of the weaknesses and vulnerabilities of dictatorial regimes so that a more effective civil resistance strategy can be developed in face of threats or attack from them.

Repression

The question of how a resistance can be sustained in the face of severe repression is closely bound up with the above discussion, since dictatorial and totalitarian regimes tend to deal ruthlessly with opposition of any kind. German response to open defiance was usually severe, involving arrest, police trials, deportations and summary executions. As a result openly defiant actions were generally of short duration. Extreme measures, like the reprisals for the assassination of Heydrich in Czechoslovakia, achieved a period of sullen and resentful compliance, but overall the repression in occupied Europe served to increase the hatred of, and opposition to, the Axis powers. Non-compliance also took forms that were less easy to trace and punish — the go-slows, obstructions, administrative sabotage and so on. Haestrup gives one example from Denmark where a German minesweeper took 26 months to be built instead of the normal 9 months and in the end never did go into service because of successive acts of sabotage.[31]

Occasionally mutiny and disaffection may deprive a regime of the means of carrying out repression, whether the regime is an occupying power or an internal dictatorial regime. In the Iranian agitation of 1978–9, during which some 10,000 people are estimated to have lost their lives, the armed forces were at first loyal to the Shah. However, defections were reported during the latter part of 1978, mainly in the Air Force, and as the unrest continued disaffection spread until in February 1979 the heads of the armed forces declared their neutrality and recalled their men to barracks.[32]

In the case of foreign invasion and occupation, however, there is usually less contact between the population and the forces involved, and there may be barriers of language, culture and ideology. Moreover it is more difficult for the individual soldier to melt into the population and avoid detection and punishment.

Units and individual soldiers in an army of occupation have refused orders to fire on unarmed crowds, but this, if it happens at all, is unlikely to be on a scale sufficient to render a policy of repression inoperable. On the other hand mass nonviolent resistance to invasion and occupation would create a dramatic and unusual situation in which many of the normal expectations would be overturned, and in the longer term at least the repression might be blunted. However, while the repression continues it may be necessary to use less overt forms of resistance while efforts are made to divide the opponent and bring international pressure to bear.

In principle extreme repression can always be applied; in practice its extent and ruthlessness can be influenced by the tactics and strategy of the resistance. Civil resistance which avoids the use of violence is less likely to encourage violent reprisals and increases the moral and political cost of using brutality. Its tendency is to inhibit violence by the opponent, though of course there is no guarantee that it will always succeed in doing so.

VII. *Civil resistance as a substitute for military defence and the process of transition*

Two important reasons for Britain or Western Europe relying substantially on civil resistance for defence are that a major conventional war fought with modern weapons would be immensely destructive and that there would be a serious risk of any such war escalating to the nuclear level. But this in itself does not tell us anything about the viability of alternatives, or about the strengths and limitations of civil resistance as a defence policy.

Civil resistance is, generally speaking, a form of protracted struggle, particularly suited to defending moral, political and cultural values. But in terms of the other roles that a defence policy is normally expected to play it has limitations. The sanctions that it invokes tend to be cumulative and slow-acting rather than swift and decisive, so that it may not be able to prevent the forcible seizure of territory or attacks upon communities or individuals. In general it is not good at defending territory or recovering it quickly, though it will aim to do so over time through political pressure interspersed with mass direct action. It cannot easily protect interests outside the national territory, for instance to ensure supplies of raw materials. Finally it does not readily lend itself to bi-lateral or multi-lateral defence arrangements which, in a military context, may provide collective security.

These limitations do not rule out the notion of a defence based solely on civil resistance. Any defence strategy will be better at doing some things than others, and in choosing a given strategy one is in effect making a statement about defence priorities. Thus by opting for civil resistance, or making this the main feature of defence, one would be giving priority to the maintenance of ideas and values and saying that these are what it is most important to defend.

Two different approaches can be adopted to try to make good the deficiencies of defence by civil resistance. One, obviously, is to think of combining it with forms of military defence — an option that we consider in the next section. The other is to imagine new concepts and structures within a non-military framework.

Possibilities for extending civil resistance

A specially trained and equipped nonviolent force or 'peace army', supported by the state or by regional and local bodies, could form a spearhead of resistance in time of attack and carry out peacekeeping work and constructive activities, or be assigned to the UN, under more normal circumstances. Such a body was in fact proposed by Gandhi for India shortly before his death, and a peace army, the 'Shanti Sena', was subsequently established under voluntary control. This body intervened successfully in several communal riots and provided a corps of workers for the campaign against government corruption led by Jayaprakash Narayan in the early 1970s.[33] With proper funding and means of transport, such a body might cross national frontiers to support allied countries under attack, send large numbers of resisters to obstruct the occupation of remote but strategically important locations, or send a nonviolent armada to defy a blockade. Here we are moving away from the notion of resistance conducted solely by the civilian population to a broader concept of nonviolent defence in which the resistance by civilians would be spearheaded by specially trained nonviolent forces who could be moved quickly to deal with emergencies. We return to this idea later, to the possible role of a trained corps in UN peace-keeping operations, and to ways in which mutual security arrangements in a nonviolent context might be strengthened.

The process of transition

Britain is of course a long way from even considering a defence system based solely on nonviolent resistance; it is not a defence option at the present time in the sense that strengthening territorial forces as a *quid pro quo* for jettisoning nuclear weapons is an option. But the fact that it could not be instituted overnight means that one has to think in terms of a process of transition and acclimatisation in which civil resistance would come to be accorded an increasingly important place in defence policy. This process is sometimes referred to as transarmament, to indicate that the intention is not to weaken the defence of the country but to meet at least certain security needs in a different way.[34]

In practice transarmament is bound to be accompanied also by debate and confrontation between advocates of different policies, among them people committed to a totally nonviolent approach. And in fact the process of change requires there to be people with this kind of commitment who can maintain pressure for the adoption of nonviolent methods and who illustrate its possibilities by their activities. In this sense the existence of organisations and groups 'demanding the impossible' is essential to the process of broadening the options that are available to society. Transarmament then is likely to be a dialectical process. It could be, for instance, that mass direct action will by example contribute most to the process of acclimatisation, and that the capacity for civil resistance by society will develop from below. Official recognition of the notion and interest in its possibilities might not come until a much later stage following a change or several changes of government.

Because change is bound to take time, the question of how far the process should go can be to some extent left open-ended. However, one does then have to consider what changes in the existing defence arrangements ought to be regarded as steps along the way. We return to this in the next section dealing with mixed military and nonviolent strategies.

VIII. Combining military and nonviolent strategies

Two sets of questions are central to this discussion. (1) Does the moral basis and social dynamic of civil resistance allow it to be combined with military methods? (2) If there is a mixed strategy, what are the most appropriate military forms to operate in conjunction with civil resistance, and what would be the organisational and other links between the two methods? Chapter 8 discusses questions about the relationship between military and non-military forms of defence if, in the long term, a total changeover to civil resistance is envisaged.

Can civil resistance be combined with military methods?

Civil resistance may be supported for a variety of reasons and from various moral and political perspectives. Pacifists, who reject any resort to organised lethal violence, might welcome any shift in defence policy which substantially reduced reliance on military means and granted a significant role to civil resistance. For all the contradictions and incompatibilities they may see within such a policy, the move itself would open up debate and could begin a process of more radical change.

Support for civil resistance need not imply commitment to a pacifist ethic. It is possible to believe that in some circumstances the use of military force is justified while acknowledging the value of refraining from violence even in self-defence in the particular social context of an organized campaign of civil resistance. From this perspective there would then be no moral problem about combining nonviolent and military defence in some way — the question would be a strategic and tactical one.

The tactical and strategic calculations are complicated by the fact that civil resistance operates at a variety of levels, and may be adopted for different reasons. If it is chiefly seen as a means of obstruction and harassment, it could fit in very well with a strategy that included conventional or guerrilla warfare, though one would still have to take into account that in a state of warfare, reprisals against civilians would be more likely. If on the other hand the moral and psychological impact of civil resistance is emphasised, and in particular the impact of disciplined nonviolence on the morale of the opponent's armed forces and administrators, then the value of combining civil and military resistance is more questionable. But even where the nonviolent aspect is emphasised, one might not want to rule out altogether the idea of a mixed strategy, though one would need to look carefully at the form that military resistance took and at the relationship between it and the civil resistance.

How could military and civil resistance be combined?

Having a defence policy with both military and nonviolent elements in it does not necessarily commit one to using a mixed strategy in the event of conflict: sometimes one form of resistance may be more appropriate than another; sometimes one may be followed by another; and sometimes, perhaps, the two can occur simultaneously in different areas, organised separately. The role of the military forces could, for instance, generally be protecting fishing and mineral rights, ensuring internal security, and resisting small or medium-scale incursions. In the event of a massive attack, however, or of nuclear blackmail, accepting occupation but responding with a well planned civil resistance could provide an alternative to capitulation.

An obvious scenario might follow approximately the sequence of events in Norway in World War II. The Norwegian forces capitulated and the British Expeditionary Forces withdrew in 1940; later the occupation was faced with civil resistance. A military defeat obviously runs the risk of demoralisation — the Norwegians were, in the words of one account, "on the verge of surrender"[35] — and in these circumstances civil resistance may have to begin in far from ideal conditions. On the other hand, a heroic military defeat may boost morale, like the Dunkirk episode or the Finnish resistance to Soviet aggression in 1939. If it was clear from the start that the function of military resistance was chiefly to deter attack but that successfully resisting an all-out invasion by a super-power was not possible, then military defeat in some circumstances might be more readily accepted.

Another role that has been suggested for civil resistance would involve the simultaneous use of military and civil resistance; this is where defence in depth is being conducted in the countryside and villages but where the towns and cities would be declared non-military zones and would offer only nonviolent resistance to occupying forces. In these circumstances the civilians undertaking resistance would be more at risk than where there was no military resistance or where it was only a marginal factor. This fact might make it advisable to avoid, for instance, large-scale demonstrations which could lead to bloodshed, and to concentrate on symbolic protests, strikes, go-slows or other forms of passive resistance.

In the previous chapter we touched upon the possibility of combining civil and guerrilla resistance in the long-term struggle against occupation. This form of mixed strategy seems at first sight an obvious one, since the two methods share many political and strategic assumptions about conducting protracted resistance. Moreover, guerrilla and civil resistance have frequently occurred in parallel, though not necessarily under a unified direction. In Norway during the German occupation, Milorg and Sivorg, which co-ordinated respectively the military and civil resistance, remained organisationally distinct. Guerrilla attacks can have a symbolic and mobilising function, convincing the population that the established order is neither pre-ordained nor indestructible and thus encouraging civil resistance. In occupied Denmark there is evidence that it was generally the violent resistance that sparked off the civil resistance, not the other way round,[36] though there as in Norway the military resistance was restrained and consisted mainly of acts of sabotage. Guerrilla and civil resistance occurred together (though usually with the guerrilla warfare being dominant) in Ireland in the independence struggle, in Cuba (where a general strike was timed to coincide with the arrival of Castro's forces in Havana), in Algeria in the struggle against French colonialism, in Nicaragua in the campaign that ousted Somoza, in various parts of occupied Europe, and in many other instances.

But there can be drawbacks to a strategy of combining armed and civil resistance. Civil resistance is more likely to be sustained and to achieve a certain psychological and moral impact in situations where there is an absence of generalised violence. It often depends on a reluctance by the authorities to resort to wholesale repression, a reluctance that may itself spring from an uncertainty about the effect on the morale of their troops and security forces of being ordered to attack civilians. But these inhibitions and constraints can quickly break down where there is the constant danger of ambushes, assassinations, bomb attacks and so on, and above all where the distinction between combatant and non-combatant begins to disappear.

Again much depends on what one is looking to civil resistance to achieve and on the strategic context of the resistance. In terms of maximising physical disruption in the short term, combining civil and guerrilla resistance would be the most effective approach, and it made sense militarily to do this for instance when resistance was timed to occur in conjunction with Allied offensives during World War II. However, if there is no possibility of rescue from outside or of seizing the military initiative so as to limit the risks to the civilian population, there is a strong case for avoiding action that would lower the threshold on the use of violent reprisals by the opponent.

Civil resistance involves the population *as civilians* refusing their co-operation as a way of pressing for political and economic rights, and self-determination, and its success may depend crucially on the distinction between the status of civilians and combatants being kept very clear. Protracted guerrilla warfare however, especially in an urban setting, tends to break down that distinction. This arguably is the strategic contradiction at the heart of trying to combine guerrilla and civil resistance. They will often occur together simply because people respond to intolerable situations in different ways, but this does not mean that it is a sound strategy deliberately to combine them.

However, some of these objections would not apply, or would apply less forcibly, where the guerrilla activity was kept deliberately low-key, perhaps confined to acts of sabotage against military and industrial targets, or targets of special symbolic significance, meticulously avoiding political terrorism. Such activity might help, as in Denmark, to spark off or sustain resistance, and provide dramatic evidence to the population and the outside world of continuing opposition during periods when civil resistance had to take less visible forms.

IX. *Defence of Britain by civil resistance*

The advantages of a strategy for Britain of relying solely on civil resistance are considerable: Britain would pose no military threat; attempts at nuclear blackmail would be blatantly unjustifiable. Defence by civil resistance would aim to provide a disincentive to attack, but if it did nonetheless occur, the destruction and loss of life would be much smaller than with any kind of military resistance, and of course infinitely less than with nuclear war. It would cost much less, and this would release resources to build a sounder domestic economic structure and to undertake positive peace-making tasks at the international level. Another advantage of civil resistance is that it can draw upon almost all sectors of the population, mobilising the skills and commitment of those normally excluded from armed service, for example women of all ages and older men.

Some of the disadvantages and limitations have also been touched upon. Its deterrent or dissuasive capacity remains uncertain; for this reason, and because it involves a radical departure in ways of thinking about security, it is more difficult to present to people as a convincing alternative on its own. It involves being prepared to endure if necessary a military occupation and engage in a prolonged struggle. It is less well suited than military methods for certain defence tasks, such as ensuring the security of outlying areas of possible strategic importance to an opponent, and it does not easily lend itself to arrangements for collective security.

Some of these limitations are particularly relevant to Britain. An opponent able to mount an effective blockade to cripple the economy might not need to invade in order to force concessions from a British government. Nonviolent methods of running the blockade might be devised, but the opponent would be in a much stronger position than in trying to rule directly a population that was refusing to co-operate. Britain would be unlikely to achieve success using military methods to break a blockade by a major power, but the military argument here is that if Britain contributed to the effective defence of Europe the Soviet Union would be less likely to be in a position to impose a blockade in the first place. Furthermore, it is argued, since there is no obvious nonviolent equivalent to a collective security arrangement, a disarmed Britain would be sheltering behind the defences of the rest of Europe and its preparations for civil resistance would be largely irrelevant.

These arguments have some weight. However, mutual assistance is possible within the framework of defence by civil resistance even if it cannot take as strong a form as that of a military alliance. A mutual aid agreement for civil resistance would be roughly equivalent to the form of military agreements that fall short of an alliance with an integrated command structure and troops stationed outside the territory of some member states; thus, each country could be mainly responsible for its own defence, though pledged to support each other in specific ways in the event of an attack; this is the kind of loose structure that would be suitable if in-depth defence by territorial or militia forces became the dominant strategy in a number of states.

Within that kind of structure a country which shifted the emphasis of its self-defence decisively in a non-military direction would not necessarily be regarded by the other states as having opted out of its responsibilities, especially as the debate on the viability of civil resistance has a European dimension and by the time any one state is in a position to opt for civil resistance as the main element in a defence strategy, it is likely that several other European states will have moved some way along the same path. In a transition stage one can envisage a loose security pact which had both military and non-military dimensions, with some states pledging and asking in return only non-military forms of support, and others agreeing to support each other militarily.

A blockade would present a formidable problem for Britain if the Soviet Union controlled Western Europe. However, there are limit-ations to a blockade, as there are with any economic sanctions. As a prelude to invasion, a blockade is a powerful instrument. As an *alternative* to invasion, i.e. as a means of indirectly manipulating the policy of a country, it has serious disadvantages. It takes time to operate; the interruption in trade tends to injure both parties, and it is not something one can keep applying and lifting every time the country that is the object of pressure steps out of line.

If the Soviet Union had occupied Western Europe, a blockade of Britain would have repercussions throughout Europe and could multiply the problems that the USSR would surely already have in trying to control such a large and densely populated area. Prior agreements for mutual assistance could have some effect. If Britain was, for instance, providing a sanctuary for governments in exile as well as broadcasting and other facilities for the opposition move-ments in Europe, then perhaps these movements would threaten to escalate their campaign in the event of an attempt to blockade Britain.

If serious preparations had been made in Western European countries for prolonged civil resistance (possibly alongside the military defence system), Soviet control might be extremely shaky and the formal extension of its power prove in practice to be a dangerous weakness. Thus the political upheaval that would accompany a Soviet drive across Europe, and the vast over-extension of its forces, could provide the opportunity for Poland, Czecho-slovakia and other countries in Eastern Europe to loosen Soviet control; indeed unrest might easily spread to the Baltic States and other non-Russian republics in the USSR. If anything this would be more likely to occur if Soviet expansion was met purely with non-military resistance, since a war by creating a common danger tends to cement alliances. Thus the political disincentives to the Soviet Union launching an attack on a Western Europe that had reached the point of making thorough preparations for civil resistance could be powerful.

One strategic consideration that might lead a country to opt on pragmatic grounds for civil resistance as a defence policy does not apply to Britain, that is an inability to mount anything more than a token military defence. This, approximately, was the position of Denmark in relation to Nazi Germany in the late 1930s. Britain has the industrial muscle and military experience and hardware to inflict a high cost on an invader. On the other hand, the relationship of forces if Britain alone faced an all-out attack by a superpower such as the Soviet Union would be so unequal that opting for civil resistance might be both more prudent and more effective.

Another consideration concerns the likely reason for an attack on Britain. If the aim was to seize certain assets like ports and military bases of strategic importance (or of potential strategic importance to the other side), then civil resistance would probably not be effective, at any rate in the short run. This point would apply particularly if some of the remoter outlying areas were involved, for instance the Shetlands, which could be seized without any attempt to occupy the whole country.

Finally it is obvious that if Britain opted for defence by civil resistance it would not be able to give proper protection to overseas dependencies, such as the Falklands, Hong Kong and Gibraltar, or former colonies such as Belize with whom we have defence agreements. However, even if Britain retains very considerable military forces, its capacity to defend overseas territories is likely to diminish, as we pointed out in Chapter 1.

The limitations of defence by civil resistance point to the case that can be made for retaining at least some element of military defence. How important a role preparations for civil resistance would then have in the overall defence plan would depend on a number of factors: whether it is viewed only as a last resort or as a preferable option to either in-depth defence or guerrilla warfare; and whether civil resistance is taken seriously as an option should Britain be faced by overwhelming military power or the threat of nuclear attack. The case for adopting civil resistance depends also on whether British political and social conditions are suitable to a civil resistance strategy and whether convincing plans for conducting it can be developed.[37] It is to these questions we now turn.

Is British society suited to civil resistance?

It can be argued that the most successful examples of civil resistance to military occupation are drawn from small states with a socially homogeneous population which is relatively united in its political values. Thus the most impressive examples of civil resistance to Nazi rule come from Norway, Denmark and Holland. In contrast, France was deeply divided between collaborators and those who supported the resistance; and the resistance in turn was split between contending political groups. India, of course, was neither small nor homogeneous, a fact reflected in its eventual partition, though in this case the civil resistance was directed not against a recently established occupation force but against an entrenched colonial power.

In these terms British society is far from ideal for a strategy of civil resistance. Britain is still a deeply class-divided society. Moreover a young generation now experiencing mass unemployment may be especially alienated from the traditional values and institutions of British society, as the rioting in the summer of 1981 in many decaying inner city areas demonstrated; these social divisions overlap with the ethnic divisions in British cities and towns. There is also a tendency in some sectors of the community to reject central organisational authority or reliance on individual leaders and this could create difficulties for a national resistance council seeking a coherent and unified strategy.

The existence of a separate national consciousness in Scotland and Wales is also a potential source of difficulty for any attempt at a co-ordinated policy of civil resistance for Britain as a whole. These divisions may prevent a unity of goals and organisation, and could tempt an occupying power to try to buy off opposition by concessions to the national groups. The role of the Slovaks following the Soviet occupation of Czechoslovakia may illustrate how separate national consciousness and interests can prevent unity in civil resistance. The political and practical difficulties of co-ordinating a joint resistance between mainland Britain and Northern Ireland would be so great that it would almost certainly be necessary to devolve responsibility for non-military resistance to the Protestant and Catholic communities in Northern Ireland.

Some radical pacifist critics of the notion of civil resistance as the defence policy of the state and Government also argue that it could not function in a society as divided, hierarchical and unjust as that in Britain. Their conclusion however is not that nonviolent methods should be rejected in favour of military ones but that they should be used in the first instance to transform existing society and to defend social gains against any attack whether coming from inside or outside the national territory. Nonviolent social defence is the term sometimes used to describe this approach, emphasising that it is not the nation-state itself that needs to be defended but values, freedoms and autonomous institutions created from below.

Nonetheless there are times in history when the immediately important task is to resist foreign invasion and domination as the precondition for defending and extending social gains. And where this is true, the pressure for people to unite in a common cause in spite of serious political, social and cultural divisions is strong. Moreover, the continued strength of nationalist sentiment ought not to be underestimated; if so much fervour could be generated over the Argentinian military takeover of the Falkland Islands 8,000 miles away in April 1982, how much stronger would be the reaction if part of mainland Britain were to be occupied?

Many aspects of British experience, and some contemporary developments, favour the adoption of a defence by civil resistance. This country has a long tradition, established to a great extent by struggle and agitation from below, of democracy and with it the habit of voluntary organisation and local initiative. It has an unusually strong tradition of trade union organisation and activism, and it has experienced a large number of movements of popular resistance incorporating forms of direct action and civil disobedience. Moreover, during the last twenty years there has been a great increase in movements relying primarily on forms of nonviolent resistance, including environmentalist campaigns, rent strikes and squatting, widespread non-co-operation and civil disobedience by Welsh nationalists, and nonviolent direct action by the peace movement.

The move away from reliance on established forms of authority and the suspicion of national leadership also has positive benefits, if it takes the form of an unwillingness to obey an occupation regime and of self-reliance on local initiative. Too much popular trust in individual representatives or leaders can undermine rather than promote resistance, if these leaders themselves compromise with an occupying power.

How far existing national or social divisions would undermine resistance to an occupying power depends on several factors. First, it depends on whether different groups and factions would respond to the occupation by a willingness to work together on the basis of a demand for independence and autonomy, and accept whatever discipline was necessary for an effective struggle.

Second, it would depend on the nature of the occupying power. A United States intervention to prevent a major change in British defence policy (which would in any case probably take the form of manipulation rather than direct military intervention) could split British society on a right versus left basis. But a Soviet attack and occupation could be expected to unite the majority of the population against the occupying force. No doubt the Soviet Union could find a few collaborators on an ideological basis, and rather more operating out of self-interest or a conviction that they should help to keep the society functioning, but there would be no significant political or social support for a Soviet-imposed regime. In this sense a Soviet-occupied Britain would not be comparable to occupied and Vichy France, although in the case of US intervention the analogy might be more exact.

Third, the organisational structure of the resistance could be geared to resolve or minimise some forms of disunity; for example resistance organisations in Scotland and Wales could be partially or wholly autonomous. Almost inevitably too, organisations and groups participating in the overall campaign of resistance would have considerable freedom of action; the function of any national or regional Resistance Council would be to hammer out agreed strategies wherever possible, so that local initiatives, or initiatives by particular groups, would fit into a broader pattern of activity. On some occasions initiatives from below would be a signal to the Regional and National Resistance Councils of new possibilities.

Unity in a population is always a relative concept. Even the cohesive societies of Norway and Denmark had small pro-Nazi parties before and during the occupation. Moreover, while unity is something to be striven for in a civil resistance campaign, it is not a *sine qua non* for success. In occupied Denmark political differences, and differences over questions of strategy, led to the successive formation of two resistance councils, the *Council of Nine* which was an all-party parliamentary group leading the 'indirect' resistance from July 1940 on, and the *Freedom Council*, a seven-person coordinating committee which organised sabotage from September 1943 on, but which also helped to guide two major episodes of spontaneous nonviolent action — the rescue of 95% of Danish Jews by spiriting them away to Sweden in October 1943, and the nine-day General Strike in Copenhagen in July 1944. Upon the surrender of German forces in Denmark in May 1945 a Danish Cabinet was reinstated with leadership drawn from both the Council of Nine and the Freedom Council.[38]

It is important to distinguish in any conflict between positive and negative goals. Provided there was unity or a broad consensus over the negative goal of ending occupation and foreign rule, very wide differences over the positive social and political goals of the liberation struggle would exist without constituting a fatal weakness. The positive goals would develop and mature in the course of the struggle, as happened in many countries during World War II resulting in a swing to the Left in much of post-war Europe. Even where there are fundamental divisions in society, united action by key sectors may still be effective, a point underlined by the role of the power workers in the 1974 strike in Northern Ireland that brought down the power-sharing executive.[39]

Organisational aspects

The organisational requirements for advance planning and co-ordinating civil resistance in Britain need detailed investigation; here we confine ourselves to a few suggestions aimed at encouraging discussion and the development of more precise plans.

Our assumption is that the base for civil resistance would be existing political trade union, cultural and religious bodies. It would make sense for these to be brought together in a Co-ordinating Committee for Civil Resistance similar to the body set up in Norway at the beginning of the German occupation on which many independent organisations were represented to co-ordinate their opposition to the creation of a corporate state on National Socialist lines. In the UK, separate national committees would probably be needed for Wales, Scotland, Northern Ireland and England, and indeed the aim should be to create a network of organisations at regional and local level.

In addition one would need a quasi-official body that would act as a link between the organisations of the base and the central government and parliament — some kind of Civil Resistance Council. This could be a semi-autonomous body with an independent director which would liaise with the Cabinet and present an annual report for debate in Parliament. This would probably be preferable to setting up a government department, or a body that was directly subordinate to an existing department such as the Ministry of Defence, since it would be important to ensure that the Council retained a capacity for spontaneous initiative and planning.

In the event of an occupation, the key considerations would be the need to maintain a government with a strong claim to legitimacy, probably in the form of a government in exile; the need for an authoritative decision-making body inside the country to co-ordinate resistance on the spot; and the need for a balance between central-isation and devolution in the resistance.

Advance plans should be made to set up a government in exile in a country sympathetic to Britain's adoption of a non-nuclear defence policy. This might be a Commonwealth country which might also be asked to accept political refugees and provide facilities such as broadcasting stations. A government in exile would be responsible for mobilising international support, making clear the illegitimacy of any client regime that was established, collecting funds to aid the internal resistance, and representing the British people at the United Nations or other international bodies.

The primary and long-term responsibility for organising resistance within the country would, however, rest with the Civil Resistance Council, acting in close conjunction with the network of committees that had been established. The Council would presumably have to work underground and it might be necessary to enlarge it to give it a more representative character.

These are the kinds of structure and arrangement one should probably aim for. They assume that, at least in the initial stages of resistance, there are advantages to central planning and co-ordination, though this kind of centralisation is compatible with a considerable degree of individual and local initiative, and indeed the network structure of regional and local committees allows for initiatives from below in response to particular circumstances.

Mutual security in a nonviolent context: a European Treaty Organisation and other proposals

Civil resistance is *par excellence* a defensive strategy; it normally comes into operation precisely at the point that unacceptable demands are being made upon a society. The corollary of that, however, is that, like territorial defence, it can exert only limited pressure on behalf of others. It could easily therefore become iso-lationist in its political thrust. Yet the motivation and vision of the concept of nonviolence is strongly internationalist, and it is important to consider ways in which civil resistance could be extended to contribute to collective security and meet obligations to people in other societies under attack.

The internationalist commitment can be signalled by allocating resources to world economic development. Funds and resources would become available if a programme of radical disarmament was adopted, and some at least of the pressures for maintaining the present inequitable structure in the global economy would be removed. Major political and diplomatic initiatives could also be undertaken to secure new political agreements, especially in Europe, to lower international tensions and achieve measures of detente and disarmament, and Britain could give more active support to such bodies as the United Nations and the International Court of Justice.

But Britain could also pledge direct help of various kinds to countries faced with aggression, and in the first instance to those with whom it has especially close ties, such as the countries of Western Europe and the Commonwealth. Sir Stephen King-Hall proposed a European Treaty Organisation (ETO) comprising Western states committed to a nonviolent form of defence.[40] He argued that its defence plans should be determined by the following principles: (1) the main foundation of its strategy should be switched from reliance on armed force to reliance on political and moral force; (2) these political and moral forces would be organised to operate in three theatres — the home fronts; the uncommitted nations' fronts and the enemy fronts. The object on the home fronts would be to create a sense of democratic unity among the ETO peoples and also to train and prepare them for nonviolent resistance in the event of an enemy occupation; the object of the uncommitted nations' fronts would be ''to win those nations for the free way of life and encourage them to resist penetration by Communist ideology''; the object on the enemy fronts would be ''the creation of pro-democratic opinion in the Soviet Union and satellite states''; (3) ETO states would maintain conventional forces sufficient to maintain internal security; (4) as an interim measure the conventional forces should be large enough ''to put up a token resistance to Russian non-nuclear armed aggression across ETO frontiers''.

One does not have to endorse completely all of King-Hall's underlying assumptions to find interesting and challenging his suggestion for a European defence association centred on a strategy of nonviolent defence, and his approach to the problem of transition at the European level. Thus if NATO, or an alternative European alliance, did begin to move towards a non-nuclear strategy in Europe following British nuclear disarmament, this approach of maintaining sufficient forces to put up a token resistance while concentrating on building up the capacity for nonviolent resistance is an alternative to either increasing conventional forces or backing these up with a major programme of in-depth defence. King-Hall also envisaged that the conventional forces retained by ETO countries would be highly mobile and could provide contingents for UN operations.

Direct help of a non-military kind could also be given to a country under attack, including providing a base for a government in exile; accepting political and other refugees; sending in equipment such as transmitters and printing equipment; sending in personnel with special skills and experience relevant to civil resistance; providing broadcasting and other facilities to governments and resistance movements in exile; actively seeking to subvert the government that had initiated the aggression. Economic and other sanctions could also be taken against the aggressor state.

However, if in addition countries adopting defence by civil resistance were to train special mobile Nonviolent Action Corps, this could broaden the scope of international action. There could be direct action on a dramatic scale with thousands of resisters, where appropriate, going into an aggressor state. There is in fact one precedent for this kind of 'unarmed invasion' which took place in 1955 when several thousand Indian nonviolent activists crossed the borders into the Portuguese enclaves of Goa, Daman and Diu in an unsuccessful attempt to secure their liberation.[41] In other circumstances more symbolic forms of action would be appropriate, such as flying an international team, including well known and respected individuals, into a city or area threatened with bombardment to act as a kind of voluntary hostage team. Clearly in some situations steps of this kind would not be as effective as military action; on the other hand they could be a means of exerting pressure in situations where the risks of using military force would be too great.

Mutual security agreements involving forms of nonviolent action need not of course be confined to Europe. King-Hall himself suggested the possibility of a similar Asian Treaty Organisation. Britain might also conclude agreements with Commonwealth countries, or the Commonwealth as such might be the basis of a non-military defence association .

If Britain moved to a non-military, or mainly non-military, system of defence but had trained nonviolent forces at its disposal, these could also be put at the disposal of the United Nations for peacekeeping operations. Since the interventions in Korea and Katanga, UN operations have generally aimed to provide a buffer force between contending parties and been armed only with light weapons for self-protection. Their effectiveness derives not from the fact that they are an armed force, since they would not be in a position to withstand a major attack, but from their political and moral authority as representatives of the United Nations and as members of the armed forces of the contributing states. The notion of unarmed peace-keeping forces has been proposed from time to time, and if trained people were available this idea could be put to the test.

It is in ways such as these that the international dimension of non-violent defence could be extended.

X. *Summary of the argument*

Civil resistance operates by virtue of the fact that governments and economic systems require the compliance of the majority of the population. With the integration of national and international economies brought about by industrialisation, and with improved communications, education and political literacy, its potential in regulating power within and between states has increased. Civil resistance can also exert a powerful moral and psychological impact where there is a commitment to nonviolence or a courageous refraining from the use of violence.

Civil resistance has played an important role in anti-colonial struggles, in thwarting attempted coups, in resisting dictatorships, and in opposing military invasion and occupation. Thus it has been used with varying degrees of success in situations where armed struggle and military defence are traditionally employed.

As a total substitute for military defence it has limitations. Its capacity to deter attack is uncertain. Nevertheless well laid and publicised plans for civil resistance could provide a powerful dis-incentive to an attempt to take over a country, particularly in Europe, where the problems of holding down and controlling a very large and populous area are already well understood. But it involves a willingness to accept the possibility of occupation and endure the hazards and suffering of a prolonged struggle. There is no guarantee that it will prove successful against a repressive or dictatorial opponent, although it has sometimes produced results in the face of extreme repression. It is not well adapted to meeting limited threats to outlying areas which might be of strategic importance and it provides less scope than military defence for collective security arrangements.

However, there are moral and strategic reasons in favour of opting for a system of defence by civil resistance. A country that had renounced nuclear weapons would ultimately be vulnerable against a nuclear superpower prepared to use its nuclear weapons; a major conventional war in Europe would be immensely destructive and might escalate to the nuclear level; the inherent political and economic disincentives to a Soviet attempt to take over Western Europe would be enhanced by preparations for civil resistance, and if an occupation did take place there would be at least a reasonable prospect of conducting a successful struggle for emancipation; and radical disarmament would release resources and provide opportunities for positive peace-making. Choosing this option could also reflect the conviction that alternatives to resorting to war, and preparations for war, must be explored, even though this is bound to involve risks.

Alternatively civil resistance could provide a parallel or back-up system to military defence, enhancing deterrence by making the task of retaining control in occupied territory more difficult. Its relative importance in the overall defence system would depend on the role it was expected to play. If it was regarded simply as a last-ditch resort in the event of military resistance being unsuccessful, it would probably remain a relatively marginal element in the defence system. But it could become more central to the policy if it was seen as a serious alternative to using military force in particular circumstances or against particular types of threat, for instance where a country is faced with overwhelming odds or threatened with nuclear attack, or as a complementary strategy to military resistance, for example as a way of obstructing the control of cities that had been declared non-combat zones and occupied by the opponent's forces.

There are problems about a defence strategy involving both armed and nonviolent resistance, especially if one attaches importance to the moral and psychological impact of a nonviolent approach. But making preparations for both kinds of resistance would permit a choice of using one or the other according to circumstances, or for military resistance to be followed by civil resistance. It seems desirable, however, for the military and civil resistance to be kept organisationally separate; the two might also be separated in terms of place and time.

The strategic position in which a nuclear-disarmed Britain would find itself does favour in some respects the adoption of defence by civil resistance. On the other hand, some of the limitations of this approach are relevant in the British context, especially if the probable motive for an attack is thought to be the seizure of locations of strategic importance.

British society is in some ways not ideal for a policy of civil resistance because of the social and economic divisions, and the divisions related to nationality (English, Welsh, Scottish and Irish) and race. But the organisational structure for conducting civil resistance could take account of some of these divisions, and there might also be a coming together of different groups and interests in face of a common danger. The strength of the democratic tradition, and especially the tradition and experience of independent political, trade union, cultural and religious organisations, are positive and important factors. A few preliminary suggestions for an organisational framework for preparing defence by civil resistance have been put forward.

Finally the international dimensions of a policy of defence by civil resistance have been briefly considered, including the suggestion for a mutual aid agreement between European or other states committed to this approach, and the training of special unarmed forces which could support resistance in Britain or in other countries, and could be put at the disposal of the United Nations for peacekeeping operations.

XI. *Conclusions*

The Commission agreed that civil resistance had potentially a significant contribution to make to the defence of the country and favoured further research into its possible role in the British and European context. Government backing for such research, at least at the level at which this has already occurred in Holland and Sweden, is desirable, not only because funding is important, but because this would indicate that the idea was being taken seriously at an official level.

A minority of the Commission favoured moving to a system of exclusively nonviolent defence, while recognising that the process of change would take time. This judgement was based on the moral and strategic considerations summarised in the previous section.

Most of the Commission, however, thought that a military capability was essential to defence, and that for the foreseeable future it would remain the predominant element. It was needed for a variety of reasons — to enable Britain to contribute significantly to the defence of Western Europe, to provide a deterrent that would be more credible than nonviolent defence, and to perform a number of tasks for which civil resistance was not particularly well suited, such as defending territory or protecting outlying areas like the Shetlands that might be of strategic interest to an opponent.

Nevertheless, it was agreed that civil resistance could have a significant and perhaps in time a major role. It could provide a fall-back strategy in case, for whatever reason, an occupation occurred, and it might also be seen as an option to be used in particular circumstances or against certain types of threat.

Notes to Chapter 7

1. Various terms have been proposed for this concept, usually with differing nuances of meaning. 'Defence by civil resistance' is adopted here because it is clear and relatively neutral. 'Nonviolent defence' might suggest too close an identification with a strictly pacifist approach, and 'civilian defence', a term which has been used in the past, has somewhat fallen into disfavour because of the frequent confusion with civil defence. 'Social defence' is the term widely used in Germany and France and is intended to convey the notion that this method can be used to defend social gains against internal threats as well as against external aggression; however its connotation in English is somewhat weak. The American scholar Gene Sharp has proposed 'civilian-based defence' and this term is now beginning to be more widely used in the United States; however, we felt that 'defence by civil resistance' would probably be more readily understood.

2. Several of these cases are discussed in *The Strategy of Civilian Defence*, A. Roberts, ed. (London: Faber and Faber, 1967). A Penguin edition of this book was published in 1969 under the title *Civilian Resistance as a National Defence: Non-Violent Action Against Aggression*, with a revised introduction by Adam Roberts taking into account the nonviolent resistance in Czechoslovakia to the Soviet and Warsaw Pact invasion of 1968. But as this version is out of print, references are given here to the earlier version. For a discussion of events in Poland during 1980 from the point of view of their significance for civil resistance, see R. Polet, *The Polish Summer* (London: War Resisters International, 1981). See also C. Arbor, *A Study of Civilian Defence*, MA Dissertation 1980, Bradford, University of Bradford, which examines the concept of nonviolent defence with particular reference to the resistance in Hungary in 1956 and Czechoslovakia in 1968. The Commission is grateful to Christine Arbor for a paper she wrote for us based on part of her dissertation. A research project on civil resistance in Denmark from 1940 to 1945 is being undertaken by Lennart Bergfeldt at the Department of Peace and Conflict Research, Uppsala University, Sweden. Again the Commission would like to thank Lennart Bergfeldt for sending us a copy of a draft chapter covering the period 1940–1943.

3. The idea of nonviolent defence goes back at least to 1852, when it was proposed by Elihu Burritt in the United States. In 1915 Bertrand Russell in his essay 'War and Non-Resistance', published in *Atlantic Monthly* in August of that year suggested that "after a generation of instruction in the principles of passive resistance", Britain might disband its armed forces and respond to any invasion with a campaign of non-co-operation. In the period between the two World Wars, writers like Aldous Huxley in Britain, Richard Gregg in the US, and Bart de Ligt in Holland, partly influenced by Gandhi's campaigns in India, made similar proposals.

4. Sir Stephen King-Hall, 'The Small Countries', *Free Denmark*, 1, 5 (August 1942)
   1. Cited by G. Keyes, 'Strategic Non-Violent Defense: The Construct of an
   Option', *Journal of Strategic Studies*, 4, 2 (June 1981), 125–51.
5. A key event was the international conference at St Hilda's College, Oxford, in
   1964 which led to the publication of Roberts's, *The Strategy of Civilian Defence*.[2]
   From the late 1960s onward, studies appeared in a number of countries, notably
   G. Sharp's *The Politics of Nonviolent Action* (Boston: Porter Sargent, 1973); A.
   Roberts's studies for the National Defence Research Institute, Stockholm, *Total
   Defence and Civilian Resistance* (1972), *The Technique of Civil Resistance* (1976), and
   Occupation, Resistance and Law (1980); A. Boserup and A. Mack's *War Without
   Weapons: Non-Violence in National Defence* (London: Francis Pinter, 1974)
   originally published in Danish and commissioned by the Danish government;
   and various essays and studies notably by Theodor Ebert (West Germany),
   Jean-Marie Muller (France), Johan Galtung (Norway) and Gene Sharp (USA).
6. In Holland, government interest goes back to 1974 when the defence paper 'On
   the Security of our Existence' included a government policy statement that
   attention would be given to the problems of social defence (defence by civil
   resistance). In 1977 the government set up a Commission charged with
   proposing a detailed research programme into nonviolent conflict resolution and
   defence by civil resistance. Its proposals were published in 1982, but only one of
   the ten projects it proposed is to be funded by the Dutch government, and the
   Commission itself was dissolved in May 1982. However, some of the other
   suggested projects may be backed by research institutes or universities.

   In Sweden, the studies by Adam Roberts[5] were commissioned by National
   Defence Research Institute. In 1972 the Swedish Ministry of Defence financed
   an International Conference in Uppsala on Non-Military Forms of Struggle.
   The most significant development, however, was the decision of the Swedish
   Cabinet in December 1980 (at the request of the Conservative Minister of
   Defence) to create a working body under a special investigator to present a
   proposal "for the tasks etc. for a Swedish non-military resistance as a
   complement to other total defence measures".

   Smaller initiatives have been taken by other European governments. In
   Norway, at the request of the Norwegian Cabinet, the Norwegian Defence
   Research Establishment prepared a 49-page report 'Non-Military Defence and
   Norwegian Security' which concluded that nonviolent forms of defence were not
   an alternative to military defence but that the potential of nonviolent means
   could not at that time be determined. (However, the Norwegian Defence
   Commission of 1974 in a brief section on defence by nonviolence concluded that
   it would lack the desired deterrent and defence capacity and might increase the
   chances of attack). In Denmark the study by Boserup, *War Without Weapons*[5] was
   prepared at the request of the Working Group on Disarmament Questions of the
   Foreign Ministry. Among the distinguished military men who have become
   advocates of a system of defence through nonviolent resistance is General de
   Bollardière in France.
7. C. Von Clausewitz, *On War*, J.J. Graham trans. (Harmondsworth: Penguin,
   1968), p. 119.
8. G. Sharp, *Social Power and Political Freedom* (Boston: Porter Sargent, 1980) has a
   chapter entitled ' "The Political Equivalent of War" ' — Civilian based
   Defense', pp. 195–261.
9. Numerous articles and books on the resistance in Czechoslovakia have appeared
   since 1968. See for instance A. Roberts and P. Windsor, *Czechoslovakia 1968:*

Reform Repression and Resistance (London: Chatto & Windus for the Institute for Strategic Studies, 1969) or Z. Mlynar, *Night Frost in Prague*, (London: Hurst, 1980).

10. The *Le Monde* correspondent in Poland in a report on 1 April 1982 stated that according to reliable sources some 1,700 clandestine broadsheets and bulletins were being published and as many clandestine groups existed to reproduce and distribute them. May 1982 also saw the resurgence of mass demonstrations in favour of Solidarity in Warsaw and several other Polish cities.

11. There is now a vast literature on the Indian Independence struggle which includes accounts and analyses of the Salt March. See for instance G. Sharp, *Gandhi Wields the Weapon of Moral Power: Three Case Histories* (Ahmedabad: Navajivan, 1960) and G. Sharp, *Gandhi as a Political Strategist* (Boston: Porter Sargent, 1979). Other titles are to be found in *Nonviolent Action: A Selected Bibliography*, A. Carter, D. Hoggett and A. Roberts (London: Housmans, 1970), though of course more has been written since this bibliography was published.

12. J. Haestrup, *Europe Ablaze* (Odense: Odense University Press, 1978), p. 132.

13. Haestrup, *Europe Ablaze*:[12] "The Axis powers had to live with the law that in the eyes of Europe they were ruthless invaders, and had to accept the conditions of invaders. Among these conditions was the dilemma that the captured territories were so vast, and the captured communities so complicated that the Occupying Powers had to seek support to a great extent in the machinery of society in the defeated countries, regardless of how reliable or unreliable they believed them to be. This applied to state as well as regional administration; it applied to the production apparatus; it applied to the transport system and communications network; and it applied to the forces of law and order. In principle, the Occupying Powers had to rely upon the assistance which, in spite of everything, was to be had from these citizens."

14. Haestrup, *Europe Ablaze*,[12] p. 90.

15. Keyes in 'Strategic Non-Violent Defense'[4] (p. 139) suggests that the German administrators by 1943 in the face of Danish national integrity had become somewhat half-hearted and allowed themselves to bungle the pogrom of the Jews in Denmark while the Danes carried out the rescue.

16. For further discussion of strategy in civil resistance see A. Roberts, 'Civilian Defence Strategy' in *The Strategy of Civilian Defence*;[2] Boserup & Mack, *War Without Weapons*,[5] who propose a strategic theory derived from Von Clausewitz and argue that unity is the 'centre of gravity' of civil resistance; Keyes, 'Strategic Non-Violent Defense',[4] whose approach is close to that of Boserup, but who argues that morale is the key factor for both the offence and the defence (rather than unity as such), and links this to the proposition that action from principle must be the core of a civil resistance campaign. Keyes sums up his view as follows: "the fast track to failure in nonviolent defense is to use tactics without strategy, strategy without principle, and principle without tenacity".

17. Keyes, 'Strategic Non-Violent Defense',[4] p. 136.

18. Sharp in *Social Power and Political Freedom*[8], p. 242. The phases of resistance, and the strategy appropriate to them, outlined here are based on Sharp's chapter "The Political Equivalent of War" — Civilian-based Defense'.

19. See Haestrup, *Europe Ablaze*,[12] pp. 129–31; G. Sharp, 'Tyranny Could Not Quell Them' (London: Peace News, 1963); T. Gjelsvik, *Norwegian Resistance, 1940–1945* (London: Hurst, 1979), especially chapter 3, 'The Struggle to Stand Fast'. For further titles see Carter *et al. Nonviolent Action*,[11] pp. 44–46.

20. See Keyes, 'Strategic Non-Violent Defense',[4] who discusses the problem of 'the weak majority' and the appropriate direction for nonviolent strategy to take in order to take account of it, pp. 139–40.

21 Haestrup, *Europe Ablaze*,[12] pp. 129–131

22. See A. Roberts, 'Civil Resistance to Military Coups', *Journal of Peace Research*, XII, 1 (1975), 19–36, which examines both the Kapp putsch and the Generals' revolt in Algiers.

23. Haestrup, *Europe Ablaze*,[12] p. 69.

24. M. R. D. Foot, *Resistance: An Analysis of European Resistance to Nazism, 1940–45* (London: Methuen, 1976), p. 239, notes that the Vichy regime in France did have overwhelming support among the population at first but that the situation had completely changed by the later stages of the war.

25. See Haestrup, *Europe Ablaze*,[12] pp. 101–4 for accounts of both the students' strikes in Leiden and Delft, and the strikes in Amsterdam and elsewhere in February 1941.

26. B.H. Liddell Hart, 'Lessons from Resistance Movements: Guerrilla and Non-Violent', in Roberts, *The Strategy of Civilian Defence*.[2].

27. J. Bennett in 'The Resistance of Denmark 1940–5', Roberts, *The Strategy of Civilian Defence*,[2] footnote 11, p. 165.

28. Haestrup, *Europe Ablaze*,[12] p. 69.

29. This is the judgement of, among others, Mlynar, *Night Frost in Prague*.[9]

30. A view cogently argued by Jean-Marie Muller in 'Les Accords de Moscou: Comment fut Brisée la Resistance des Tchécoslovaques', *Alternatives Non-Violentes*, 33 (April 1979), 16–35.

31. Haestrup, *Europe Ablaze*,[12] p. 132.

32. See *Keesings Contemporary Archives*, XXV (1979), 29733.

33. See Narayan Desai, *Towards a Nonviolent Revolution* (Varanasi: Sarva Seva Sangh Prakashan, 1972), where the work of the Shanti Sena during the riots in Baroda is described.

34. On transarmament see for instance A. Roberts, 'Transarmament to Civilian Defence' in *The Strategy of Civilian Defence*,[2] pp. 291–301. For a critical assessment of the notion see M. Randle, 'Radical Change or Technical Fix?', *War Resisters International Newsletter*, 177 (July 1980), 5–8.

35. Gjelsvik, *Norwegian Resistance, 1940–1945*.[19]

36. Bennett in Roberts, *The Strategy of Civilian Defence*,[2] p. 165.

37. Clearly what is also needed is a detailed consideration of strategies for civil resistance in the British context. We have not attempted this here, but it is one of a number of topics touched upon in this Report which requires further study.

38. Keyes, 'Strategic Non-Violent Defense',[4] p. 136.

39. Whether the Ulster Workers' Strike of 1974 was politically and morally justified is a separate issue. Civil resistance can of course be used by powerful sections of a society for unjustified and undemocratic ends. An obvious example is the civil resistance by segments of the population in Chile which paved the way to the military overthrow of the elected Allende government in 1973 and the establishment of the brutal Pinochet dictatorship.

40. Sir Stephen King-Hall discusses the notion of a European Treaty Organisation (ETO) in *Defence in the Nuclear Age* (London: Gollancz, 1958); see especially pp. 145–72, the chapters headed 'Defence Without Arms' and 'E.T.O. in Action'.

41. See *Keesings Contemporary Archives*, X (1955–1956), 14401. Demonstrations and direct action in India against continued Portuguese rule in the enclaves of Goa, Daman and Diu in June and July 1955, culminated in a mass march across the

borders by approximately 3,000 'satyagrahis' on 15 August 1955, Indian Independence Day, during which at least 13 people were killed by Portuguese forces who opened fire. In Bombay on 29 July the Transport and Dock Workers' Union boycotted all foreign ships bound for Goa, and on 12 August, 500,000 workers in Bombay took part in a one-day strike called by the Goa Liberation Aid Committee. The direct action was organised by the ruling Congress Party and on 7 September 1955, the Bombay Government issued instructions to the police to prevent satyagrahis, whether individuals or groups, from crossing the border into Goa and Daman, and similar instructions were issued in Saurashtra to prevent satyagrahis from entering Diu. Goa was eventually united with India in December 1961 when Indian forces invaded and took over the enclave.

Chapter 8
Transition

I. Introduction

For over 30 years, Britain's defence and foreign policies have been framed around the possession of nuclear weapons and membership of a nuclear alliance. Moving away from such policies will involve changes and adjustments — economically and technically, and above all in the political and diplomatic sphere. In this chapter we consider certain aspects of this process of transition.

It is the political and diplomatic aspects that are undoubtedly the most crucial. First, care has to be taken not to give misleading signals to either friends or potential adversaries, or to cause unnecessary panic or over-reaction which could have a de-stabilising effect. Second, the political initiatives accompanying a change in British or European defence policy could make the difference between its having only a marginal influence in the world outside and its contributing in an important way to the process of detente and disarmament. Moreover, as we noted earlier, foreign policy, and success in achieving certain political and economic changes in the world are likely to be even more central to future British and world security than defence policy as such. The demilitarisation and neutralisation of both East and West Germany for instance, if it could be achieved, is likely to enhance the prospects of European security at least as much as any changes in defence strategies.

In this report we are not able to examine in detail the question of what foreign and development policy a nuclear-disarmed Britain should pursue. We recognise, however, the central importance of this issue and do indicate the broad direction such a foreign policy should take and a few of the major goals it should be seeking to achieve. In this chapter we also suggest some of the diplomatic initiatives and procedures that might accompany British nuclear disarmament in the early stages in order to enhance its impact and reduce the attendant risks.

Two important considerations always arise whenever important

policy changes are being considered. First, how quickly should one
try to implement them; second, should one attempt to operate within
existing structures in an effort to change them or seek to create new
institutions and a new framework?

Clearly there are risks in making far-reaching changes very
rapidly; in this instance other countries might become alarmed and
take counter-measures against Britain — or the USA, for example,
might introduce still more nuclear weapons into Europe to compensate for what it perceived as NATO weaknesses resulting from
Britain's nuclear disarmament and the closure of US nuclear bases in
this country. On the other hand, if one moves too cautiously the
policy changes may have little or no effect on the world outside.
Canada's very gradual withdrawal from involvement in nuclear
defence has certainly caused no crisis either within NATO or outside
it, but it has had no very positive influence either and has not affected
the direction of NATO strategy. Something bolder and more decisive
than this is required if Britain's nuclear disarmament is to have a
wider impact and significance.

The question about whether or not to work within existing
institutions applies most importantly in this instance to membership
of NATO. For reasons which were explained in Chapter 3, the
majority of the Commission favour a nuclear-disarmed Britain
retaining NATO membership on a conditional basis and seeking to
end NATO's reliance on nuclear weapons within a stated period.
However, it is possible that NATO as a whole would reject these
conditions, and therefore alternative options, such as British non-
alignment, or the setting up of a non-nuclear European Defence
Association, have to be given some attention. Moreover some
members of the Commission, and many people in the nuclear disarmament movement, believe that Britain ought to withdraw from
NATO rather than seeking to change its policy from within.

There are of course a good many imponderables in considering the
steps that a future British government committed to nuclear disarmament should take. Much would depend on the character of the
government, on the attitudes of current allies, on the international
developments that had taken place in the intervening period, and on
the political changes and climate of opinion within Britain. If such a
government were voted in at the next election, the international
context might be much as it now is, but if this did not happen until,
say, 1990, the context might have changed considerably, especially if
pressures for nuclear disarmament continued to grow throughout
Europe, perhaps leading to the withdrawal of some of the smaller

countries like Holland, Belgium or Norway from NATO. To keep the discussion manageable, however, we assume, unless otherwise stated, that the situation has not drastically changed at the international level, and focus on the objectives a British government might set itself in a five-year term of office.

These objectives would include:

(1) Dismantling British nuclear weapons, and the nuclear disarmament of all British forces. This would include the withdrawal from service of US nuclear weapons, such as the Lance short-range missiles, which are deployed with British forces under a system of dual control.

(2) The removal of US nuclear weapons from Britain and ensuring that if other US facilities remained in Britain these were not related to its nuclear strategy.

(3) (a) Negotiating the conditions on which Britain would stay in NATO, assuming a policy of conditional membership were adopted; or

(b) Negotiating British withdrawal from NATO if the conditions were rejected, or if a policy of withdrawal had been decided from the start.

(4) Furthering detente and disarmament, and seeking to check the spread of nuclear weapons, through political initiatives that would accompany British nuclear disarmament and the adoption of alternative defence strategies.

(5) Holding a thorough defence review, introducing new defence policies, and setting up a research project to investigate the possible role of nonviolent civil resistance.

(6) Establishing a framework for the redeployment of personnel, the alternative uses for land released by nuclear disarmament and base closures, and other problems of economic conversion.

(7) Moving towards greater support for the UN and Third World development.

Transition, however, is not only a matter of action by government. The raising of people's consciousness about the dangers of nuclear war, the acclimatisation of the population to the notion of relying on different defence strategies, or radically different forms of defence, measures of economic conversion, and many other initiatives can be taken by individuals and popular or specialist organisations and are an essential part of the transition process. Without such initiatives from below, governments would be unable to bring about radical political and economic change. In this sense transition has to begin, not from the time an anti-nuclear government is elected, but here and now.

It is important in this connection to distinguish between the options available to a government operating within a relatively short time-span, and the demands which radical movements for disarmament and peace can and should be making. The government of the day has broadly speaking to act within the constraints imposed by public opinion; it can give a lead, but only to a limited extent, as for instance over the issue of capital punishment. Radical movements can press for the fundamental changes they regard as politically and morally essential, even if at times little heed is paid to them. Thus if government is the art of the possible, the role of popular movements is to widen those possibilities by altering the context in which political decisions are taken.

This Commission has been principally concerned about the options for a future British government committed to nuclear disarmament. For this reason there is an emphasis in the report on options which are politically realistic in the short to medium term. But the Commission is also conscious of the importance of a broad vision concerning future possibilities, and it has looked at some of these and at the processes through which radical change might come about.

There will be those who regard as genuine options only those strategies with a strong emphasis on conventional military defence, at least while the international situation remains broadly as it is at present. Others who are committed to a nonviolent approach would accept a military strategy with a strongly defensive emphasis only in so far as it represents a move away from reliance on weapons of mass destruction and could be seen as part of a longer-term transition programme. The experience on the Commission, however, has been that even those who have very different views about the longer-term possibilities were able to reach a consensus about many of the steps that are urgently needed in the short and intermediate term.

II. International steps

Declaration of intent and the ending of a British independent deterrent

As soon as Britain opted for a non-nuclear defence and rejected reliance on nuclear strategies (as well as renouncing unconditionally any resort to chemical or biological warfare), there should be an official statement explaining this decision and its implications. The statement would point out that the logic of this decision is that Britain could not accept NATO's current nuclear strategy but nevertheless intended to retain close links with the USA and Western Europe. It would announce that it would allow time for the US nuclear bases and facilities in Britain to be removed in an orderly way.

At the same time, however, it should give a clear signal of its determination to move away from any reliance on nuclear weapons by cancelling Trident, withdrawing forthwith the Polaris submarine fleet, and announcing a timetable for the phasing out of nuclear weapons research work in Britain.

The declaration would underline the fact that Britain sees its own nuclear disarmament not as an act taken in isolation from the world outside but as an initiative aimed at promoting a wider programme of nuclear disarmament, arms control and detente.

Top-level conference with the US government

The purpose of this conference would be to allay US fears while presenting British policy clearly and seeking to negotiate on certain objectives. The most important of these would be the removal of the US nuclear and related bases from Britain or the removal of the US military presence altogether if Britain were adopting a non-aligned policy.

The British government has listed 56 US bases in Britain, though, as noted in Chapter 1, Duncan Campbell of the *New Statesman* claims to have identified 103, the majority of which relate at least as much to US global military strategy as to European defence.[1]

Many of the US bases would clearly be unacceptable to a nuclear-disarmed Britain, whatever its relationship to NATO—the nuclear weapons dumps at Macrahanish and Burtonwood, the Poseidon base at Holy Loch, the air bases for the F-111s in the Midlands and East Anglia. Other air bases may be earmarked to receive further nuclear bombers from the United States in an emergency, or nuclear-capable aircraft that would be withdrawn from West Germany in the event of war.

The British government would have to review the functions of all the US bases. Where they served no purpose in a system of non-nuclear defence, they should be closed. (Advances in satellite equipment may in any case render some of the US surveillance bases superfluous). Britain should propose a timetable for phasing out nuclear bases, to be completed within three years—a length of time which should be adequate for the USA and also sufficient to minimise economic disruption in Britain. Where early-warning and communications bases are deemed necessary for the security of Britain and Western Europe in a system of conventional defence, Britain should seek agreement with the USA to take them over.

If Britain remained in NATO, it would probably continue to house US conventional forces assigned to Europe, and to provide facilities for US reinforcements to use Britain as a staging post in the event of war. Britain in this case would clearly continue to be a prime target for Soviet attack in wartime, at any rate at the conventional level. Moreover, it might be difficult to convince the Soviet Union that the USA was not stockpiling any nuclear weapons in Britain while it retained military bases here, or that it would not rapidly move them into Britain in an emergency. These again are considerations that a British government would have to take into account in making its decision about NATO membership, and would have to be set against the advantages of working for change within the Alliance.

As long as Britain remained in NATO it would continue to allow US ships harbour facilities; however, it should insist that no nuclear-armed ships should enter British territorial waters — the position formally adopted by Japan.

Negotiations with NATO on conditional membership

If Britain decided to remain conditionally in NATO, it should take the first opportunity to put its proposals for a non-nuclear NATO, simultaneously impressing on its allies its resolution to reject nuclear weapons and reassuring them of Britain's continued willingness to contribute to the collective security of Western Europe. We suggest the convening of a special conference of NATO political leaders to put these points, thereby indicating the importance Britain attaches to its decision and to the discussion with its NATO partners. Britain would indicate at this conference that it would not take part in any future exercises where the use by NATO of nuclear weapons is envisaged, and would propose a time-scale for phasing out NATO's nuclear strategy.

The four principal stages in the process of de-nuclearising NATO strategy are:

(1) the adoption by NATO of a no-first-use of nuclear weapons policy;

(2) the withdrawal of the short-range 'battlefield' nuclear weapons from Europe;

(3) the withdrawal of 'theatre' nuclear weapons;

(4) the decoupling of the US strategic nuclear deterrent from NATO.

The first stage, a no-first-use policy, could be achieved relatively quickly. A British government committed to non-nuclear defence should require this change of policy within a year of the conference with NATO allies as a sign that progress was possible in meeting the other conditions.

As battlefield nuclear weapons are largely first-use weapons, to be employed against a Warsaw Pact conventional attack, a no-first-use policy should logically lead to a decision to withdraw them. However, as they have been deployed in order to compensate for the perceived weakness of the West's conventional defences, their actual withdrawal might be delayed by discussion on the form a non-nuclear defence of Western Europe should take. There is also the problem that battlefield nuclear weapons are deployed by the Warsaw Pact, and mutual withdrawal of such weapons would be preferable. The Olof Palme Commission on Disarmament and Security Issues has proposed the removal of battlefield nuclear weapons from a 300 kilometre-wide European zone centred on the border between East and West Germany;[2] if this was accepted it could be the first step in a phased withdrawal of these weapons. Nevertheless, if agreement cannot be reached with the Soviet Union, the NATO states should be prepared to act unilaterally.

The distinction between 'battlefield' and 'theatre' nuclear weapons is not in practice clear-cut, since a number of medium-range systems (for example Pershing 1A) can be regarded as falling into either category.[3] NATO's longer-range theatre forces comprise chiefly at present the US F-111 bombers based in Britain, though the Poseidon-carrying submarines based in Holy Loch also have a theatre aspect, as do Britain's own nuclear forces. Britain's proposed three-year limit for the removal of US nuclear weapons from its own territory could be linked to a demand for removal of the battlefield and theatre nuclear weapons based in Europe within three or four years. We suggest that unless there has been substantial progress towards the removal of these weapons from Europe within three years, Britain should consider withdrawing from the Alliance.

If however cruise and Pershing II missiles had been stationed in Europe, it is assumed that priority would be given to removing them, since they represent a dangerous escalation in the nuclear arms race. Their removal has not been included among the conditions because the Commission hopes that they will not be deployed.

Decoupling the US nuclear deterrent from NATO would be the longer-term objective of these steps, so that a genuinely nuclear-free Western Europe would be established. Britain itself should make it clear from the outset that it no longer wanted a US 'nuclear guarantee', and should seek to persuade other European members of NATO to accept the full implications of a non-nuclear approach. The USA too could be asked to accept that its obligations to Western Europe under the NATO treaty were confined to support at the conventional level.

How likely it is that these conditions will be met depends crucially on future developments in the rest of Europe and how far the anti-nuclear campaigns can influence the policies of their governments. Quite conceivably one or two European members of NATO will be pressing for similar changes in policy by the time Britain repudiates nuclear weapons, and it may be possible to form an anti-nuclear caucus within NATO; in this case Britain's negotiating strategy should be drawn up in consultation with the other countries concerned.

If progress towards de-nuclearising NATO strategy came to a standstill, Britain's first step would be to withdraw from the integrated military command structure while remaining on NATO's North Atlantic Council. If subsequently NATO accepted the ideas of a non-nuclear strategy, Britain could resume full membership; if on the other hand it became clear that there was no realistic possibility of this happening, Britain should withdraw altogether from the Alliance.

Reactions in NATO

There is no exact precedent for a country rejecting NATO's nuclear strategy. However, in assessing possible reactions to this change in British policy, it may be instructive to look at the cases of France and Greece which have both withdrawn from NATO's integrated military command, and at Canada which reversed its nuclear policy in 1969.

France

France withdrew from NATO's military command in 1966. Since then, however, it has continued to participate militarily through the early-warning systems and in NATO exercises; it remains a member of the North Atlantic Council, pays regularly towards NATO's civilian costs, and has a say in appointing the NATO secretary-general. It is also generally assumed that France would commit its troops to NATO in the event of war with the Warsaw Pact.

The French withdrawal was not sudden. De Gaulle had indicated his own opposition to the integrated military command in 1959, refused to adopt the Athens Guidelines in 1962 which relate to consultation among the NATO allies before nuclear weapons are used, and withdrew the remainder of the French fleet in 1963. Nor could the French move be seen as pro-Soviet in view of De Gaulle's conservative nationalism, his domestic policies and the country's continuation on the North Atlantic Council. At that time, however, France was not as strategically important to NATO as Britain is today.

Nevertheless the French withdrawal was disruptive. 26,000 US soldiers had to be moved from four American bases in France, NATO headquarters had to be moved from Paris to Brussels, and NATO supply lines were restricted.[4] After a dispute with the USA, France finally agreed to pay for the relocation of US bases, but otherwise France has not been penalised for its withdrawal from the integrated military command.

Greece

Greece withdrew from the NATO military command in 1974 in protest against the Turkish invasion of Cyprus. US bases were 'called into question', but never actually expelled, and Greece re-joined NATO in 1980. In the circumstances the USA was not alarmed by Greek withdrawal, especially as it coincided with Greek endeavours to join the EEC.

The election of the Pasok government, headed by Papandreou, in October 1981 has again raised doubts about Greece's future relationship with NATO. Papandreou is actively seeking a Balkans nuclear-free zone and has declared his intention of negotiating for the withdrawal of US nuclear weapons from Greece. However, at the moment Greece depends on the USA for 90 per cent of its military supplies and, although it is seeking to expand domestic arms production and co-operation with Britain or France, it remains vulnerable in the event of a break with NATO.[5]

For the time being, Papandreou will accept three conditions for remaining in NATO: that US bases will not be used to launch a military attack against a country friendly to Greece; that intelligence from US monitoring stations in Greece will not be accessible to Turkey; and that US weapons should be equally as available to Greece as to Turkey.[6] He is also seeking a NATO guarantee of Greek borders from Turkish invasion and refuses to co-operate in NATO exercises which do not recognise Greek jurisdiction over the Aegean Sea.[7]

Greece is considered strategically important to NATO, but it has a history both of anti-American feeling and of US involvement in its internal politics. Papandreou clearly hopes that by proceeding with caution and in conjunction with the other Balkan states, he can avoid the worst consequences of a split with NATO.

Canada

Canada has never possessed nuclear weapons of its own, but it has in the past been more closely integrated with US nuclear policy than it is now. Until 1969 Canada made a nuclear contribution to NATO in the form of nuclear-armed aircraft, surface-to-air missiles, and 'Honest John' rockets.[8] It began its de-nuclearisation by phasing out its nuclear capabilities in Europe, meanwhile reducing its European troop commitment from 10,000 to the present 3,000. Gradually US nuclear warheads and delivery systems have been removed from Canada, although during emergencies US tankers may refuel at Goose Bay and US planes on alert may fly over Canada.

The Canadian decision was taken during the period of detente and caused no great upset in the US or other NATO states. At the same time, neither has it made any impact on NATO nuclear strategy, and Canada remains fully integrated into NATO's military command.

Comparison with Britain

Could Britain expect a different response from NATO, and from the USA in particular, if it adopted a non-nuclear policy, insisted on the removal of US bases, or withdrew altogether from the Alliance? Britain's renunciation of a nuclear capability is not in itself likely to arouse major objections and might indeed be regarded in some NATO circles as a sensible move. But because of Britain's strategic importance, the USA would certainly take a much more serious view of having to remove its nuclear weapons from Britain than it did in the case of Canada. And if Britain were to leave NATO, for example following a breakdown of the attempt to get a non-nuclear strategy adopted, this would certainly constitute a more damaging blow to the

Alliance than the partial withdrawal of France in 1966. (In a sense France's decision makes any subsequent defections that much more serious a problem for NATO).

It could not be expected therefore that the USA would accept with complacency the new British policy. While it is unlikely that it would try by force to retain its bases in Britain, it could exert political, diplomatic, and no doubt some degree of economic pressure, and could be expected to give support and encouragement to those forces within Britain opposed to the non-nuclear policies of the government. The CIA has funded organisations in Britain in the past, and, given that the new policies would undoubtedly be controversial, it is clear that there would be no shortage of candidates opposed to nuclear disarmament.

If a propaganda campaign against non-nuclear policies is the most likely form of US opposition, 'covert operations' cannot be ruled out if the USA perceived the British government as being anti-American. There is little point at this stage in speculating on the possibilities of conspiracies between disgruntled British military officers or other groups and the CIA: whatever the likelihood of this being attempted, Britain is very different from a country like Chile or Guatemala and a military take-over in this country would be much more difficult to organise or sustain.

No doubt the US government could bring economic pressure to bear on Britain but unless it could persuade the rest of Western Europe to join with it in applying economic sanctions, it would probably not be able to cripple the British economy. The USA is less well placed than at certain periods in the past to apply pressure of this kind, and moreover Britain, unlike Greece, does not depend on the USA for arms.

The best safeguard against reprisals, including political de-stabilisation, is an unwavering firmness on the part of the British government — patiently explaining changes in policy and questioning the perceptions behind current NATO strategy while at the same time insisting on its rejection of nuclear weapons — and a population prepared, in the majority, to support the new policies and if necessary to resist by mass non-co-operation any illicit attempt to seize power or thwart the democratic process.

Establishing alternative options if Britain withdraws from NATO

The conditional membership of NATO could be rapidly foreclosed by several possible developments — for instance if the USA insisted that while it remained part of the Alliance and deployed troops in Europe it could not accept a no-first-use of nuclear weapons policy, or the withdrawal of battlefield nuclear weapons, or agree to dissociate its conventional alliance with Europe from its own nuclear deterrent strategy; alternatively, or additionally, the majority of European members of NATO might make it clear at an early stage that they would not go along with the programme for ending reliance on nuclear weapons.

The timetabling of British withdrawal from NATO if it failed to move in a non-nuclear direction could not be too hard and fast. We suggested that the first stage should be for Britain to withdraw from NATO's integrated military command system, and that total withdrawal would follow if it became clear that NATO would not alter its strategy.

The two main options open to Britain in the case of withdrawal are (*a*) to seek to establish, or become linked to an alternative collective security system in Western Europe, or (*b*) to adopt a non-aligned position.

(*a*) *Alternative European collective security arrangements*

A non-nuclear European defence association is perhaps most likely to come about if the USA decided to withdraw from NATO and Europe because it could not accept the demands for a non-nuclear policy, and if the European members of NATO wanted nonetheless to maintain a collective security system. The problems and disadvantages of a purely European defence association were considered in Chapter 3. It was agreed that an association of this kind might have to be considered, especially if NATO in its present form began to disintegrate, and that it might take the form of guarantees of mutual aid without any attempt to establish a unified military command, and without the stationing of any troops outside their respective countries.

It is difficult to set a timetable for establishing an alternative military alliance of this kind, since it depends so much on what countries other than Britain might want to do. However, if Britain decided that the time had come to explore this possibility seriously — for instance if it became clear that NATO was on the verge of breaking up — it could put forward a set of proposals in conjunction with others interested in the idea, suggest an initial exploratory period of say one year, followed, if the response was positive, by a further two-year period to establish a new system.

There are a number of situations in which the establishment of a non-nuclear defence association covering most of Western Europe would be ruled out, or might prove impracticable, but where mutual security agreements between particular groupings of states might prove attractive. If NATO continued in existence, for instance, but one or two other states in addition to Britain decided to pull out of it — say Holland and Norway — then these might wish to be linked together by some kind of loose defence agreement. It is also possible that even in the event of NATO breaking up, a network of bi-lateral or other agreements might be established more easily than a single European defence association. Arrangements of this kind could be made quite rapidly, given the appropriate context, but it is impossible to predict the timing with any degree of assurance given the variety of possibilities that could arise.

Although the adoption of a fully fledged system of defence by civil resistance is not an immediate possibility, we have argued earlier that preparations for civil resistance ought to be put in hand so that it could provide at least a fall-back strategy for countries adopting a non-nuclear defence. European states which took this idea seriously could begin not only preparing their own populations but making arrangements with other like-minded countries to extend political support and practical help if this kind of resistance had to be resorted to. Even if preparations for civil resistance were regarded as a relatively minor aspect of defence planning, it would be important to make provision for such assistance on a transnational basis, both within Europe and beyond it.

Agreements to provide assistance in nonviolent struggles need not be confined to the government level; political groups, trade unions, religious bodies and so on in different countries could arrange to assist each other in a variety of ways should the need arise.

(b) British non-alignment

Non-alignment is the other obvious choice for a Britain outside NATO. By non-alignment we mean not being formally linked to either of the military blocs and being free to pursue an independent foreign policy. It does not have to mean strict neutrality in all disputes and can involve taking sides politically according to the merits of the case. There is an argument, based on a calculation of self-interest, for a stricter form of political as well as military neutrality, but that is not what is being considered here.

Clearly a non-aligned status does not bring any guarantee of security, as the history of the last 20 years in a number of Third World countries has amply demonstrated; indeed in specific situations it may leave a country isolated and vulnerable. It is in no way to be considered a substitute for a defence policy, but defines rather a political context in which, by deliberate choice, or as the result of a failure to secure a non-nuclear European NATO, or some alternative collective security system in Europe, Britain would be re-fashioning its defence policy.

In principle Britain could adopt a non-aligned position as soon as a government committed to this policy was elected; similarly at any point at which Britain decided to withdraw from NATO, non-alignment would in a sense present the least complicated alternative.

In practice, as we have suggested, Britain should — whatever the context — act with deliberation and allow time for other countries to adjust to the changed circumstances. We have already suggested the procedure we think should be followed if Britain's attempts to work inside NATO proved unsuccessful. If Britain had decided from the start to pursue the non-aligned option, it should give the statutory one-year's notice to NATO, and be willing to extend this by another year or eighteen months if this could avoid undue friction with our allies. At the same time Britain's departure from the Alliance should not be delayed for too long or the momentum of the new policy might be lost.

It would be particularly important if Britain were to leave NATO, for whatever reason, to make it clear that this was not a retreat into isolationism. Britain's continued concern for European security could be indicated, for instance, by serious efforts in conjunction with other European states to establish nuclear-free zones in Europe, to promote a new political settlement, and to bring to an end the confrontation between the two military pacts. Continued membership of the EEC, even if the British government in question had serious doubts about its economic advantages for Britain, might also be taken as a positive indication of British intentions in relation to Europe. Similarly Britain's concern for global security could be indicated by an increased commitment to the UN, and by its initiatives related to detente, disarmament and development.

Promoting detente and disarmament

European security

Britain's nuclear disarmament, especially if there were also moves towards a non-nuclear strategy by other NATO countries, might create an opportunity for reaching a new political and military agreement in Europe; the creation of nuclear-free zones, the withdrawal of foreign troops, perhaps even the neutralisation of East and West Germany. The growing strength of the peace movement in West Germany, and the emergence of an independent peace movement in East Germany are encouraging signs, especially as public opinion in the two halves of Germany will be a factor of key importance in achieving any new European political settlement.

In the longer term, the aim of peace in Europe requires an end to the rigid division between East and West and the dissolution of the two opposed military blocs. If these developments also meant a reduction in Soviet and US influence over their respective allies, Europe would gain greater political independence as well as greater hopes for peace. In the foreseeable future, it would not be realistic to envisage Eastern Europe becoming wholly independent of the Soviet Union; however, it is conceivable that, provided it was satisfied that its own security was not endangered, the Soviet Union would be prepared at some point to contemplate a relationship with the countries of Eastern Europe similar to that which now exists between it and Finland, i.e. one which would give the countries concerned a far greater measure of political and economic independence than they now have. The growth of independent peace movements and other political and trade union organisations within Eastern Europe could make Soviet control in the old style more difficult to maintain and thus put pressure on the Soviet Union to look for a new arrangement.

What diplomatic steps Britain and other Western countries should take to enhance the possibilities of unilateral nuclear disarmament contributing to detente and creative political change is difficult to specify at this stage. One possibility would be to call for an East/West European security conference at an early date; however, if this occurred too soon, for instance at a time when the USA was suspicious of, or hostile to, developments in Britain, and the Soviet Union was determined to maintain its present control of Eastern Europe, it might prove counter-productive and be used as a propaganda exercise by both sides. At some point, nonetheless, a conference involving the superpowers would be necessary, since any new political settlement in Europe, or the creation of de-militarised zones would have to be supported by them. On the other hand certain steps, such as the creation of nuclear-free zones, could be established.

Britain might best be able to contribute to detente in Europe in the early stages by promoting simultaneously an adequate defence policy and limited diplomatic measures to reduce tension and armaments in Europe which have some reasonable prospect of success. This means, for instance, that a defence policy should be designed to avoid exacerbating the military confrontation in Europe and should, as far as possible, be easy to adapt to the creation of a disengaged zone, or to limitations on some types of conventional armament. Indeed, adopting such a defence posture might ease the way to political negotiations.

An obvious step in negotiations with the Soviet Union if some agreements had proved possible — for example on no-first-use of nuclear weapons and perhaps on some confidence-building measures — would be to try again to agree a reduction in conventional arms in Europe. The Vienna negotiations on mutual force reductions have dragged on since 1973, bogged down in attempts to reach 'balanced' reductions and disputes about present force levels. While a reduction in total armed forces on both sides would be politically desirable, and might be more likely if the West had taken radical unilateral steps to alter its defence philosophy and force structure, it might be more fruitful to pursue other goals. One possibility would be to follow up the 1981 UN Convention restricting the use of inhumane conventional weapons by seeking agreement between NATO and Warsaw Pact members to ban completely the manufacture of these weapons or their deployment either in Europe or elsewhere; this would be a logical extension of renouncing nuclear and chemical weapons. Another possibility, which would follow naturally from the adoption by the West of a strictly defensive military stance, would be to explore agreement to renounce weapons with a primarily offensive role such as long-range bombers, and to limit the numbers of tanks.

Disarmament and security in general

A number of developments, as we noted in Chapter 1, are tending to undermine the always precarious equilibrium of deterrence. One of these is the increasing deployment of 'battlefield' nuclear weapons and the emergence of nuclear war-fighting doctrines. For this reason the Commission has placed considerable stress on the importance of linking British nuclear disarmament with a no-first-use agreement and the withdrawal of battlefield nuclear weapons from Europe.

A major effort is also needed to prevent the further spread of nuclear weapons to other states and areas of the world. Of itself Britain's action in renouncing nuclear weapons would not necessarily affect the calculations of those states currently planning to acquire them, though it would strengthen public movements in many countries. But Britain's action could free it to campaign more actively for better safeguards against proliferation, and might give more authority and credibility to the existing Non-Proliferation Treaty, which in principle obliges those states possessing nuclear weapons to move rapidly towards nuclear disarmament. Other steps that could help to freeze proliferation would be the conclusion of a Comprehensive Test Ban Treaty, and the creation of further nuclear-free zones similar to that established in much of Latin America by the Tlatelolco Treaty of 1967.

Britain's nuclear disarmament may have most impact if it is envisaged not as one sweeping gesture but as a series of leads, almost as an agenda for further disarmament moves and negotiations. Thus efforts could be made to persuade the Soviet Union to respond to moves on Britain's part in specific ways — for instance the withdrawal of British battlefield nuclear weapons might be met by a reduction in the number of Soviet battlefield weapons deployed, or the British cancellation of Trident and withdrawal of Polaris by a proportionate Soviet reduction in the numbers of its missile-carrying submarines. Of themselves these moves would not have any great military significance since, as we have argued, exact military balance has little meaning in the context of the nuclear confrontation between the superpowers. But they would signal a willingness to accept reductions in the numbers of nuclear weapons deployed and to raise the nuclear threshold, and they could create a more favourable climate for the negotiation of political settlements or of measures of arms control and disarmament.

Halting the arms trade

Britain, along with the Soviet Union, the United States, and France, is among the top four exporters of major weapons to Third World countries, many of them governed by repressive and bloody dictatorships. The war with Argentina over the Falklands has focused attention on certain aspects of this situation. President Carter stopped the supply of arms to Argentina in 1978 because of its appalling record on human rights, but other Western countries, notably West Germany and France, took its place; Britain until the Falklands war provided 10 per cent of Argentina's arms.

However, the problem is not simply that the arms exported may be used to further aggressive adventures, or to suppress the civilian population; a heavy expenditure on imported arms can seriously distort the economies of developing countries and can create long-term dependence on the supplier country. Hard currency to pay for expensive armaments has to be obtained by producing the goods and raw materials needed by the industrialised countries, which makes it more difficult for the developing country to achieve a rational economic structure geared to meeting the needs of its own people. Excessive arms expenditure in fact can contribute to the economic and social instability that often leads to military and authoritarian rule.

What is not always recognised is that the armaments industry in the West is heavily dependent on exports. In European countries especially, where the home market is restricted, arms exports are necessary to make possible longer production runs; even Sweden has not altogether escaped from this situation. This could be an argument for producing simpler and cheaper weapons and shaping one's military strategy accordingly.

A unilateralist government should at an early stage review Britain's whole arms exports policy, and an all-party watchdog committee of the House of Commons might be set up to scrutinise arms transfers. At a suitable moment Britain could propose a conference of arms-exporting countries aimed at drastically curtailing, even if it could not hope to eliminate altogether, the international trade in arms.

III. Internal measures

Ending the British deterrent and removal of nuclear bases

We suggested earlier that some of the first steps a unilateralist British government should take are to cancel Trident and withdraw the Polaris fleet from service. At the same time nuclear weapons would in general be withdrawn from British forces.

But if Britain remained conditionally in NATO, it might delay the withdrawal of the battlefield nuclear weapons deployed with BAOR in Germany — the Lance missiles and nuclear artillery — and phase them out in conjunction with all battlefield nuclear weapons deployed by NATO. Britain might, however, set a limit of three years for the withdrawal of battlefield nuclear weapons from its own forces in Europe, and this could have the effect of giving greater urgency to NATO's deliberations on its nuclear policies.

We also suggested that the USA should be asked to withdraw the F-111 bombers and cease to base Poseidon submarines at Holy Loch in Scotland within three years. But if cruise missiles have been deployed in Britain, we would expect a unilateralist government to ask for their prompt removal, perhaps allowing twelve months at the outside for this to be done.

Dismantling Britain's nuclear weapons

Technically this would pose few problems. Aldermaston already has considerable experience of dismantling nuclear warheads, either because they are obsolete or during periodic checks, and in the mid-1970s the Windscale reprocessing plant (now known as Sellafield) was believed to have a plant for recovering the plutonium from old warheads.[9] The technical problems of storing or disposing of highly radioactive materials are much greater, but these are familiar to nuclear scientists; they are not different in kind to those presented on a larger scale by the nuclear energy programme.

Most of Britain's nuclear-capable weapons systems can also be conventionally armed. During the Falklands war, the Vulcan bombers — originally designed as exclusively nuclear bombers — were adapted to carry conventional bombs, leaving Polaris and the battlefield Lance missiles as Britain's only all-nuclear systems. Polaris would simply be retired, as would Trident if it had come into commission. The Lance missiles are assigned to the British Army of the Rhine where they are deployed on a dual key basis with the USA; their nuclear warheads are supplied by the US and these would be returned at the point at which it was decided to withdraw battlefield weapons from British forces in Europe; the missile itself could be conventionally armed.

As so many British weapons systems are dual-capable — from helicopters up to jet bombers, from field artillery up to missiles — Britain will need to make some effort to reduce, even if it cannot altogether eliminate, doubts about the reality of its nuclear disarmament. We discuss below a proposal for international inspection.

It would be difficult, however, to allay altogether suspicion about the military potential of Britain's nuclear energy programme, especially if it included fast-breeder reactors. This is one of the arguments against the further expansion of Britain's nuclear energy programme which is considered in a supplementary paper to be published by the Commission.[10] In any case Britain should publish a full inventory of its nuclear weapons and of its production, use of, and trade in fissile materials from the beginning of the nuclear programme in Britain. As the history of decision-making on nuclear weapons has been one of secrecy and at times deception, the government should aim to set the record straight. Certain papers for instance have not been released under the 30 years rule,[11] while many other documents and facts have been withheld. Release of this information and the commissioning of a full, up-to-date, official history of the nuclear weapons programme would add credibility to a government declaration that it had forsworn the nuclear option permanently.

Inspecting British nuclear disarmament

A British declaration that it had jettisoned its nuclear arsenal and delivery systems might be viewed with some scepticism by the Soviet Union and other countries. It is important therefore not only that Britain should disarm at the nuclear level but that it should be seen to disarm.

One possibility would be to invite an inspection team from the United Nations and the International Atomic Energy Agency to Britain to witness the process of nuclear disarmament. There are problems about ensuring complete nuclear disarmament because of the possibility of concealment. But inspection and control of the dis-mantling of Britain's strategic nuclear forces in the shape of its Polaris (or Trident) system would not present a problem, and the same would be true for the closing down of its nuclear weapons establishments at Aldermaston, Burghfield and Cardiff. The test would be whether these measures, and the additional control that an inspection team could exercise, would be sufficient to reassure other states that Britain had indeed abandoned a nuclear strategy. The organisation of its forces, and the pressure it was prepared to exert on NATO countries to move away from a nuclear strategy, would be further indications of its seriousness of purpose.

International inspection of British nuclear disarmament could be something of a pilot operation, showing both the problems and possibilities involved. Inviting such inspection would be another signal that Britain did not see its action in isolation from the need for nuclear disarmament and arms control on a wider basis, and if the process was successful it could help to remove an important stumbling block to the acceptance of disarmament.

British defence review and the introduction of new strategies

An early review of British defence policy would clearly be needed. Initially Britain would simply switch to conventional defence, retaining its present forces, but over time it would become possible to introduce more radical strategies and redeploy conventional forces. How much British defence strategy could be expected to change during the five year period under discussion would depend on a number of factors, among them whether or not Britain continued to be a member of NATO. If it did, the pace of change would probably be less rapid since British strategy would have to dovetail with NATO plans, whereas a non-aligned Britain would have greater freedom of manoeuvre. Moreover, Britain's departure from NATO would radically change the context of its defence planning and therefore entail a thorough-going re-assessment of its strategies.

British force levels and costs under various options

Staying in NATO

The defence posture that a non-nuclear NATO would probably adopt would be what we have defined as 'defensive balance' — i.e. having forces sufficient to provide a reasonable prospect of thwarting a Soviet conventional attack, thereby making such an attack less likely (see Chapter 5). Because of the advantages inherent in the defence, this would not require NATO to match soldier for soldier and tank for tank the forces of the Warsaw Pact, though obviously the overall relation of forces would have to be taken into account and reviewed periodically.

Such a review would naturally follow any unilateral withdrawal of battlefield and theatre nuclear weapons by NATO from Europe. We do not suggest that there should be any attempt to match in conventional terms the enormous destructive capacity of the nuclear weapons being withdrawn; but as these weapons have been seen in the past as a way of making good perceived deficiencies at the conventional level, their withdrawal would inevitably lead to a reassessment of the conventional balance.

It is far from self-evident, in spite of frequent assertions to the contrary, that NATO lacks an effective conventional defensive posture at the moment, even on the Central and Northern fronts. The larger numbers of Warsaw Pact tanks, for example, have to be seen in the context of NATO's much greater investment in anti-tank missiles; and it is doubtful whether on any front the Warsaw Pact enjoys a degree of numerical advantage that would make it rational for the Soviet Union to attempt a major offensive drive against Western Europe — except possibly as a pre-emptive measure if it came to the conclusion that the West was about to attack.[12] In view of the great importance of avoiding a conventional arms build-up in Europe, one possibility that ought to be seriously examined upon the withdrawal of nuclear weapons from Europe would be to maintain present force levels but perhaps to carry out some reorganisation to improve effectiveness. This would not involve any significant additional defence burden for Britain.

It might be decided however that some strengthening of NATO defences would be required. This might take the form of a modest increase in front-line forces. An alternative would be to maintain something like the existing level of front-line forces but to build up the capacity throughout West Germany and Western Europe as a whole for territorial in-depth defence. Possible ways of doing this are discussed in Chapter 5. Britain might increase its own territorial forces to some extent, though in-depth defence is of less potential importance here than in mainland Europe. However, we suggested the possibility that Britain might make a somewhat larger contribution to NATO's conventional forces, especially during the initial phase of the strengthening of territorial forces, in order to release some German professional forces to train and stiffen the new territorial units; BAOR, for example, might be reinforced by something like 15,000–20,000 troops for this purpose.

Britain could, of course, increase its contribution to NATO in a different way, for instance by providing a greater naval presence in the Eastern Atlantic. But however it was carried out, an increased British contribution to NATO would be an added burden on the defence budget. However, against this extra expense has to be set the considerable savings that would be made by the cancellation of Trident and other projects related to Britain's nuclear forces. Further substantial savings would be made if Britain, presumably along with other NATO states, moved away from reliance on ultra-sophisticated weapons systems such as the Tornado Multi-Role Combat Aircraft.

A European defence association

If a purely European defence association replaced NATO at some point, we would have to assume that US forces would be withdrawn and that Western Europe could no longer count upon US intervention on its behalf in the event of war. If the association wished to maintain something like the present balance at the conventional level in Europe, it would have to raise larger forces, and train many more reserves, to compensate for the withdrawal of the USA. This would be expensive for all the European states involved, including Britain, and this country might have to re-introduce conscription to raise larger forces.

Because of the costs of such a policy, a European association might well be forced to re-think its strategy and opt for a more modest military capacity. Thus it might switch the emphasis of its strategy to territorial in-depth defence, and might also seek to build up the capacity for civil resistance. If there was a major shift of emphasis towards territorial defence within a West European alliance, Britain too might extend the scope of its preparations for defence in depth; alternatively it might be thought more appropriate for Britain to strengthen its naval, coastal and anti-aircraft defences. The extent of Britain's contribution to any continuing multinational force in Europe would be a matter for negotiation with Britain's partners and would greatly depend on how large a multinational force it was decided to maintain.

British non-alignment

A non-aligned Britain could only aim for a 'high entry price' policy. This means that it could not expect to withstand an all-out attack from a superpower, but could, like Sweden and other neutral countries in Europe, raise the cost of aggression and operate on the assumption that it was unlikely to be singled out for an all-out attack. Given this more limited aim, there could be substantial cut-backs in some of the armed services, and the cost of defence could be greatly reduced. In Appendix 2 we give examples of three possible force structures for a non-aligned Britain, and their estimated cost. Even the largest estimate represents a major saving on present British defence expenditure.

Conscription

Of the various options and strategies discussed above, only British membership of a European defence association would seem at all likely to require the re-introduction of conscription in this country, and then only if the association sought without the benefit of US assistance to maintain the present balance of conventional forces in Europe.

The NATO option, if territorial defences were strengthened,

might require Britain to raise larger forces, but not on a scale that would justify conscription. On the other hand, it can be argued that since the Warsaw Pact has far larger trained reserves than NATO, and since the bulk of NATO reserves are in the United States and could not be moved quickly to a European battlefield, Britain could at least help to solve this problem by bringing back conscription.

There are however serious questions even from a military perspective about switching to a conscript system in Britain. It is not at all evident that Britain would make a more effective contribution to European defence by such a change; it would raise larger forces but these might be less efficient than the highly professional forces we now have. The efficiency of reserve forces is often highly questionable. Thus the net result of re-introducing conscription could actually be a loss of military effectiveness, and for this reason, among others, military circles in Britain have shown little enthusiasm for the idea.

Two other arguments of a mainly political nature are put forward. Firstly, it is argued that re-introducing conscription would signal Britain's continued determination to defend itself following its renunciation of nuclear weapons. Secondly, taking this step might be regarded as a significant gesture of solidarity with the rest of European NATO states, all of which have conscription. These considerations on their own, however, could hardly be decisive, and there would need to be a clear and essential role for the additional forces produced by conscription to justify taking this step.

If Britain, either independently or together with its partners in Europe, decided that force levels should stay approximately as they are, or should be reduced, in conjunction possibly with an increasing emphasis on preparations for nonviolent resistance, then clearly conscription would not be necessary. The Commission agreed that the re-introduction of conscription in Britain was not in itself desirable, though some felt that it was a step that might have to be considered in certain circumstances.

Exploring defence by civil resistance

At the beginning of its term of office, the government should sponsor a research project, similar to those which have been officially sponsored in Holland and Sweden, into the possible role of civil resistance in defence policy. It should also give serious consideration to setting up at some point a Civil Resistance Council as proposed in Chapter 7.

Civil resistance could be assigned a recognised though subsidiary role in defence planning, a situation which by and large obtains in Sweden at present. However, one might want to keep open the possibility that it would in time play an increasingly important role, and this would require giving some careful thought to the kinds of mixed strategy that would be appropriate. It would be difficult, for instance, to place a major emphasis simultaneously on territorial in-depth defence and civil resistance, since the dynamics of nonviolent resistance may make it preferable for people to be less inclined to resort to arms, while territorial defence would probably mean involving the bulk of the population in military training.

A Ministry of Disarmament

We suggest that a future British government committed to detente and disarmament should establish a properly staffed Ministry of Disarmament. The Minister would have Cabinet rank, and the role of the department would be to formulate proposals for disarmament and arms control, and to study and evaluate those put forward by other states. One of the subsidiary problems concerning dis-armament at present is that it is simply not taken sufficiently seriously or given adequate time and attention either by individual governments or international agencies. This would be a small step in the direction of redressing the balance and might encourage similar moves by other countries.

Economic adjustment and redeployment

A non-nuclear defence policy would entail as a minimum the redeployment of workers at Aldermaston, Burghfield and Cardiff where nuclear weapons are produced, and also the civilians who service the Polaris fleet. In addition, the withdrawal of US Forces personnel from Britain, whether partial or total, and the closure of at least some US bases would require economic adjustment. Certain weapons programmes would also have to be cut back or cancelled — most notably the Tornado Multi-Role Combat Aircraft if it was still applicable, and Trident.

In the longer term, the British government should seek to end the military domination of industrial production and scientific research and use the skills and labour released to meet social needs. Just how this would proceed would obviously depend on the defence options taken up.

In general six steps are necessary in planning conversion of defence facilities to other industrial uses:

(1) identify assets (plant, land, equipment, people);
(2) survey the market, forecast demand, analyse consumption patterns, assess needs;
(3) identify new products;
(4) consider constraints (e.g. transportation, shortage of skills);
(5) overcome constraints (e.g. road-building, re-training);
(6) convert the defence installation.

The first three steps do not need to wait for a change in government policy. Shop stewards' committees in firms heavily dependent on military production have already taken these steps in some places. In general we would suggest that an anti-nuclear government should stipulate that alternative use committees should be set up in advance of any closures, with a third of the committee named by management/administration, a third by employees, and a third by the local community. For while conversion must be viewed as part of national planning for economic recovery, it will best be worked out regionally and locally and with the participation of the people most directly involved. The government must also ensure advance notice of any base closure or cancellation of contracts, and offer guarantees to the workers affected, including provision for re-training.

In the short term, the scale of conversion is not too daunting. Some 5,000 workers are employed at Aldermaston, including up to 1,200 graduates, with perhaps around 1,000 at each of the associated factories at Burghfield and Cardiff.[13] There are many alternative products they could manufacture and they should be canvassed for their ideas for new products and designs. The Clydeside area, where unemployment currently stands at about 18 per cent, clearly needs a development programme. The Clyde Submarine Base provided work directly for 2,800 civilians in 1975 and for a further 2,000 workers in surrounding service industries. As there is evidence that the base may have actually stood in the way of the area's development in recent years, its closure could in fact open up new opportunities.[14]

There are around 27,300 US military personnel in Britain and a further 2,000 American civilians employed on US bases, plus 29,000 dependents.[15] The government estimates that US bases create either directly or indirectly, 25,000 jobs for British civilians.[16] As many of these bases would be phased out in the first five years, Britain should seek to learn from the US Department of Defense's Office of Economic Adjustment. Although it should be criticised for planning after the closure of bases rather than in advance, in the period 1970–77 the OEA helped to create 110,000 new jobs where previously defence installations had employed about 90,000 civilians.[17] The economic climate in Britain today is less favourable than in the USA at that time, but nonetheless this experience should be a source of confidence. The Office of Economic Adjustment found that "the imagined disasters that a base closing portends can actually become catalysts for community improvements never before thought possible".[18]

Thus while nuclear disarmament and the closure of bases, or more substantial cut-backs in defence spending if radical alternative strategies were adopted, would cause some problems of adjustment in the short run, there is no reason to think these would be insuperable and there is solid evidence that in the longer term a major shift of expenditure and resources towards the civilian sector would help to put the British economy on a sounder footing.

IV. Summary and recommendations

In this chapter we have focused on the process of transition from a nuclear to a non-nuclear strategy during the (presumed) five-year term of office of a British government committed to nuclear disarmament.

The most important aspect of the management of transition is at the political and diplomatic level to ensure both that Britain's actions were not misunderstood and did not create unnecessary panic or instability, and that the maximum positive repercussions flowed from the change of policy. However, a full consideration of the foreign and development policies that might accompany British nuclear disarmament is beyond the scope of this report and no more is attempted here than a broad indication of the kinds of policy Britain ought to pursue. In the short term an important goal would be to raise the nuclear threshold in Europe by trying to secure the removal of battlefield and theatre nuclear weapons and the adoption of a no-first-use of nuclear weapons agreement; some of the broader aims would be the de-militarisation of East and West Germany, the creation of nuclear-free zones intended eventually to cover the whole of Europe, the eventual disbandment of the two military alliances in Europe and the encouragement of detente and disarmament. Strengthening the UN and diverting resources to development would be an important aspect of this wider programme.

Among the early political and diplomatic moves should be a declaration of intent by the new government, and negotiations at the highest level with the USA and with Britain's other NATO partners.

In the option in which Britain remains conditionally within NATO, Britain would press for the Alliance to adopt a no-first-use of nuclear weapons policy within a year of the conference with its allies. A period of three to four years could be suggested for phasing out battlefield and theatre nuclear weapons in Europe, leading to the decoupling of European NATO from the US nuclear deterrent. Attempts would be made at every stage to reach agreement with the Soviet Union for the mutual withdrawal of nuclear weapons, but if necessary NATO would take these initiatives unilaterally.

If NATO resisted the pressure to move away from a nuclear strategy, Britain would have to begin the process of withdrawal from the Alliance. The first step in this process would be for Britain to withdraw from the integrated military command system, while remaining on the North Atlantic Council; however, if it became clear that there was no real possibility of changing NATO strategy, Britain would eventually have to withdraw from the Alliance.

If Britain did, at whatever stage, withdraw from NATO it could explore the possibilities of alternative collective security arrangements in Europe, or adopt a non-aligned position. Whatever course of action was chosen, sufficient time should be allowed to avoid creating unnecessary panic or misunderstanding, though it would also be important to maintain the momentum of change and to make it clear that Britain would not be diverted from its decision to move away from reliance on nuclear weapons.

A unilateralist government would aim to set Britain firmly on a new course within its five-year term of office. Its first step would be to abolish the British independent deterrent by cancelling Trident, withdrawing Polaris from service, and withdrawing other nuclear weapons from British forces. (Battlefield nuclear weapons, however, deployed with British forces in Europe might be phased out in conjunction with other NATO battlefield weapons). The USA would be asked to withdraw its F-111 bombers from Britain, and its Poseidon submarines based at Holy Loch, within three years. US surveillance systems related exclusively to a nuclear strategy would also be withdrawn in this period; those that could serve a useful function in a system of conventional defence might be taken over by Britain and operated on behalf of NATO. Britain should also consider inviting to this country an international inspection team, perhaps under UN and IAEA authority, to monitor the process of its nuclear disarmament.

A review of defence strategy would take place at an early stage following the election of a unilateralist government. The degree of change in defence strategy that could be expected to occur during the five-year period would depend to a considerable extent on whether Britain remained in NATO (or was part of an alternative European alliance) or adopted a non-aligned approach; changes in strategy would tend to be more gradual where they had to be agreed upon by several countries. A serious investigation into the possibilities of non-violent resistance should be sponsored at an early stage.

The implications for British defence in terms of force levels and costs under the various options and strategies were briefly reviewed. *In the conditional NATO option,* if the Alliance adopted a posture of 'defensive balance', substantial increases in force levels should not be necessary. But Britain might make some additional contribution to NATO defences while the Alliance was re-organising itself during the phasing out of battlefield and theatre nuclear weapons, especially if there was a decision to build up territorial forces for in-depth defence. But the additional cost to Britain of increasing its contribution to NATO could be offset to some extent if the Alliance moved away from its reliance on ultra-sophisticated technology. *In a European defence association* there would be enormous problems about attempting to maintain the present balance of forces in Europe without US support; it would mean raising larger forces and would impose a heavy financial burden on all the countries involved, including Britain. For this reason a European defence association might adopt a more modest posture, perhaps switching the main emphasis to territorial in-depth defence, and preparations for civil resistance. *A non-aligned Britain* which adopted a 'high entry price' policy could make substantial cut-backs in some of the services and greatly reduce the cost of defence.

Conscription is likely to be necessary only if Britain were to become a member of a European defence association that was aiming to maintain the present balance of forces in Europe. In the NATO option, depending on the strategy adopted, Britain might need to raise some extra forces but not on the scale that would warrant conscription. Conscription would probably not be necessary either if Britain adopted a non-aligned approach.

Finally the government should establish a framework for managing the various aspects of economic conversion, including the re-deployment of people engaged in the nuclear weapons industry, and the alternative use of assets released by nuclear disarmament and the closure of bases.

Notes to Chapter 8

1. See Chapter 1, p. 34 and note 18 of Chapter 1.
2. O. Palme, *Common Security: A Programme for Disarmament* (London: Pan, 1982). pp. 146–150. It is worth noting that Palme's Commission included both a Polish and a Soviet representative.
3. For an analysis of theatre nuclear forces on both sides, see Sverre Lodgaard, 'Long Range Theatre Nuclear Forces in Europe', in *World Armaments and Disarmament: SIPRI Yearbook 1982* (London: Taylor & Francis, 1982), pp. 3–50. Long-range theatre nuclear aircraft on the NATO side, in addition to the US F-111s based in Britain, include various bombers deployed with the US Navy. There are also medium range theatre systems in Europe, including Pershing 1A missiles (range 740 km) and F-4 Phantom bombers (combat radius, 1,100 km). See also Frank Barnaby, 'The Effects of a Global Nuclear War: The Arsenals', in *Ambio,* XI, Number 2–3 (1982), pp. 76–83. Future US plans include not only the deployment of cruise and Pershing II missiles in Europe, but the placing of cruise missiles on submarines and surface ships.
4. On De Gaulle's withdrawal from the NATO Command Structure, see Eliot R. Goodman, 'De Gaulle's NATO Policy in Perspective', *Orbis,* X, 3 (Fall 1966), 690–723.
5. *The Times,* 2 February, 1982; *The Financial Times,* 3 March, 1982.
6. *The Times,* 26 October, 1981.
7. *The Times,* 3 June, 1982.
8. C. Hitchens, 'Canada's Nuclear Departure', *New Statesman*, Vol. 99, No. 2569, 13 June 1980.
9. M. Stott and P. Taylor, *The Nuclear Controversy: A Guide to the Issues of the Windscale Inquiry* (London: Town and Country Planning Association/Political Ecology Research Group, 1980), pp. 100–101.
10. The paper on the implications of a non-nuclear defence policy for nuclear electricity by Howard Clark is to be published, among other supplementary material produced by the Commission, by the Lansbury House Trust Fund, London. For the view that energy policy could become a vital element in a wider process of realignment and disarmament, see M. Spence, 'Will Gas Pipeline Set East and West Alight?', *E. N. D. Bulletin,* 9 (May/June 1982), 12–19.
11. Thus Sir Henry Tizard, Chief Scientific Advisor on Defence in the latter part of the war and during the Attlee administration, wrote a confidential paper in 1949 arguing that Britain should not attempt to have an independent nuclear deterrent but should rely on the US deterrent. The paper is referred to in Gowing's official history, *Independence and Deterrence.* However this paper has not been made available under the 30-year-rule.
12. See for instance Jonathan Alford 'NATO's Conventional Forces and the Soviet Mobilization Potential', *NATO Review,* 28, 3 (June 1980), 18–22. Alford argues that Warsaw Pact forces are probably aimed at deterring attack by means of an evident capacity to launch a pre-emptive strike, but are unlikely to appear to the Soviet Union anything like sufficient to secure Western Europe or even West Germany. Alford, however, is concerned about the far larger pool of reserves available to the Soviet Union than to NATO.

13. D. Fishlock, 'Aldermaston's Nuclear Role: Where Trident's Punch is Packed', *The Financial Times,* 16 October 1980; and 'Inside Aldermaston', BBC Television programme, 12 January 1982.

14. D. Greenwood and T. Stone, 'The Clyde Submarine Base and the Local Economy', paper for Scottish CND Conference, February 1975.

15. Public Affairs Office, USAF, Mildenhall.

16. The Prime Minister, Mrs Thatcher, Written Answer, 17 November 1981, *Hansard,* Sixth Series, Vol. 13, Session 1981–82, Written Answers section, p. 85.

17. P. Wallensteen, 'The Politics of Base Closing: Some Swedish Experiences', in P. Wallensteen, ed., *Experiences in Disarmament* (Uppsala: Department of Peace and Conflict Research, Uppsala University, 1970), p. 116.

18. Quoted in Labour Party Defence Study Group, *Sense About Defence* (London: Quartet, 1977), p. 82.

Appendix 1
British military forces in 1982

Army

Total strength[1]	163,100	(including 9,750 recruited overseas)
Combat strength[2]	112,300	56,800 in British Army of the Rhine
		3,000 in Berlin
		37,500 in UK
		4,200 in Mediterranean
		9,200 in Hong Kong and Far East
		1,600 other areas
Regular reserves	139,600	
Territorial Army	70,200	(to rise to 86,000 by the early 1990s)
Home service force	4,500	(set up in September 1982)

Notes

1. This is the figure for April 1982 given in the Statement on the Defence Estimates, 1982.
2. This figure is based on the functional analysis of personnel, using the average strengths provided for in the 1981–82 Defence Estimates (including locally recruited personnel), given in the Statement on the Defence Estimates. 1982

Navy

Total strength	73,100	(including 7,900 Marines)
Regular reserves	28,000	(including 2,100 Marines)
Volunteer reserves	6,400	(including 1,000 Marines)

Vessels (excluding 4 submarines armed with Polaris)

Submarines	27	(11 nuclear powered, 16 diesel)
ASW Carriers	3	
Destroyers	12	
Frigates	44	
Patrol Craft	21	(including 9 offshore patrol craft)
weepers/hunters	34	
Fleet Air Arm Aircraft	15	combat aircraft and
	102	armed helicopters

ASW Carriers Anti-submarine warfare aircraft carriers.

Air Force

Total strength		91,700	
Regular reserves		29,500	
Voluntary reserves		600	

Aircraft (front-line units)[1]

About a third of Britain's aircraft are capable of carrying nuclear weapons (the Vulcan bombers, the Tornado multi-role combat aircraft, the Buccaneer, the Jaguar and the Nimrod) and under present policy many of them have a nuclear role. But as they are all capable of being used in purely conventional warfare these aircraft are included in the totals below.

Strike/attack	3 squadrons with Vulcan[2]	54	
	1 squadron with Tornado	12	
	4 squadrons with Buccaneer	50	
	4 squadrons with Jaguar	48	164
Ground support	3 squadrons with Harrier	44	
	2 squadrons with Jaguar	24	68
Maritime patrol	4 squadrons with Nimrod	28	28
Reconnaissance	1 squadron with Canberra[3]	20	
	2 squadrons with Jaguar	24	44
Air defence	2 squadrons with Lightning (plus 24 in reserve)	24	
	7 squadrons with Phantom	87	111
Airborne early warning	1 squadron with Shackleton (with 5 in reserve)	6	6
Total combat and reconnaissance			421
Air transport	5 squadrons fixed wing	56	56
	4 squadrons helicopters	70	70
Tanker	2 squadrons	16	16
Search and rescue	2 squadrons helicopters	32	32
	Total aircraft		595
Surface-to-air missiles	8 squadrons		

Notes

1. This list of aircraft excludes communications, training and some other squadrons which go to make up the total of 700 aircraft listed by I.I.S.S. It follows the headings of Annex E of the Statement on the Defence Estimates, 1982, Cmnd 8529–I, 51–2.
2. Two more squadrons of Vulcan are being phased out and replaced by Tornado.
3. Canberra is being phased out.

The sources for these figures on British forces are Statement on the Defence Estimates 1982, London, HMSO, Cmnd 8529–I and Cmnd 8529–II, modified and amplified where relevant by *The Military Balance 1982–1983* (London: I.I.S.S., 1982) which appeared slightly later and takes account of losses of ships in the Falklands.

Appendix 2
Possible force structures for an independent British defence policy

This Appendix presents three possible force structures for a non-nuclear Britain pursuing an independent defence policy. These force structures all start from Britain's present military strength; they all assume that Britain would move towards abandonment of its residual global role, which would allow a reduction in ocean-going ships; and they all represent possible interpretations of a 'high entry price' policy. Structure 1 represents a Swedish-style force structure for Britain, taking into account that Britain's land mass is smaller than Sweden's but its population much larger, and that a purely professional army should be more efficient than a largely conscript army. Structure 2 lays less stress on ground forces, while maintaining a significant air and sea defence. Structure 3 sets lower levels for the army and for air defence and reduces the number of large vessels in favour of more patrol craft. Structures 1 and 2 posit a stronger air defence and maritime air support than the present forces allocated specifically to the defence of Britain itself.

The forces are presented in outline only, and exclude army equipment. They are targets; it is assumed that a five-year period of adjustment would be required for the army, ten years for the air force and twenty for the navy; and the process of adjustment for the navy is shown in table 1.

The force levels and estimated costs in this Appendix are based on a submission by Dan Smith to the Commission, published as: Dan Smith, *Non-Nuclear Military Options for Britain* (Bradford: Bradford School of Peace Studies and London: Housmans, 1982), which examines the rationale for the force levels and costings in more detail. The figures given here include additionally the Swedish-style force structure I, and have been updated to take account of 1982 force levels and defence costs.

Table 1 Three possible force structures for a non-nuclear Britain.

	Force structure 1	Force structure 2	Force structure 3
Army (by Year 5)[1]			
Regular army	160,000	80,000	50,000
Ready reserves[2]	350,000	70,000	70,000

	Force structures 1 and 2	Force structure 3
Airforce (by Year 10)	60,000	48,000
Aircraft (Front-line units)[3]		
Strike/attack	0	0
Ground support	48 (Harriers)	48
Maritime patrol	28	28
Reconnaissance	36 (Jaguars)	24
Air defence	112	64
Airborne early warning	11	11
Maritime support	48 (strike)	24 (strike)
	36 (air cover)	24 (air cover)
Total (combat and reconnaissance)	319	223
Air transport		
Fixed-wing	0	0
Helicopters	54	54
Tanker	0	0
Search and rescue	16	16
TOTAL	389	293
Surface-to-air missiles	12 squadrons	6 squadrons

	Year 1	Year 10	Year 20	Year 1	Year 10	Year 20
Navy			35,000			28,000
Vessels[4]						
Submarines	27	16	16	27	16	16
Destroyers	12	8	0	12	6	0
Frigates	44	24	21	44	24	12
Patrol craft (large)	12	20	26	12	25	40
Minesweepers/ hunters	34	36	38	34	36	38

Notes

1. These force structure projections cover the period from Year 1 of a non-nuclear Britain to year 20 (assuming consistency of defence policy and planning).
2. 'Ready reserves' cover both Regular and TA reserves, but implies the forces are *actually available* and assigned to a particular role.
3. The aircraft represent front-line strength only; there would be additional training, communications and liaison light aircraft.
4. No provision is made for anti-submarine warfare carriers on the grounds that these are very vulnerable and an inefficient way of conducting ASW.

Table 2   Estimated costs of defence policies with structures 1–3, compared with budgeted 1982 figures.

All figures are in £ million.

	Force structure 1	Force structure 2	Force structure 3	Defence estimates 1982
Army	2000	890	630	2235
Navy	910	910	710	1861
Air Force	1990	1990	1530	2729
Reserves	530	270	270	287
Research & development	1300	1170	620	1833
Training	1000	650	490	1162
Repair	750	610	500	869
War and contingency stocks	350	270	230	403
Other support	1780	1380	970	2307
Nuclear strike force				327
Miscellaneous expenditure				78
TOTAL	10610	8140	5950	14091

Notes

Price basis is that used in 1982 Defence White Paper, Volume 2, Table 2.3 (Cmnd 8529-II, p. 12)

The costings are very rough, and only indicate the main headings used in the Statement of the Defence Estimates, although calculations have been made for subheadings. The estimated costs relate to the force levels indicated in Table 1 at the end of the 20-year period. As regards elements not explicitly listed in Table 1 but covered by the present defence budget (e.g. shore-based early-warning equipment), the nature of the exercise does not warrant an appearance of great precision.

Possible force levels have been related to existing force levels and the costs then estimated upwards to play safe. The results are therefore a rough indication of the kind of expenditure required.

Appendix 3
Balance of conventional forces in Europe

There are a number of problems in assessing the balance of conventional military forces between NATO and the Warsaw Pact. Both major powers in each alliance, the USA and the USSR, have military concerns outside Europe, and so it is necessary to estimate (especially in the case of the USSR) how many of their total forces might be committed to a war in Europe. Moreover, adding up total forces available in Western and Eastern Europe does not provide a clear picture of the forces likely to be involved in a war on the Central Front, since both geographical and political factors indicate that only some NATO and Pact countries would commit their forces in a war centred on Germany.

Another problem is that counting up forces and weapons now deployed in Europe by both sides does not take account of the reinforcements available to each, or of the speed with which such reinforcements may be brought into the battle area, questions which require complicated assessments. Finally, a table of figures conveys no idea of what may be crucial factors: the morale and efficiency of the troops, the quality of the equipment and the adequacy of the strategic planning. In the past, NATO has been able to count upon the technological superiority of its equipment. However, this technological gap has narrowed over time as the Soviet Union has modernised its forces, and to this extent the balance has shifted somewhat in favour of the Warsaw Pact. But NATO does still have an edge at the technological level and the extent of the change should not be exaggerated.

Some of the main problems involved in assessing the military balance in Europe are briefly discussed in the accompanying notes to the tables in this appendix.

Table 1   Overall comparison of NATO and Warsaw Pact forces

	NATO				Warsaw Pact		
	N. Europe	S. Europe	US	Total	USSR	E. Europe	Total
Total forces	1,670	1,211	2,117	4,998	3,705	1,116	4,821
Reserves (all services)	2,050	2,129	900	5,079	5,200	1,938	7,138
Total ground forces	998	931	791	2,720	1,825	793	2,618
Total ground forces in Europe	975	931	219	2,125	871c	793	1,664

Notes

All figures are thousands of troops.

c: Estimated figures.

Both US and Soviet forces are of course deployed partly to defend their own territory, and both have commitments outside Europe. The bulk of Soviet ground forces not assigned to Europe would probably be deployed along the frontiers with China, with Iran and Turkey, and in Afghanistan.

Source: International Institute for Strategic Studies, *The Military Balance, 1982–83* (London: I.I.S.S., 1982).

Calculating the balance of forces in a war in Central Europe

There is no satisfactory way of producing a straightforward table of the forces likely to be deployed in actually waging war in Central Europe because there are so many elements of uncertainty. The first problem is to clarify the balance of forces in place in Central Europe. The I.I.S.S. *Military Balance* does not address itself specifically to this question. The British Statement on the Defence Estimates produces a simplified statement of the balance on the Central Front as follows:

	NATO	Warsaw Pact
Total soldiers	790,000	960,000
Soldiers in fighting units	600,000	720,000
Main battle tanks	7,100	17,700
Artillery	2,700	7,700
Fixed-wing tactical aircraft (i.e. all tactical aircraft excluding helicopters)	1,250	2,700

Source: Statement on the Defence Estimates 1982, 1, London: HMSO, 1982, Cmnd. 8529-I, p. 22

This calculation includes some Warsaw Pact tanks in training units and storage, and excludes anti-tank missiles in which NATO has clear superiority.

The second problem is to estimate what proportion of the Warsaw Pact forces in place would be used in an attack. It is not certain that all Soviet forces in Eastern Europe would be launched against West Germany — their present role is in part to secure the Soviet presence in Eastern Europe. It is very unlikely that a high proportion of East European forces would be used in an attack, though some might be.

The third problem is to estimate what the total Soviet attacking strength is likely to be. What forces could the Soviet Union muster and how quickly could it mobilise them? The IISS *Military Balance* calculates that the 74 divisions now stationed in the European part of the USSR might be available plus the 31 divisions already in Eastern Europe (the other 82 divisions would presumably be deployed on the border with China, in Southern USSR bordering Iran and Turkey, and in Afghanistan). When at full strength, there are 11,000 men in an armoured division and 14,000 in a mechanised division in the Soviet army, so around 1,250,000 combat troops might be available for a Soviet attack.

Estimates which have been made of Soviet attacking strength include the following: Brigadier General Robert Close has suggested the Pact could put 39 divisions into the front line for an offensive within 48 hours, and a further 60 Soviet divisions reinforced by Czechoslovak troops within 6 days.[1] Les Aspin cites a US Defense Department calculation that it would take the Pact about 30 days to mobilise 90 divisions on the West German border.[2] Colonel Jonathan Alford suggests the USSR could (depending on the time of year) mobilise about 150 divisons to join the 20 in East Germany.[3]

The fourth problem is to assess the reinforcements and reserves which NATO could make available for fighting in Central Europe. The West German Army can call on about 500,000 regular reserves and the German TA after mobilisation is about 480,000 strong. The USA has $7\frac{1}{3}$ divisions assigned to reinforce its forces in Europe in the event of war. Since there are 18,300 men in a US armoured division and 18,500 in a mechanised division, this would mean about 135,000 combat troops plus logistic support. After mobiliation further US reserves could be available, perhaps another $14\frac{1}{3}$ divisions.[4] In addition British, French, Belgian and Dutch reinforcements would be mobilised. While some of these reinforcements should be available within a few days, bringing over all US forces potentially available together with their equipment would take weeks, especially as most of the equipment would have to come by sea. Therefore estimates of the real balance between Pact and NATO forces in a war depend considerably on how much time it is assumed NATO forces have to get into place.

Therefore the fifth question is whether a Soviet surprise attack is at all likely.[5] An attack out of the blue is extremely improbable. Field Marshal Lord Carver argues that it would be out of character for the USSR to launch a limited operation, and is sceptical about a surprise attack except as a pre-emptive strike.[6] It has also been argued that the USSR "seems to take about three months to set up a major attack force, whether against Czechoslovakia in 1968 or Afghanistan in 1979".[7] It is almost incredible that the Soviet Command would spearhead an attack on West Europe relying only on the 20 divisions in East Germany now or that it would rely heavily on East European divisions for the crucial breakthrough. Moreover, Western satellite monitors should pick up any evidence of troop movements. It is possible that NATO might fail to interpret evidence of a Soviet build-up correctly, and also possible that NATO governments might hesitate to mobilise in a period of tension for fear of provoking a military response. But the likelihood of NATO being taken totally by surprise is not a reasonable basis for NATO planning.

Notes to Appendix 3

1. Evans and Novak, 'NATO Fears of Soviet Superiority', *Washington Post*, 31 December 1976.
2. L. Aspin, 'A Surprise Attack on NATO — Refocussing the Debate', *NATO Review*, 25 4 (August 1977), 6–13.
3. Colonel J. Alford, 'NATO's Conventional Forces and the Soviet Mobilisation Potential', *NATO Review*, 28, 3 (June 1980), 18–22.
4. International Institute for Strategic Studies, *The Military Balance, 1982–83* (London: I.I.S.S., 1982), p. 132.
5. See e.g. S. Nunn, 'Deterring War in Europe', *NATO Review*, 25 1 (February 1977), 4–7. See also R. K. Betts, *Surprise Attack: NATO's Political Vulnerability and Hedging Against Surprise Attack*, Brookings General Series Reprint 384, (Washington: The Brookings Institution, 1982).
6. Address by Field Marshal Lord Carver printed in *Survival*, XIX, 1 (January/February 1977), 36.
7. R. Stubbing, 'The Soviet Megalith Under a Microscope', *The Guardian*, 22 February 1982 cites William Kaufmann on this point.

Appendix 4
Guerrilla warfare and international law

Note: This Appendix relies extensively on Adam Roberts's duplicated monograph *Occupation, Resistance and Law — International Law on Military Occupations and on Resistance*, especially Chapter 5 on 'the Legal Status of Resistance' (published by Forsvarets Forskningsanstalt, Huvudavdelning 1, Stockholm). A revised version of the monograph is due to be published in 1983 by Oxford University Press. The treaty provisions quoted are available in Roberts and R. Guelff (eds), *Documents on the Laws of War* (Oxford: Clarendon Press, 1982).

Some of the difficulties and ambiguities surrounding guerrilla warfare are reflected in the state of international law on the subject. However, developments in the laws of war in the post-war period, embodied in the four 1949 Geneva Conventions and the 1977 Geneva Protocol I, testify to the increasing importance of guerrilla war. The agreements named in this appendix relate mainly to guerrilla activities in *international* armed conflicts. Where a conflict is internal in character, different legal considerations apply.

The basic text is Article I of the Regulations annexed to the 1907 Hague Convention IV Respecting the Laws and Customs of War on Land. This article reads:

"The laws, rights and duties of war apply not only to armies, but also to militia and volunteer corps fulfilling the following conditions:
1. To be commanded by a person responsible for his subordinates;
2. To have a fixed distinctive emblem recognisable at a distance;
3. To carry arms openly; and
4. To conduct their operations in accordance with the laws and customs of war.
In countries where militia or volunteer corps constitute the army, or form part of it, they are included under the denomination 'army'."

The intention here of maintaining the distinction between belligerents and civilians is clear. The conditions set out were deliberately stringent, so much so that in many conflicts the activities of guerrillas were considered by one or both parties as outside the scope of the laws of war.

These conditions outlined in the 1907 Hague Regulations were retained in the 1949 Geneva Conventions, but with some significant modifications and innovations. The effects of these were, first, to expand the category of lawful belligerents to include organised resistance movements in some circumstances, second to extend some protection to other resisters, thus effectively creating a category of what were subsequently and unofficially termed 'unprivileged belligerents' (who would not be able to claim prisoner-of-war status), and third to impose some general restrictions on all parties including absolute prohibitions on hostage-taking and collective punishment.

The 1977 Geneva Protocol I, which has so far been ratified by only about twenty states, takes us a step further along the path of bringing guerrillas within the scope of the laws of war under certain conditions. The Protocol broadens the scope and application of the 1949 Conventions, stating in Article 1 that both conventions and Protocol apply in "armed conflicts in which peoples are fighting against colonial domination and alien occupation and against racist regimes in the exercise of their right of self-determination". This is a significant extension of the type of conflict considered to fall within the legal framework governing international armed conflicts.

The Protocol also further enlarges the category of lawful belligerents — termed 'combatants' — giving further scope for recognition of some 'national liberation front' types of forces as lawful belligerents. Article 44 modifies two of the conditions which militias etc were required to fulfil under the 1907 Hague Regulations and the 1949 Geneva Conventions, namely those relating to the wearing of a distinctive emblem recognisable at a distance and openly carrying arms. Combatants are now obliged to carry their arms openly immediately before an attack.

Commenting on the overall implications of the 1977 Protocol I, Adam Roberts observes on pages 168–69 of the monograph mentioned in the introductory note to this Appendix:

"It has sometimes been criticised as creating rights but no obligations for guerrilla soldiers. This is not correct. Under Article 44, such soldiers are obliged to comply with the rules of international law applicable in armed conflicts; and under paragraph 3 of Article 96 any 'liberation movement' seeking to bring the Protocol into force would assume all the obligations as well as rights, which are assumed by other parties to the 1949 Geneva Conventions and 1977 Protocol I. The obligations involved are very extensive, and would require guerrilla movements to refrain from a wide range of activities including attacks on civilians and non-defended localities."

How far these provisions of international law are likely to be observed or could be enforced is another matter. They are nevertheless significant in so far as they represent steps towards a consensus about the occasions when resort to guerrilla warfare is justified, the constraints within which it should operate, the measures that may, within the framework of international law, be taken in combatting it.

Appendix 5

List of those who sent comments or submissions to the Commission

Horst Afheldt
P. C. Alcock
Jonathan Alford
Nils Andren
Christine Arbor
Armament and Disarmament
  Information Unit
John Baylis
Lennart Bergfeldt
John Biggins
Richard Body, MP
Ken Booth
Anders Boserup
Jeffrey Boss
John Bradbrook
Hans Gunter Brauch
Brighton Anti-Nuclear Group
Rt. Rev. David Brown, Bishop
  of Guildford
John Brunner
Communist Party of Great
  Britain
Charles Constable
Bob Cryer, MP
P. C. da Silva
Rev. Victor de Waal
Rev. Brian Duckworth
Ted Dunn
Theodor Ebert
Ecology Party
Philip P. Everts
John Ferguson
David Fernbach

Lawrence Freedman
Ronald Gaskell
James George
A. J. R. Groom
Bjorn Hagelin
Rev. John Holdsworth
David Holloway
Michael Howard
Gene Keyes
M. J. Knottenbelt
R. D. Leakey
Leeds Diocesan Justice and
  Peace Commission
Simon Lunn
Scilla McLean
Jeff McMahan
Jennifer Macias
Brian Martin
Medical Campaign Against
  Nuclear Weapons
Margaret Melicharova
Methodist Church Division of
  Social Responsibility
Peter Nailor
Newcastle University Nuclear
  Disarmament Group
Kjell-Ake Nordquist
Jan Øberg
Theodore Olson
Mark Reader
Cynthia Roberts
Paul Rogers
Martin Ryle

Brian Salisbury
Alex Schmid
Gene Sharp
Sikh Cultural Society of Great
   Britain
Hans Sinn
Paul Smoker

State Research
Aaron Tovish
Henry Usborne
Enid Wistrich
Women's International League
   for Peace and Freedom
Steve Wright

Appendix 6
The brief of the Commission and list of members

The Alternative Defence Commission was set up in October 1980, sponsored by the Lansbury House Trust Fund in conjunction with the School of Peace Studies at Bradford University. The Commission was selected on the basis of two criteria; firstly it included people with a specialised knowledge of defence and disarmament issues; secondly it included individuals representative of a broad spectrum of views and coming from different backgrounds who had an active concern about defence policy. Mr Frank Blackaby chaired the Commission. At the time it was formed he was Deputy Director of the National Institute for Economic and Social Research (London), and since September 1981 has been Director of the Stockholm International Peace Research Institute (SIPRI).

The brief of the Commission was "to examine a comprehensive set of alternative proposals which might be adopted if Britain abandoned its present reliance on nuclear weapons" — i.e. if Britain abandoned its own nuclear weapons and refused to allow nuclear weapons or bases on its territory. The Commission's brief also excluded any reliance on bacteriological or lethal chemical weapons, but it was otherwise expected to explore the range of possible alternative strategies, both military and non-military. The Commission was asked to give particular attention to the implications of alternative strategies for Britain's alliance commitments: whether a nonnuclear policy would necessitate leaving NATO, whether there was a possibility of changing NATO from within, given the growing strength of the nuclear disarmament movements in Europe, and what would be the alternative options open to Britain if it left the Alliance.

In the course of its work the Commission wrote to political, trade union, religious and peace bodies in this country, soliciting views and submissions; it also approached defence specialists and research institutes in Britain and other countries and received a great deal of help and encouragement.

There were originally 18 Commission members. Because of the pressure of other commitments, or for other reasons, a few decided they could not remain on the Commission and in some cases were replaced by colleagues. There are now 16 members of the Commission as follows:

Viv Bingham, President of the Liberal Party, 1981–82

Frank Blackaby, Chair, Director of the Stockholm International Peace Research Institute (SIPRI)

April Carter, Politics Tutor, Somerville College, Oxford, and representative on the Commission of the Lansbury House Trust Fund

Malcolm Dando, Lecturer in Peace Studies, University of Bradford

Rt. Rev. Tony Dumper, Bishop of Dudley

Mary Kaldor, Science Policy Research Unit, University of Sussex. Member of the Labour Party Defence Study Group; author of *The Baroque Arsenal* (1982)

Isobel Lindsay, Member of the National Executive of the Scottish National Party (SNP), and Lecturer in Sociology at Strathclyde University

Terry Moran, Lucas Aerospace Combine Shop Stewards Committee

Professor James O'Connell, Professor of Peace Studies, University of Bradford

Michael Randle, Research Fellow in Peace Studies, University of Bradford (Co-ordinator).

Professor Joseph Rotblat, Emeritus Professor of Physics at St. Bartholomew's Medical College, University of London, and founder member of the Pugwash Conferences on Science and World Affairs

Elizabeth Sigmund, Co-ordinator of the Working Party on chemical and Biological Weapons; author of *Rage Against the Dying* (1980)

Dan Smith, Independent research worker on UK defence policy, member of the Labour Party Defence Study Group. Author of *The Defence of the Realm in the 1980s* (1980)

Walter Stein, until 1981 Senior Lecturer in Literature and Philosophy, Department of Adult Education and Extra-Mural Studies, University of Leeds; editor of *Nuclear Weapons and Christian Conscience* (1961, reprinted 1981)

Dafydd Elis Thomas, MP, Plaid Cymru; Member of Parliament for Meirionnydd

Ron Todd, National Organiser, Transport & General Workers Union

Selected reading list

Emphasis on British Defence

D. Fernbach and L. Mackay (eds) *Nuclear Free Defence* (London: Heretic Books, 1983)

D. Smith, *Defence of the Realm in the 1980s* (London: Croom Helm, 1980)

D. Smith, 'Non-Nuclear Military Options for Britain', *Peace Studies Paper No. 6*, (Bradford: Bradford University School of Peace Studies, and London: Housmans, 1981)

G. Prins (ed.) *Defended to Death* (Harmondsworth: Penguin, 1983), especially the chapter headed 'Alternatives'.

Emphasis on Alternative Strategies for Europe

F. Barnaby and E. Boeker, 'Defence Without Offence: Non-Nuclear Defence for Europe', *Peace Studies Paper No. 8* (Bradford: Bradford University School of Peace Studies, and London: Housmans, 1982)

M. Kaldor and D. Smith (eds), *Disarming Europe* (London: Merlin Press, 1982), especially chapters by Ben Dankbaar 'Alternative Defence Policies and Modern Weapon Technology' and Anders Boserup, 'Nuclear Disarmament: Non-Nuclear Defence'

H. Afheldt, 'Tactical Nuclear Weapons and European Security' in SIPRI, *Tactical Nuclear Weapons: European Perspectives* (London: Taylor & Francis, 1978)

On Territorial/In-Depth Defence

A. Roberts, *Nations in Arms* (London: Chatto & Windus, 1976)
See also the paper by H. Afheldt cited in the previous section.

On Nonviolent Civil Resistance as a Basis for Defence

S. King-Hall, *Defence in the Nuclear Age* (London: Gollancz, 1958: available from Housmans Bookshop, London)

A. Boserup and A. Mack, *War Without Weapons* (London: Frances Pinter, 1974)

A. Roberts (ed.), *Civil Resistance as a National Defence Policy* (Harmondsworth:

Penguin, 1969 — a slightly revised version of *The Strategy of Civilian Defence* (London: Faber & Faber, 1967)

G. Sharp, *Making Europe Unconquerable* (New York: Institute for World Order, 1983, forthcoming)

On Nuclear Weapons and Strategic Arms Limitation

Lord Carver, *A Policy for Peace* (London: Faber & Faber, 1982)

L. Freedman, *Britain and Nuclear Weapons* (London: Macmillan, 1980)

J. McMahan, *British Nuclear Weapons: For and Against*, (London: Junction Books, 1981)

M. Dando, P. Rogers, P. Van Den Dungen, *As Lambs to the Slaughter* (London: Arrow Books, 1981)

Church of England Working Party, *The Church and the Bomb* (Sevenoaks: Hodder & Stoughton, 1982)

O. Palme, Common Security: A Programme for Disarmament (London: Pan Books, 1982)

SIPRI, *The Arms Race & Arms Control* (London: Taylor & Francis, 1982)

SIPRI, *World Armaments and Disarmament, SIPRI Yearbook 1982* (London: Taylor & Francis, 1982)

Additional papers published by the Lansbury House Trust Fund (6 Endsleigh Street, London W.C.1) on behalf of the Alternative Defence Commission, and available from the Commission:

'Non-Nuclear Defence and Civil Nuclear Power'.

'Some Aspects of Economic Conversion'.

'Economic Defence'.

'Domestic Political Implications of Non-Nuclear Defence'.

Index